Internationalism, National Identities, and Study Abroad

Internationalism, National Identities, and Study Abroad

France and the United States, 1890–1970

Whitney Walton

Stanford University Press

Stanford, California

Stanford University Press
Stanford, California

© 2010 by the Board of Trustees of the Leland Stanford Junior University. All rights reserved.

No part of this book may be reproduced or transmitted in any form or by any means, electronic or mechanical, including photocopying and recording, or in any information storage or retrieval system without the prior written permission of Stanford University Press.

Printed in the United States of America on acid-free, archival-quality paper

Library of Congress Cataloging-in-Publication Data

Walton, Whitney.
　Internationalism, national identities, and study abroad : France and the United States, 1890–1970 / Whitney Walton.
　　　p.　cm.
　Includes bibliographical references and index.
　ISBN 978-0-8047-6253-3 (cloth : alk. paper)
　1. Foreign study—France—History.　2. Foreign study—United States—History.　3. Educational exchanges—France—History.　4. Educational exchanges—United States—History.　5. National characteristics, French—History.　6. National characteristics, American—History.　7. France—Relations—United States.　8. United States—Relations—France.　9. Internationalism—History.　I. Title.
　　LB2376.6.F8W35　2009
　　370.116´20944—dc22　　　　2009015730

Typeset by Westchester Book Group in 10.9/13 Adobe Garamond

*To Charles Whitney Walton III and
in memory of Patricia Coryell Walton*

Contents

List of Illustrations   ix
Preface   xi
Acknowledgments   xv

    Introduction   1

§ 1   The American Quest for Knowledge and the French Quest for Americans, 1870–1919   12

§ 2   Making Internationalists? The Albert Kahn Around-the-World Scholars' Reports on France and the United States, 1898–1930   39

§ 3   Internationalism and the Junior Year Abroad: American Students in France in the 1920s and 1930s   62

§ 4   American Girls and French *Jeunes Filles*: Negotiating National Identities in Interwar France   85

§ 5   Warm Relations in a Cold War Atmosphere: Resurgence and Expansion of Study Abroad Following World War II   109

§ 6   American National Identity and French Student Life: Politicization and Educational Reform in the 1960s   141

§ 7 Sexuality, Gender, and National Identities in
     Twentieth-century Franco-American Exchanges   171

     Abbreviations Used in Notes   195
     Notes   197
     Index   253

Illustrations

Figures

1.	Albert Kahn, 1914	40
2.	First Delaware foreign study group in Nancy, 1923	63
3.	First junior year in France group from Smith College, 1925, in Paris	64
4.	Students in a French university classroom, circa 1920s	74
5.	The Delaware foreign study group, 1929–30	87
6.	Some of the first Fulbright fellows from France, in Paris, 1949	119
7.	Class of 1951, junior year abroad in France	135

Tables

1.	Americans studying in France and French in the United States, 1948–1960	111
2.	American and French Fulbright grantees, 1949–1958	120
3.	Americans studying in France and French in the United States, 1959–1971	144
4.	Leading host countries for all foreign students, 1962 and 1968	145

Preface

A young French *lycée* professor, Jeanne Darlu, described her educational visit to the United States in 1906 as "filled with new sensations and ideas." She stated also that it gave her a new understanding and appreciation of her own country: "I see more clearly than before [France's] faults and weaknesses; . . . I am more aware of the reasons behind the victory of her redoubtable competitors in world markets. But I also feel more how the weave of the national soul has delicacy, gentleness, and real humanity." Darlu's response was echoed by thousands of others who followed her in seeking a foreign experience as part of their education.

Throughout the twentieth century French and American students, teachers, and scholars came to similar conclusions about France and the United States through some form of academic work in the opposite country. They learned to appreciate another culture, and they gave more serious thought than before to what they valued in their own nation. American Louis Blum wrote of his year studying in France from 1928–29 with the University of Delaware Foreign Study Plan: "One learns to see and to judge for one's self, to have broad ideas and tolerance; one understands his country better in the light of the history and doings of another." Study abroad challenged unconscious assumptions about national superiority, as Bryn Mawr student Althea B. Avery succinctly put it in 1935: "such an experience tends to put an end to imperialism in thinking."

Study abroad links the histories of internationalism and nationalism that are usually treated separately. Akira Iriye, a leading historian of diplomatic relations and internationalism, emphasizes the goals of mostly nongovernmental organizations to establish relations of cooperation and exchange across national boundaries as a fundamental feature

xi

of internationalism. Missing from his work, and that of other important scholars, is the dynamic interaction among the persons, especially ordinary citizens, involved in such transnational relations. And while Benedict Anderson brilliantly analyzes how people unconsciously imbibe a sense of nationalism through a variety of print media, study abroad compels individuals to articulate their understanding of nationalism and even to evaluate or revise it. Accounts by French who studied in the United States and Americans who studied in France suggest a definition of internationalism that entails appreciation and tolerance for cultural difference and a conscious assessment or reassessment of national identity.

Looking back on his year as a Fulbright exchange student shortly after World War II, American Richard T. Arndt noted that study in France not only enhanced his appreciation for that country but also provided him with a larger perspective generally. He wrote that it "rationalized and fed my love for another country, so different from mine; in doing so it internationalized me beyond repair." Parallels in the broadening and even internationalizing effects of study abroad appear in the similar language with which two students, one French and one American, articulated the significance of their experience in the other country. In a recent interview Jean-Michel Roche, now a historian of international relations, said that as a result of an academic year at Harvard University on a Fulbright scholarship in 1969–70, he learned (among other things) that, "France was not the center of the universe." Remembering his junior year in France with the Tulane University program in 1972–73, Herbert Larson, now an attorney, said: "You very quickly learn that the United States is not the center of the universe." Studying in France and the United States helped young Americans and French persons integrate internationalism and nationalism into their personal identities and outlooks.

The consistency of such responses over time offers a parallel or alternative narrative of recent Franco-American relations to the more familiar studies of French anti-Americanism and American cultural imperialism. Historians have explained how and why military alliances between France and the United States gave way to mutual mistrust and criticism on the part of particular governments and popular opinion over the course of the twentieth century. But in this book, that turbulent history serves as an important backdrop for a different story—one of mutual fascination, cultural misunderstandings, the dissolution of stereotypes, and respect for, or at least understanding of, political and cultural differences. Supporters of study abroad on both sides of the Atlantic frequently invoked national interests to justify exchange programs and educational subsidies—like trade benefits, a favorable public image abroad, and the dissemination of a national culture and sometimes ideology. And specific policies of respective French and American governments were common topics of conversations for students abroad and their hosts, ranging from French debt repayment to the United States in the 1920s to the American role in Vietnam and President Charles de Gaulle's nuclear weapons development program in the 1960s. But none of these official goals or positions overdetermined the outcome of study abroad. As visitors and hosts, French and Americans engaged with these and other differences as part of a process of understanding one's own and the other's national identities and regarding them as equally valuable.

Undeterred by the vagaries of state relations and popular national stereotypes, a steady stream of French students flowed to the United States for part of their education, and an even larger number of American students attended French institutions of higher learning throughout the twentieth century. What motivated them to undertake such an unorthodox, even daring, enterprise? What were the institutional frameworks and goals for study abroad in the two countries, and how did they change over time? How did the French and American governments influence study abroad and with what results? What are the implications of study abroad, based on the Franco-American example, for international relations? These are the questions this book will answer.

Acknowledgments

It is not possible for me to thank adequately the many people who have helped me in a variety of ways with the completion of this project. But I must try.

I am pleased to acknowledge a Spencer Foundation Small Research Grant, a Fulbright Research Scholarship, and a Center for Humanistic Studies Fellowship from the College of Liberal Arts at Purdue University for providing me with time and financial support to work on the research and writing of this book.

Staff members at the Franco-American Commission in Paris were particularly helpful in allowing me access to their archives and in other ways facilitating my research. I am glad to be able to thank Arnaud Roujou de Boubée, Amy Tondu, Françoise Gaulme, Karla Taudin, Cécile Ouziel, and Véronique Bourgerolle-Jungbluth. I spent many happy days descending into the basement at 9, rue Chardin, pulling out whatever dust-covered packets of files I wished, and hauling them upstairs for perusal in the library. I wish to note here that in order to protect the privacy of the Fulbright grantees whose records I consulted at the Franco-American Commission, I invented the names cited in this book.

Many thanks to the helpful staff at the Smith College Archives, Northampton, Massachusetts, notably Nanci Young and Deborah Richards. The staff at the University of Delaware Archives, Newark, Delaware, including Jean Brown and Ian Janssen, was equally accommodating. I am very grateful to the assistance from several persons at the Musée Albert Kahn in Boulogne-Billancourt, France, and especially from Nathalie Clet-Bonnet. She and the staff allowed me to join them for lunch in the gardens or in the kitchen, where I enjoyed the food and, especially, the conversation.

I cannot thank enough the American and French women and men who shared with me their memories of studying in the other country. Whether or not I included their statements in this book, I enjoyed every moment of our face-to-face or telephone conversations, and I value each and every oral interview and collection of letters provided. At the request of some individuals who wished to remain anonymous, I invented names for them in this book.

Some material in this book was previously published as articles in *Diplomatic History*, *Gender & History*, and *Clio: Histoire, femmes et sociétés*. I acknowledge the kind permission to reprint it; the review process with these journals helped me to focus different parts of the argument.

Countless friends and colleagues contributed their time, expertise, and encouragement to this project. I benefited greatly from feedback and conversations at many annual meetings of the Western Society for French History and the Society for French Historical Studies. The same applies to the research seminar at the Université Marc Bloch in Strasbourg, France; the Colloquium on International Cultural Relations in the Twentieth Century in Paris, France; the seminar on the History of Immigration of the École Normale Supérieure in Paris; the seminar of GERME (Groupe d'études et de recherche sur les mouvements étudiants) in Paris; and panels at the Organization of American Historians and the American Historical Association. Among those who read all or parts of my work are Rebecca Boehling, Nancy L. Green, Sally Hastings, Lloyd Kramer, Rebecca Rogers, and Michael G. Smith. I am grateful for their insights and support. Excellent questions, encouragement, suggestions, and feedback also came from Tithi Bhattacharya, Tom Broden, Susan Curtis, Charles Cutter, Natalie Zemon Davis, Nicole Fouché, Ellen Furlough, Danielle Haase-Dubose, Anne Knupfer, Robert May, Bill Mullen, Pascal Ory, Mary Louise Roberts, Marcia Stephenson, Natalia Tikhonov, Ludovic Tournès, and Lee Whitfield. I thank Janet Polasky and the other, anonymous reader for Stanford University Press for their constructive and detailed suggestions on the manuscript. Thanks also to Norris Pope and Sarah Crane Newman at Stanford University Press for shepherding this project through the publication process. I apologize to those whom I have failed to mention by name. Any errors that remain are my own.

My husband Tom and daughter Sarah have put up with me and supported me during this long process (it has been a longer process for Tom than for Sarah), and I thank them with love. For the subject of this book, I owe a great deal to my parents. They provided all of their children with love and a good education, among many other things, and they allowed me to sail off to France for a year of study when I was a sophomore in college. I am pleased to dedicate this book to them.

Internationalism, National Identities, and Study Abroad

Introduction

In the beginning of the twenty-first century, study abroad is booming, both because of and despite the terrorist attacks of September 11, 2001. According to the Institute of International Education (IIE) publication *Open Doors*, numbers of American students studying abroad have increased since the day that has become known as 9/11. In the academic year 2006–2007, a record high of 241,791 Americans earned college credit studying abroad, an increase of 8 percent over the previous year. An IIE press release attributes this growth to a realization that the United States indeed operates within a global framework, and it is in Americans' best interest to understand more about the rest of the world.[1] Colleges and universities throughout the United States are emphasizing or requiring study abroad experiences. Many of these programs are relatively short—a few weeks in the summer—and run by American faculty in a foreign setting, while others last for a semester or a year and expose American students to foreign faculty, institutions, and students.

In the opposite direction, students from other countries have been flocking to the United States for higher education since the beginning of the twentieth century. As early as 1922, according to one study, 8,357 foreign students attended American colleges and universities, representing "the largest enrollment of foreign students of all countries in the world."[2] More recently, in 2007–2008, 623,805 internationals studied in the United States, a number exceeding the former all-time high of 586,323 reported in 2002–2003. This suggests that recent efforts to ensure that international students feel welcome in the United States have succeeded, following three years of declining enrollments and increased security measures in the aftermath of September 11, 2001 .[3]

The change in terminology in the United States from "foreign student" to "international student" and "foreign study" to "international programs" reflects a notable development in thinking about study abroad and internationalism. A recent communication from the Institute of International Education suggests that this change occurred around 1990 and that the reason for it may be that "international" has more inclusive and less divisive connotations.[4] To call a student from another country "foreign" implies difference or strangeness, one who is not native born, not "one of us." "International" suggests more of a state of mind than different national origins, though it is used also to mean the latter. An international student might be a citizen of the world, one who crosses borders for personal, national, or international benefit and who sees his or her own country and other countries from an internationalist perspective. This raises these questions: What is an internationalist perspective, or what is internationalism?

Historians have recently addressed the latter question and devised different answers to it. For diplomatic historian Akira Iriye, internationalism is the belief or practice of cooperation among nations as opposed to the more common subject of the history of international relations—national power rivalries.[5] In the context of global feminist movements of the early twentieth century, historian Leila Rupp defines internationalism as a "phenomenon and a spirit rather than a formal ideology" and "a response to the tension between the pervasiveness of nationalism and the increasing integration of the world through trade, communication, and other forms of interaction."[6] Writing of a transatlantic literary and political movement of black authors and activists encompassing Africa, Western Europe, and the United States in the 1920s and 1930s, literary scholar Brent Hayes Edwards describes internationalism as a pointed critique of national and colonial race discrimination and the assertion of an alternative, transnational practice of black expression.[7] Several historians (for example, Frank Costigliola, Emily S. Rosenberg, and Christopher Endy, to name only a few) have identified "internationalism" in the context of early twentieth-century U.S. foreign relations as nongovernmental efforts to influence other countries to adopt American economic, cultural, or political practices.[8] Similarly, French scholars have examined French government and nongovernmental international relations in the form of cultivating a positive image of France abroad to promote diplomatic alliances, commercial relations, and French cultural authority.[9] Despite such real aspirations within the United States and France to engage each other primarily by propagating national ways, historians recognize that this form of international relations is never simply one way. Surveying historical scholarship on the cultural influence of the United States in Europe and the world during the Cold War era, Jessica C. E. Gienow-Hecht concludes that, "Many scholars no longer interpret the spread of American and Western culture as 'imperialism' but as a continuous process of negotiation among ethnic, regional, and national groups."[10]

These various definitions of internationalism reflect particular historical contexts and subjects, including individuals, organizations, and governments. They represent a new and lively interest in the multiple ways that culture constitutes relations between and among different countries and their citizens. This book proposes yet another definition of internationalism based on the students, institutions of higher education, and governments involved in study abroad between France and the United States in the twentieth century. In both countries, government officials, academic leaders, private foundations, and organizers of study abroad programs charged study abroad with different purposes over time, including spreading one's own culture, promoting peace, serving national economic and political interests, solving global problems, enhancing professional skills, and combating communism. Many participants shared these objectives, but along with and often superseding these more historically specific purposes, study abroad increasingly became a process of dismantling stereotypes, accepting and appreciating national differences, reassessing one's national identity, and constructing a more cosmopolitan self. I call this process and its results cultural internationalism.

Students who experienced this cultural internationalism through study abroad were no less patriotic or identified with their country because of it. They did, however, reevaluate (or in many cases, consciously analyze for the first time) their understanding of Americanness or Frenchness. This reflective sense of national identity extends historian Benedict Anderson's definition of nationalism as a seemingly "natural" common narrative that unites people into a collective, imagined community to a particular individual consciousness.[11] Study abroad often contributes to what philosopher Kwame Anthony Appiah calls "rooted cosmopolitanism," being at once identified with, and having as an individual constituted, a life that is local, national, and international.[12] Only by analyzing students' accounts of study abroad, along with institutional and governmental objectives and structures, is it possible to discern the process of "internationalization" and how it has become embedded in study abroad programs.

The United States has a long history of study abroad in both directions—Americans abroad and other nationals in the United States—but few scholars have examined this subject as it has evolved in the past century. Several historians of international cultural relations mention students as an important vector of transnational cultural exchange, but thus far none has pursued it. On the other side of the Atlantic, scholars are only beginning to study the history of French youth seeking higher education in the United States, focusing primarily on the period immediately following World War II. Surprisingly, the importance of France in American study abroad history is practically unknown. Yet, in the early 1920s there were more student fellowships for Franco-American exchanges than for any other nation paired with the United States, and the first Junior Year Abroad programs from the United States were established in France. In addition, for several years in the late 1950s and 1960s, France ranked as the top destination for Americans studying abroad.

Many scholars have documented the pervasive influence in France of American mass culture before and especially following World War II, along with the anxieties and adaptations it engendered.[13] At the same time, France exerted a unique appeal to American tourists who went there to practice an ideal of modern, democratic leisure and to seek traditional culture, romance, freedom, and social status, as Christopher Endy and Harvey Levenstein, among others, have shown.[14] Study abroad participates in these diplomatic and cultural phenomena, but it also differs from them. The young French persons and Americans who lived and studied in the other country for an extended period of time—usually one year—gained an understanding about their hosts and about themselves that was not available to tourists and travelers. Study abroad reveals both the official objectives of cultural appreciation, if not cultural imperialism, at an institutional level, along with the actual responses of participants that fulfilled these expectations and generated new forms of nationalism and internationalism.

This book analyzes the history of study abroad between France and the United States during the twentieth century at the intersection of diplomatic and cultural history. I define study abroad generously—usually as organized academic programs whereby Americans studied, researched, or taught in French institutions, and vice versa. This transnational and comparative approach to study abroad based on archives, print sources, and oral histories from France and the United States analyzes cultural relations between the two countries at the levels of governments, institutions of higher learning, and individuals, thereby linking social and cultural developments with national politics and international relations. This work offers an alternative to the Americanization or anti-American narratives of modern Franco-American relations and a new approach to cultural internationalism that emphasizes the important role of ordinary individuals in a form of international relations that paralleled state diplomacy but was distinctly different.

Throughout a long twentieth century of interaction between the two countries, France lost its prominent position in international affairs, and the United States became a superpower. This transformation is evident in the evolving policies and practices surrounding study abroad and in the imaginings citizens of each country developed about the other. At least since the 1920s America loomed large in France as the center of technology, materialism, uniformity, and monotony, while Americans imagined Frenchness as historical, traditional, aesthetically dominant, and sexually permissive.[15] These and many other stereotypes accompanied students from both the United States and France to be tested against personal interactions, daily life, and classroom learning in the opposite country. Thus, students returned with new understandings derived from new foundations in lived experience. Although institutions of higher learning and the French and American governments charged study abroad with purposes that changed over time, ultimately students' own aspirations for knowledge and experience helped shape programs and policies.

The focus on France and the United States in particular reveals a mutual fascination, even appreciation, often at odds with formal diplomatic relations between the two countries.[16] This study also complicates theories of travel as reinforcing nationalism through predictability and repetition, because study abroad adds elements of surprise and confusion from the educational focus and students' participation in daily life.[17] To be sure, study abroad did reinforce nationalism in interesting ways—for example, putting students in an unfamiliar position of defending their country and articulating exactly the national features of which they are most proud—as well as acknowledging some less attractive characteristics. But it also entailed some measure of learning about and adapting to a foreign but more or less equally valued culture. Personal accounts of study abroad offer insights into the process of cultural exchange, including the construction and breakdown of stereotypes; experiences of misapprehension and understanding; and the limits and possibilities of tolerance, self-knowledge, and appreciation of difference. At the same time documentation of study abroad in both French and English reveals the distinctive national approaches and responses to changes in international relations, society, and culture.

Existing literature on the history of study abroad focuses almost exclusively on the nineteenth century. Historians of education in the United States have examined study abroad in Germany as a major factor behind late nineteenth-century reforms of universities in the United States.[18] Other historians have studied the backgrounds, motivations, and results of young American men and women who studied in Europe to obtain professional training or advanced degrees unavailable to them in the United States in the nineteenth century.[19] Study abroad has also figured in intellectual histories of the historical profession and of social policy in the United States.[20] Focusing on Europe, historians of higher education have noted the importance of foreign students to French and German leaders as a source of revenue, an indication of national prestige, and a means of disseminating national values, ideas, and culture, up to World War I.[21] Specialists in American higher education produced a large body of literature on study abroad from the 1920s through the 1970s, mostly providing evidence of its success for foreign language learning, the personal growth and maturation of students, and a developing sense of internationalism.[22] Mine is the first comprehensive historical approach to study abroad as a case study over the long term in the twentieth century, from a comparative perspective, in the context of debates over the purpose and curricula of higher education, and through the prism of international relations.

Letters, reports, personal narratives, interviews, and other accounts by students are central to this project and will balance documentation of the policies and procedures of institutions of higher learning and governments. The personal accounts contain some inherent biases, including the predisposition of individuals to regard study abroad positively, the overdetermining effects of mandatory self-reporting, and nostalgia for the excitement and freedom of youth. Letters written by students abroad to their families at home are not likely to reveal behaviors sure to elicit parental disapproval, and oral interviews conducted twenty to fifty years after the study abroad experience include illuminating and obfuscating filters of hindsight and memory. But such sources are also rich with details about the process of engaging stereotypes, interacting with others, assessing experience, and articulating new understanding that are absent from institutional and governmental sources. An essential component of this study is to account for students' notions of the other country, the different sources and media of communication of such notions, and, especially, how those notions interact with and shape students' experiences in the other country.[23]

Additionally, it addresses the importance of gender in the history of study abroad and in international relations.[24] Women's and men's experiences differed as numbers of women in higher education and in the labor force increased in both countries, and they differed because gendered national stereotypes underlay expectations, motivations, and policies of study abroad. How students, especially women, dealt with these stereotypes shows the pervasiveness of gender at the levels of policy and practice in foreign relations. In addition to gendered national stereotypes, fantasies of sexuality also permeated French perceptions of the United States and especially American imaginings of France. Negotiating sexual stereotypes and different cultural practices surrounding sexuality and youth sociability was an important aspect of study abroad and reveals the salience of sexuality and gender in international relations.

The chapters that follow chart the history of study abroad between France and the United States chronologically and thematically. Chapter 1 opens in the late nineteenth century when hundreds of American postgraduates sought advanced scholarly training in Europe, especially Germany. At a time when American universities lacked the library resources, laboratories, and research methods of Europe, ambitious young scholars crossed the Atlantic to obtain skills and credentials that aided them in securing academic positions in the United States. As a number of historians have shown, many of these men and, occasionally, women, became leaders in the professionalization of academic disciplines, the establishment of research universities, and social reform efforts in the United States. At the same time, however, they gained a new understanding of themselves, a more tolerant view of cultural difference, and a more skeptical sense of their national identity. Germany was the favored destination of these students abroad, and French educational reformers worked hard, but not very successfully, to make French universities more attractive to Americans. The outbreak of World War I and the eventual Franco-American alliance represented a golden opportunity for strengthening and transforming academic relations between the two countries.

The next chapter addresses the Albert Kahn Around-the-World Scholarships, a philanthropic initiative by a French banker to provide recent graduates with international experience to serve French national interests and to help solve global problems. Between 1898 and 1930, forty-nine French men and twenty-four French women, along with seventy-six men from Germany, Japan, Britain, Russia, and the United States, traveled the world on these scholarships. Focusing on French *boursiers'* (fellows) reports of the United States, and American fellows' accounts of Europe, this chapter charts how young French teachers assessed the role of France in the face of growing American economic, military, and cultural power. While most considered France to have an important role as a cultural and intellectual guide to the newer nation, women especially engaged in a real exchange of ideas regarding female education in the two countries. They saw much to emulate in educated American women, in contrast to the often disparaging views that French male travelers to the United States articulated. Charged with more explicitly internationalist objectives than the French *boursiers*, the fifteen American fellows were inspired by their travels to suggest ways of improving transnational cooperation and conflict resolution. Undaunted, even galvanized, by World War I, fellows from both countries acted to uphold Kahn's ideals through various organizations and publications and in their capacities as teachers during the 1920s. This little-known venture into educational exchange for national and international benefit—predating the better-known Rhodes Scholarships and Carnegie Endowment for International Peace projects—represents a successful precedent for subsequent governmental and nongovernmental practices.

Chapter 3 looks at the junior year abroad as an educational and international innovation directly inspired by World War I. After the war, private citizens, organizations, and colleges and universities in the United States supported study abroad in the interest of international understanding and world peace. In 1923 the University of Delaware launched the Foreign Study Plan, sending American undergraduates to study for a year in France to prepare them for careers in international business and the Foreign Service. Two years later Smith College started the Junior Year in France program, and other similar programs followed. During the 1920s and 1930s these two programs alone sent more than 1,200 undergraduates from all over the United States to study in France, and in 1928–29 estimated numbers of American students in France reached as high as 5,584. This chapter analyzes the evolution of the junior year abroad during the interwar years, including how student accounts of their personal and intellectual transformations helped shape the objectives and purposes of study abroad in American higher education and contributed to a new understanding of internationalism.

Significantly, the vast majority of American undergraduates studying in France in the 1920s and 1930s were women. Chapter 4 analyzes the unique experience of American women students who confronted gendered national stereotypes from both sides of the Atlantic during their junior year in France. They arrived in France indoctrinated with the idea of the French *jeune fille*—the submissive, chaste, sheltered daughter of the respectable bourgeoisie. In accordance with this notion, young American women were subjected to strict rules limiting their behavior and movement while studying in France. By contrast, their French hosts and, to some extent, the general French public, regarded young American women as excessively independent, outspoken, and even sexually promiscuous. Negotiating these two stereotypes led American women students to reassess American and French cultures in very particular ways and to construct original, individual feminine identities that reflected this new understanding, as well as newly acquired confidence and self-reliance from studying and living in France. Though unacknowledged by contemporaries and historians, women's participation in study abroad between the wars was crucial to its resumption after 1945.

As Chapter 5 indicates, a significant new development in study abroad after World War II was the involvement of the U.S. government, notably with the creation of the Fulbright academic exchange program and the GI Bill. Government officials in both France and the United States promoted study abroad in the aftermath of the war and in the Cold War era on behalf of their own, distinctive conceptions of national interest and national security. Yet these official goals by no means explain the enthusiasm of young French people and Americans for studying in the other country, motivated more by aspirations for cultural enhancement and professional advancement than cultural imperialism or anticommunism. Between 1956–57 and 1969–70, numbers of Americans studying in France rose from 1,252 to 6,219, while numbers of French students in the United States increased from 615 to 1,994—figures that are actually comparable considering that the overall population of the United States was roughly four times that of France. Paradoxically, the apolitical and non-ideological nature of study abroad actually served French assertions of cultural authority and American anticommunist goals better than other diplomatic and propagandistic efforts.

Chapter 6 explains how national politics and educational reforms impinged on educational exchanges in the 1960s and early 1970s to an extent not evident in earlier decades. By this time study abroad had established itself sufficiently so that in the United States especially, but also in France, many evaluations and surveys were conducted to assess the value of study abroad on a variety of measures—professional advantage, personal maturation, international goodwill, and so on. While such publications offered an overall favorable account of study abroad, relations between the governments of the United States and France were exceptionally tense under the presidency of Charles de Gaulle (1958–69). This fact alone did not staunch the transatlantic flow of students. Indeed, both French and American students expressed enthusiasm for the benefits of study abroad, sometimes in spite of and even because of negative attitudes toward the opposite country's policies. Study in France forced many American students to confront domestic issues of race relations and foreign policy, and these became the lens through which they articulated an American identity. Although politicization among students was global, more salient developments for French students and for study abroad involved reforms in higher education following the events of May 1968 that brought French universities and student life more in line with American practices. Whereas a century earlier Americans sought superior education in Europe, both Americans and Europeans acknowledged the merits, if not the superiority, of higher education in the United States. This decade of global political turbulence and frosty Franco-American relations ultimately expanded and strengthened the appeal and internationalist outcomes of study abroad.

The final chapter analyzes how sexuality figured in national imaginaries of the other throughout the twentieth century and the different ways that students confronted sexual fantasies and constructed social and sexual experiences on both sides of the Atlantic. Americans have long envisioned France as a land of sexual liberation and French men as inveterate seducers—images derived from travelers' accounts, French and American literature, veterans' stories, and movies. By contrast, while French authors commonly portrayed the United States as puritanical and averse to sensuous pleasures of all kinds, including food and drink, French people imagined American women as assertive, immoral, and even sexually promiscuous, perhaps because of the freedom of movement allowed to girls and unmarried young women and greater public visibility among married, middle-class American women. Both the power and the limitations of these stereotypes became evident as they shaped and were transformed by students' encounters with daily life. Additionally, American and French students abroad in the other country provide a rich source of information about comparative heterosocial practices and sexual norms, because, first, youth have a heightened sense of sexual awareness and discovery, and, second, as outsiders they are keen observers of intimate behaviors that may not be verbally analyzed, much less challenged, by insiders. This chapter makes clear how gender and sexuality inform international cultural relations at the levels of both discourse and practice.

Throughout this long period of Franco-American relations and changing objectives for study abroad on both sides of the Atlantic, the student experiences reveal a remarkable continuity. To be sure, particular developments in domestic politics, international relations, higher education, and youth culture inflected students' accounts of their study abroad sojourns. Nonetheless, persistent themes are a more acute awareness of national identity and a fairly in-depth understanding of and appreciation for cultural difference. This history of French and American governmental, institutional, and individual perspectives on study abroad affirms the importance of culture in international relations, and demonstrates how this particular form of cultural exchange simultaneously contributes to internationalism and to nationalism of a critical but no less patriotic sort. For anyone who has studied abroad or who works in the area of international academic programs, these findings are not new. But this long-term, comprehensive analysis of both sides of study abroad explains some of the changes as well as continuities in a project that has endured, developed, declined, and ultimately thrived over the course of a century wracked by wars, brutality, and shifting global power relations. Instead of Americanization and anti-Americanism as the dominant modes of Franco-American cultural relations, this history of study abroad narrates a relationship between equals, in which curiosity and fascination undergo reality checks, and lived experience transforms stereotypes into nuanced understanding. This work also suggests that other case studies of study abroad history might lend further support to today's current practices in a world rife with danger and fear, but also with hope and desire to overcome cultural misunderstandings and achieve greater tolerance and mutual respect.

§ 1 The American Quest for Knowledge and the French Quest for Americans, 1870–1919

John W. Burgess, political scientist and founder of the School of Political Science at Columbia University, wrote in his memoirs that in 1863 he pledged himself to a career in education with the intention of helping to avoid future wars and destruction. Graduated from Amherst College and enjoying his teaching appointment at Knox College in Illinois in the late 1860s, he nonetheless felt dissatisfied that he was not accomplishing much educationally. In his memoirs, he maintains that he said to himself: "Now is the time to interrupt your teaching and seek elsewhere the education in history, public law, and political science, which you have been vainly striving to secure in America." In 1871 he was en route to the University of Göttingen in Germany carrying a list of German scholars with whom he would study.[1] Other educated young men, and some women, in the United States shared this experience in the late nineteenth century. As Edward Alsworth Ross, professor of sociology at the University of Wisconsin, remembered of the time he was teaching in an Iowa prep school from 1886 to 1888: "I was happy in my work and setting but still restlessness grew upon me. I *must* have broader opportunities. The German University was then the loftiest thing on the educational horizon, so I resolved to be off to Germany."[2] Ross, too, made the journey to Europe, studying mostly in Berlin from 1888 to 1889.

So common was the practice of Americans spending a few years in Germany and elsewhere in Europe to pursue postgraduate studies that popular magazines offered guidance on the subject. In 1885 a *Popular Science Monthly* article titled "Studying in Germany" asserted that "there is a steadily growing class of Americans who visit Germany to spend from one to five years in study." The main reason for this was that "the center of the world's scholarship is there, and, if a young man knows that he wants learning, there is the place to get it at its best."[3] In an article published in *Century Magazine* in 1887, Morris B. Crawford wrote: "Now that multitudes of American college graduates annually migrate to Berlin, Leipzig, Göttingen, and Strasburg, it may not be out of place to call attention to some widespread misapprehensions concerning the charms and advantages to life in a German university town."[4] This popular migration of American graduate students to Germany was anathema to many French academics. But what could they do, as they also recognized the attraction of German universities?

As many historians have shown, in the nineteenth century Germany represented the acme of academic scholarship in a variety of fields in the sciences and humanities, and several thousands of American college graduates, mostly men, took courses or sought advanced degrees there to further their education and enhance their job prospects when they returned to the United States. Many of them contributed to the restructuring of American universities toward research and to the professionalization of academic disciplines. In the process a German academic model of empirical research and a seminar format of educational and scholarly discussion were adapted to American conditions.[5] The reformed American universities combined a more secular and scientific approach with the existing emphasis on moral guidance, according to historian Julie A. Reuben.[6] These institutional reforms accompanied significant social changes within and beyond the university that were all part of a broadly defined modernizing process. Konrad Jarausch asserts that universities in the United States and in Europe contributed to modernization in the late nineteenth and early twentieth centuries by enrolling more—and more diverse—students, expanding recruitment, and professionalizing newer fields, such as education, engineering, sciences, and social sciences. Jarausch argues that, because of the growing proportion of middle-class students, universities simultaneously contributed to social mobility and meritocracy, while still preserving traditional elites, culture, and status.[7]

Part of this modernization of higher education was the inclusion of women, and foreign study also played an important role. Like men, women also sought scientific training and advanced degrees in Europe that were unavailable in their own countries. For example, historian Thomas Neville Bonner charts the determination of American women to obtain medical instruction, degrees, and training in Europe when they were either barred from universities in the United States or limited to inferior women's medical colleges.[8] Because foreign students in Germany, Switzerland, and France were not required to hold that country's secondary school degree for admission into universities, and until these countries provided equal secondary education and degrees for all their citizens, foreign women were often the vanguard in gaining university access for women.[9]

Historians of higher education in the United States have emphasized the ways that study in Europe affected American institutions, professions, and scholarship in the nineteenth century. They are much less concerned with the dimensions of personal transformation and the effects of study abroad on American national identity and internationalism, with a few notable exceptions. In his book on the transatlantic circulation of ideas about social reform from the late nineteenth century to World War II, Daniel Rodgers touches on the sense of personal and social liberation that studying and living in a European country meant for young, educated Americans.[10] And Adam R. Nelson contends that study in Germany from 1850 to 1853 led American philologist William Dwight Whitney to advocate transnational cooperation in scholarship while simultaneously affirming his sense of American identity.[11] My own reading of Americans who studied in Europe from 1870 to World War I focuses on the ways that this experience fulfilled aspirations for social mobility and professional advancement, altered personal identities, and precipitated reflection on American and European cultures. Although motivations for study in Europe were primarily careerist, studying and living abroad also made some of these ambitious young Americans less provincial and more cosmopolitan. And women confronted particular challenges that men did not while pursuing similar educational and professional goals.

A second component to this examination of American study abroad from 1870 to 1918 is the semi-official French intervention. Although France was also on many academic itineraries, French educators regarded this American preference for Germany as a national affront, especially after the French defeat by the emerging German empire in 1871. Along with some American supporters, they proposed reforms for French universities to increase their appeal for students from the United States. These efforts intensified when World War I dramatically changed relations among the United States, France, and Germany. French academics capitalized on this transformation to draw American students away from presumably discredited German institutions and into French universities and thereby combat the German influence in American higher education. What began as a manifestation of French cultural imperialism actually led to a better understanding of and even appreciation for American higher education among French educators. In addition, American soldiers studying in France between the armistice of 1918 and the peace treaty of 1919 provided a foundation for a new kind of American student migration to France after the war. Thus, the history of Americans studying in Europe from 1870 to 1919 is inseparable from the history of German, French, and American international relations.

The transatlantic flow of American students to Europe in the late nineteenth and early twentieth centuries coincided with what historian Harvey Levenstein calls "the golden age of travel." He and other scholars have noted that technological improvements on steamships shortened the ocean voyage from two or three weeks before the American Civil War to about ten days in the 1870s and six days in the 1890s. At the same time capacity and comfort increased as the major transatlantic shipping lines introduced a second-class rate and accommodation between first-class luxury and steerage overcrowding. By the end of the nineteenth century, middle-class Americans could enjoy a safe, pleasant, and short voyage at an affordable price. For about $63.00 an American could purchase a second-class round-trip ticket to Europe, berth with one to three other passengers, and eat quite well in the ship's dining hall.[12]

Travel to Europe meant different things to different Americans in the late nineteenth and early twentieth centuries, and even particular countries, namely, France and Germany, represented distinctive attractions.[13] In the years before World War I, articles providing physical descriptions of France and Paris and about French literature and art proliferated in popular American magazines.[14] According to Levenstein, wealthy, upper-class Americans traveled to France to cultivate the high arts and society, while middle-class men sought pleasures of the senses, in contrast to middle-class women aspiring to cultural enrichment. Levenstein identifies this era as marking a general transition from cultural travel to leisure travel.[15] But unlike either cultural or leisure travelers, young, ambitious American graduate students journeyed across the Atlantic to enhance their academic careers and headed for Germany rather than France. For the most part, this generation of students abroad came from modest backgrounds: historian and educator Henry Johnson grew up in a small town in Minnesota; economist Richard T. Ely's father was a civil engineer, but his family lived and worked on a farm in upstate New York;

orphaned at age eight, sociologist Edward Alsworth Ross worked on family farms in Illinois as a child and young man. Travel to Europe was no lark for these men and others like them; rather, they approached study in Germany with the same forethought, concentration, and drive that characterized their entire life narratives of academic achievement.

James A. Harrison, a professor of Teutonic languages at the University of Virginia, noted in 1900 that American travelers to Germany and France divided into two extremely dichotomous groups. Whereas, Harrison states, "our student population, our elect young men, the bloom and flower of our masculine youth poured into Germany," France attracted "the fashionable, the frivolous, the modish, the voluptuary, [and] the sybarite."[16] Harrison's characterizations are overdrawn, and, in previous decades at least, hundreds of American doctors traveled to Paris to study French medical theories and practices.[17] In addition, Harrison's article is primarily about how French university reforms of 1896, as we will see below, completely changed this dichotomous pattern and drew more and different Americans to France. Among American academics, however, Germany was the place for serious study from around 1870 to 1914.

Many publications in the United States in the late nineteenth century recognized the popularity of study in Europe, especially Germany, and offered advice on how to negotiate the German university system and daily life. A supposed private, anonymous letter from an American student who succeeded in earning the highest degree of praise, *summa cum laude,* for his PhD work in chemistry, physics, and mineralogy at the University of Heidelberg in 1875 detailed the procedure for obtaining the degree. He wrote little of actual coursework and more about the administrative aspects and examination formats, because he was focused more on the degree than on anything else: "Not long after the commencement of my student-life here, I saw that it would be of great advantage to me in my scientific life to possess such a rank [PhD], which has recognized worth in all the world and is not obtained by friendship or favoritism, as is so often the case in America."[18] As he and others noted, studying in German universities was relatively easy in terms of admissions requirements and costs. Students with a diploma from an American college or university were admitted to attend lectures, though gaining degree candidacy was not automatic and entailed a specific application procedure and passing or waiving of the classics (Latin) examination. As one commentator wrote, "it is a fact that fewer difficulties beset the American in this quest [for a degree] than the German himself," because Germans had first to pass the secondary school (*gymnasium*) leaving examination, and competition for places in the university was fierce. Germans did not worry about Americans taking courses or even earning degrees because they would not compete for scarce positions in German academia.[19]

University study in Germany was easily accessible to American men, but the very different educational system presented pitfalls for the unwary. First, American students rarely knew enough German to follow lectures immediately on their arrival, and several months' study of the language alone was necessary for any meaningful coursework. Second, students in Germany were far more independent than their American counterparts; that is, class attendance was not required, and professor-student relations were distant, to say the least. These conditions meant that young American men were likely to congregate together in the most popular university town destinations (Berlin, Heidelberg, Leipzig, etc.) and spend too much of their unstructured time at concerts or in beer halls or coffee houses, often at the expense of learning German and studying their chosen subjects.[20]

One author warned parents that even the most "virtuous" and "industrious" young man might succumb to the unfamiliar freedom of student existence in Europe generally, in contrast to the United States: "He has also been accustomed to domestic and conventional restraints at home, which he will not feel in Europe." Noting that "the social instinct at this age is very strong," this author cautioned against providing American male students with too much money, because "in their anxiety to master the language they find a pretext for frequenting theaters, coffeehouses, clubs, and other places of public resort where those who spend most freely are always most welcome, and where they are beguiled into social alliances which in the main are to be deprecated."[21] For author Horace M. Kennedy, studying in Germany was a tradeoff for Americans, because German universities were "the center of the world's scholarship," but offered un-American (and contradictory) examples of overwork, authoritarianism, pedantry, excessive smoking and drinking, and immorality. Considering the overall value of studying in Germany, he concluded: "while the boy may lose promptness, alertness, manners, fluency in English, and even health, the man gains, besides knowledge, incentives and standards that may make him a better citizen."[22]

Successful American academics of the turn of the century often published memoirs of their lives, including study abroad as an important part of their careers. John W. Burgess, a political scientist who lived and studied in Germany from 1871 to 1873, modeled his own teaching after that of German university professors. As a professor at Amherst College, Burgess claimed that his students requested that he continue teaching them history after they graduated, which he did, despite faculty opposition, imitating his German mentors: "I followed in instructing them the methods of the German seminar, assigning to each a special field of investigation and bringing them together twice a week to hear the results of their researches and subject the same to discussion and inquiry by myself and the other members of the seminar." He then advised them all to go to Germany and continue their studies, which, according to Burgess, they did. Although he never realized his hope of transforming Amherst into a graduate school, he did have some success later, when he became a professor at Columbia Law School, by creating there a School of Political Science similar to those in Germany and in France.[23]

Sociologist Edward Alsworth Ross charted the excitement of his rapid and volatile intellectual growth while studying in Germany in 1888 and 1889. "I grew so fast intellectually," he wrote of his early days in Berlin, "that often on Sunday I found strange, even incomprehensible, the views I had entered in my diary the previous Sunday!"[24] In his memoir of 1939, Nicholas Murray Butler, who became president of Columbia University in 1902, emphasized the characteristics of several renowned German scholars he encountered in 1884–85, linking them to his subsequent involvement in higher educational reform:

> Imagine what it meant to an American youth who was planning to devote his life to scholarship and to university service, to come face to face with Mommsen, the historian of Rome, with Ernst Curtius, master of Greek archeology, with Wundt of Leipzig, who was revolutionizing psychology, with Klein of the same university, who had a notable group of young American mathematicians in his seminar, and to hear Vahlen at Berlin conduct his seminar in Latin![25]

He also noted the value of access to opera, theater, music, art, and the daily life of ordinary Germans that study abroad afforded young American men in the late nineteenth century. Acknowledging that "for half a century the German universities had been drawing to their libraries, lecture-rooms, and laboratories an increasing number of American youth," Butler nonetheless recommended that students take in Paris and French universities before departing Europe, because "the highly artistic and very subtle method of the French savant is a perfect complement to the patient and plodding meticulousness of the German *Gelehrter*."[26] Richard T. Ely claims that in 1877, "originally I had come to Germany to find the absolute truth," but that after studying philosophy at the University of Halle, he realized he lacked sufficient preparation, so he abandoned simultaneously the quest for truth and philosophy and moved to Heidelberg to study economics, where he successfully earned a PhD in 1879.[27] These prominent American academics did not doubt that the scholarly training they received in Europe (mostly in Germany) contributed to their successful careers after they returned to the United States, and many encouraged their own students to follow the same path.

Like these men, Martha Carey Thomas, future president of Bryn Mawr College, went to Europe to enhance her academic career prospects. Shortly after her arrival in 1879, she wrote to her mother, anticipating the import of her decision to study at the University of Leipzig: "I am sure three years in Germany will make the greatest difference in my whole power of work. I feel waked up to a new life and we are not yet in Leipzig."[28] After a few months in Leipzig, Thomas revealed not only her scholarly motivations but also her ambition behind study abroad. To her mother, she wrote: "Study, as thee knows, and influence are the two things I care about—these I can best obtain by being a professor in some women's college." To fulfill this goal, Thomas carefully plotted her pursuit of a degree in Germany in light of her knowledge of available positions in American women's colleges and the dearth of foreign degrees among applicants.[29]

Thomas confronted problems that men did not. She struggled to obtain permission from her father to travel to Europe for advanced study, writing to her friend Mary Garrett in 1879 after he had finally relented: "It made me see even with Father's liberality how tremendous a sacrifice it is for him to let me go—sacrifice of paternal responsibility, authority, traditional feeling about women, etc."[30] In 1879 she exchanged several letters with Andrew Dixon White, president of Cornell University and U.S. Minister Plenipotentiary to Berlin, regarding the admission of women to courses at the University of Leipzig, which was possible but uncertain. Although she and a few other women were admitted to university courses, Thomas found that the University had not yet granted a degree to a woman. Moreover, controversy over the admission of women generally erupted during Thomas's stay in Leipzig, deriving from fear among local officials that Russian women, if admitted to the University, would spread their radical, socialist ideas. When the leaders of Saxony appropriated to themselves the power of determining which women might study at the Leipzig University, and because of uncertainty about a degree, Thomas began looking for another German university to grant her the PhD degree, even though she was already working with professors at Leipzig. Her efforts at the University of Göttingen failed, so she and her companion moved to Zurich. Despite having to observe the particular regulations and standards of the Swiss university, and submitting her dissertation on philology to faculty whom she did not know, Thomas triumphed by earning a *summa cum laude* on her work in 1882, an honor rarely conferred and never before awarded to a woman.[31]

Thomas's sense of the value of a European degree for an academic career in the United States was affirmed in a series of articles published in the *Nation* in 1894. According to author J. B. S., studying in Germany was equally worthwhile for an American woman as for a man: "For her, as for him, the fact of having studied in Germany enhances—often quite disproportionately—her intellectual value in the estimation of those who have not done so, while, by those who have, it is accepted for what their own experience has made its worth to them. If she means to teach, her chances, like the man's, for a good position are by so much the more increased."[32] However, women's position in German universities was precarious. Although each state determined policy for its own university, J. B. S. notes that throughout Germany, "The woman student is not recognized as such except by courtesy. She is not recognized at all officially." J. B. S. details the process whereby a woman must personally cajole a university professor into allowing her to attend his lectures, cope with the astonishment and prejudices of men students, and risk being ejected from the university "if caught going into the lectures by any officer of the university or any member of its faculties who is hostile to the presence of women there."[33] Despite these difficulties, some American women persisted in their pursuit of learning and certification in Germany.[34] Writing to the *Nation* in response to J. B. S.'s articles, a reader, Adele Luxenberg of New York City, claims to have been a student at the University of Leipzig from 1889–93 and to have passed the final examination in geography administered by her professor. Luxenberg was an advocate for American women studying in Germany and opening up higher education to more women: "I can with good conscience encourage any woman who may be contemplating application to Leipzig. Every female student working together and in competition with men, helps to destroy old prejudices."[35]

Historian Patricia M. Mazón credits the German women's movement more than foreign women students with challenging the corporatist and nationalist structures that inhibited the admission of women into German universities from 1865 to 1914. She supports this position by noting widespread hostility among Germans to Russians seeking higher education in Germany because so many of them were Jewish.[36] However, Natalia Tikhonov and Pierre Moulinier argue in their recent works that foreign women students, including those from Eastern Europe and from the United States, were the vanguard in normalizing coeducation in Switzerland and France, respectively.[37] A surge of American and Russian women earned medical degrees in Switzerland and France in the 1870s, and by 1894 J. B. S., writing in the *Nation*, called the University of Paris "the paradise *par excellence* of the woman student" because it was "open to her on precisely the same terms as to men."[38] J. B. S. exaggerated here, and explained later in the article that only the public courses were completely open to women in French universities. Moulinier asserts that available statistics on French university students reveal that the numbers of women students increased tenfold after 1890, but both he and historian Carole Christen-Lécuyer indicate that women in French universities confronted prejudice and other barriers and that more substantial increases in the number of women students occurred only after World War I.[39] Despite these barriers, a small but steady stream of American women crossed the Atlantic to study in German, Swiss, and French universities and earn credentials that helped secure their professional success in the United States.

While American women and men regarded Germany as preeminent for scholarship in the sciences and humanities until World War I, in one other area France was more attractive than Germany as a place for advanced study, and that was in the arts—painting, sculpture, architecture, music, and dance. It is impossible to know exactly how many Americans studied art in France, because although the state Ecole des Beaux-Arts kept records of enrolled students, many private academies, like the Académie Julian, also provided instruction, especially for women who were barred from life drawing in the state institution.[40] Like American students in sciences and the humanities, those in art came to Europe primarily for training and credentialing. One French reporter noted in 1898 that American women art students were so exclusively focused on their careers and status that they avoided learning French or partaking in any form of French culture and life. Describing them as "cold, practical, and self-centered," in contrast to more idealistic students from Eastern Europe, Aimée Fabrègue claimed that their sole aim in coming to Paris was to get "lessons from the best masters in order to return home draped in prestige." Far from seeking to learn French and learn about France and French people, these American women sought their own kind and tried to reproduce American foods and habits in France. Many stayed at a club in Paris (the current Reid Hall) with their compatriots, and Fabrègue expressed dismay at their indifference to France, noting that after eighteen months residing at the rue de Chevreuse, one young woman did not even know the names of the French newspapers to which the club subscribed.[41] Not all American art students in France were so single-minded in their pursuit of training at the expense of learning something about French culture (American sculptor Augustus Saint-Gaudens was able to write in French and almost joined the French army during the Franco-Prussian War in 1870).[42] Nonetheless, art historian Jocelyne Rotily asserts that an important outcome of study in France for American artists before and especially after World War I was the development of an American national artistic identity.[43]

Career enhancement was the primary motive for young Americans to study in Europe before World War I, but this experience also led some to alter their lifestyles and reflect on cultural difference and national identity. Psychologist G. Stanley Hall traveled to Europe twice, once from 1868 to 1871 and then again from 1876 to 1879 before securing an academic position at Johns Hopkins University in 1881. Not only did study in Germany satisfy Hall's desire for learning and credentialing, but also it liberated him from narrow, religious provincialism. "Germany almost remade me," he wrote in 1923 of his first stay there in the late 1860s. "It gave me a new attitude toward life. . . . I fairly reveled in a freedom unknown before," he continued.[44] Specifically, he attributed his enjoyment of leisure on Sundays, moderate drinking of wine and beer, a more generous conception of religion, and appreciation of women and heterosexual awakening to his stay in Germany. Describing his close friendship with two young, unmarried German women, Hall wrote: "This experience had a profound effect upon my character. I realized that I was a man in the full normal sense of that word." Hall felt that he developed in Germany "a capacity for sentiment, *Gemüt* or the power of abandonment to the moods, feelings, ideas, and companions of the present moment."[45] Economist Richard T. Ely, who studied in Germany from 1877 to 1880, echoed this observation and even suggested that Americans could benefit from "the German manner of living." Quoting one of his letters from Germany, he wrote: "In America we would undoubtedly be healthier and handsomer if we knew how to live. If we could ever learn that when God gave us a faculty for enjoyment, pleasure and means of gratifying it, He meant we should enjoy ourselves."[46]

Cosmopolitanism and intellectual independence were related outcomes of study in Europe for many Americans. Richard T. Ely wrote of his stay in Heidelberg: "I met people from all parts of the world and learned to take what I called a 'cosmopolitan view of things in general.' I found that 'all the good in the world is not confined to the United States.'"[47] Quoting from the diary he kept while studying in Berlin in 1888–89, Edward Alsworth Ross noted many changes in his thinking: "I am losing some of that boundless confidence in the omniscience of our age that characterizes every American." Ross also noted the achievement of intellectual independence from studying abroad: "I see that I have attained my spiritual majority. I have found my own path and from now on no one will ever be my master." He wrote: "The world is under my eye and I shall see for myself."[48]

Like other young Americans of his time, writer Lincoln Steffens "got the religion of scholarship and science" while he was an undergraduate at the University of California at Berkeley.[49] But in his autobiography, he wrote that he became somewhat disillusioned with both during his studies in Germany from 1889 to 1891: "All I got out of my year of German psychology was a lead into biology on the one hand and into sociology on the other, a curiosity to hear and see what the French thought they knew about such matters, and best of all, a training in the experimental methods."[50] Steffens did, indeed, go to Paris and took courses at the Sorbonne, but it was the greater social freedom he and other Americans felt living in Germany and especially in France that he remembered most fondly. While studying in Germany, he met an American woman who became his wife, and both moved to Paris for Steffens to continue his studies. Comparing the two countries, he wrote, "We enjoyed life in Germany . . . but Paris was somehow a release from some sort of repression." Although married, Steffens took pleasure in the appearance of an unsanctioned domestic arrangement that he found common among his mostly artist friends in Paris: "I had a home, and some of our friends had homes; not all lawful, but warm, happy, domestic."[51]

Whether they came to Europe to study philology, social science, art, or science, Americans generally deemed the experience worthwhile academically, and sometimes even essential to a successful career. While the cultural differences between Europe and the United States seemed threatening to some—namely, sociability involving the pleasures of food and alcoholic drink and many other delights of the senses, such as art, music, theater, and opera any day of the week, including Sunday—others found them liberating and representative of a positive alternative to more work-oriented and puritanical American cultural values. In different ways, study abroad internationalized these individuals, usually inspiring them to reform higher education in the United States by adapting and incorporating European research methods and pedagogy. Some went considerably further, such as Nicholas Murray Butler, who maintained strong ties with Europe throughout his long career, notably promoting educational exchange and cooperation. In 1907 he became president of the American branch of the transnational peace organization, Conciliation internationale, and he influenced Andrew Carnegie to establish the Carnegie Endowment for International Peace in 1910, for which he shared the Nobel Peace Prize in 1931 with Jane Addams. Economics professor Richard T. Ely took pride in his former students who became leaders in international affairs, especially U.S. President Woodrow Wilson. However, he asserted that Wilson "did not know the world—least of all, the European world," an understanding that Ely claims came from his study abroad. "This gave me an insight into world affairs which I often wished that Wilson could have had before he was plunged into them."[52] But as American universities improved their libraries and laboratories, and adopted more rigorous research methods, study abroad became less important as an academic credential.

As early as 1899 several professors in fields of science and engineering offered differing opinions on the value of postgraduate study in Germany. They agreed that American universities provided excellent training, perhaps just within the last twenty to twenty-five years. Study in Germany could certainly provide a broader understanding of a subject and perhaps a deeper sense of "the spirit of scientific research." But by and large the value of such work was less in mastery of the discipline than in general culture. A professor of organic chemistry asserted that "residence in a foreign country . . . and the opportunity for travel . . . serve in many ways to enlarge the young man's experience, broaden his ideas, and increase his general information and culture."[53] The holder of a PhD in history from the University of Munich wrote in 1902: "Whereas twenty years ago and more it was the highest ambition of our students to obtain their second, or post-graduate degree, from Heidelberg, Göttingen, or Berlin, it is now, I believe, the desire of the majority merely to supplement

American training by a longer or shorter stay in Germany after the completion of their studies in this country."[54] Study abroad, then, was still deemed a positive thing, but more for the general cultural enhancement it provided than for essential professional skills.

While American motivations for and perceptions of study in Germany were gradually changing, French educators were fixated on the American preference for German higher education. They considered their own scholarship and pedagogy to be as good as if not superior to those of Germany, but they acknowledged the greater appeal of German universities for foreign students generally and Americans in particular. Germany drew American postgraduates for several reasons, including the reputation of German universities for scientific scholarship, the network of American students at different German universities that provided familiarity and useful information, the ease of admission into university courses, and the possibility of earning a doctorate after two to three years.[55] For much of the nineteenth century and especially after the German victory over France in the Franco-Prussian War of 1870–71, French academics sought to modernize French universities and challenge the domination of Germany.[56] They believed that modernizing French higher education would draw foreign students away from Germany in favor of France and thereby enhance national prestige. Historians including Alain Dubosclard and François Chaubet have shown that in the late nineteenth and early twentieth centuries many in and close to the French government asserted that French cultural strength might compensate for military weakness in international relations.[57] What were the strategies that French leaders proposed to woo American students? How were they implemented? And what were the results of this battle for the hearts and minds of educated Americans?

In 1895 an American sympathetic to French higher education, Harry J. Furber, sent a report to Octave Gréard, rector of the University of Paris, with recommendations for making French universities more appealing to American students. He suggested that French universities require only one exam at the end of the course and that they provide a list of American colleges and universities whose BA degrees would allow admission into French universities. Furber also noted that because most Americans' goals for studying in Europe were to acquire knowledge and earn a degree so they could successfully compete for a university position in the United States, some attainable certification of academic accomplishment was essential. Furber wrote: "When it is remembered that many of the

Americans in Europe intend in time to apply for professorships at home, it will be seen that this patent of successful effort while abroad is something more to them than a mere ornament."[58] Furber's report sparked responses in the French press, affirming his contention that it was in France's national interest to reform higher education so that future American academics would study in France and challenge the predominantly German orientation that was being perpetuated in American universities. Echoing Furber's recommendations for offering a diploma and simplifying the course structure, a French faculty member added in a report to the Paris University Council in 1896 that a friendlier and more welcoming attitude toward American students would also encourage them to choose France over Germany.[59]

University reforms in 1896 addressed some, though not all, of these recommendations and were part of a larger modernization effort detailed by historians George Weisz and Christophe Charle. Of particular relevance to study abroad was the ability of universities to create new degrees and courses and to exercise some control over private funds.[60] While these changes were modest, they achieved the goal of increasing the number of foreign students, and they contributed significantly to the general increase in the French student population before World War I.[61] Whereas in 1900 there were 1,799 foreign students attending French universities, that number rose to 4,818 in 1908 and to 6,188 in 1914; at the time of World War I, foreigners constituted 19 percent of the Parisian student population.[62] Faculties of science, letters, medicine, and pharmacy created new doctoral degrees that were easier to obtain than a state doctorate but that would not allow the holder to practice a profession in France. In this way the universities made it easier for foreigners to earn degrees but avoided additional competition for scarce positions within France. A certificate of French studies was created in 1899 exclusively for foreign students, and in 1908 a diploma of university studies represented a higher level of achievement but below that of a university doctorate.[63]

Additional practices marked French universities' commitment to attracting more foreign students. Publicity for French universities increased, and updated guides for foreign students were published on a regular basis. Many organizations to help foreign students in France were established, notably the Patronage Committee for Foreign Students at the Sorbonne in 1891. Organizations for specific nationalities and fields of study were also created, including the following ones targeting Americans: the

Franco-American Committee (1895), the American Association of Arts in Paris (1896), and an Office of Scientific Information established by the Paris medical faculty especially for North American students (1899). Universities benefited from the creation in 1883 of a private organization, the Alliance Française, which established centers all over the world for the teaching and learning of French. After 1900 French universities established scholar and professor exchanges with foreign universities, including Harvard University, Columbia University, and the University of Chicago.[64]

One American who benefited from the French university reforms and developed a positive attitude toward French higher education was Henry Johnson, an educator. While working on a postbaccalaureate degree at Columbia University, Johnson was granted permission and one year's credit for taking courses in France and Germany for a comparative study of research and education. He arrived in Paris in 1904 armed with a letter of introduction to Professor Charles V. Langlois, a paleographer, and was admitted into both open and closed courses at the Sorbonne. Open courses were, in fact, open to the public, and often gathered large crowds in big lecture rooms. Despite the fact that some of that crowd included persons looking for a warm place to sleep rather than intellectual enlightenment, Johnson interpreted the popularity of certain lectures as evidence "that interest in intellectual things was widely distributed in France."[65] Johnson was particularly impressed with Langlois's approach to teaching and scholarship. He distributed original manuscripts in Greek, Latin, Italian, and English to students and called on them to perform historical and textual analyses. "The ease with which the students did this amazed me," Johnson wrote. "They had a kind of scholarship which I had never before seen in action." He also noted the pedagogy of questioning students during their oral presentations in historian Charles Seignobos's closed research seminar: "The standards were severe and the criticism was the frankest and most fearless that I had ever heard. In the United States it would have been regarded as brutal."[66]

Johnson was less impressed with history courses he took in Berlin, finding one professor in error and unwilling to be corrected on the facts of education in the United States and another who assumed too little knowledge on the part of his students, though this was admittedly an introductory or review course in history for *gymnasium* students. He expressed dismay or scorn at an underlying Prussian assumption that primacy went to the strong, even in daily social behavior, such as boarding a streetcar.

This would no doubt have gratified French university reformers. But were they succeeding in combating German influence in American higher education and appealing to American students to forsake Germany for France? Johnson proclaims that on his return to New York harbor, he had this thought: "Having looked at Europe, I came back thanking God that I was an American."[67]

Johnson's expression of patriotism might reflect the fact that American universities had developed such that they were indeed competitive with those in Europe. French academics became increasingly aware of this as more of them visited the United States and taught courses in American universities. They were no less committed to combating Germany's sway over Americans, and a better understanding of American universities and students led to additional proposals for attracting American students to France. The repetition and expansion of recommendations for appealing to American students reveal both the difficulties of coordinating two very different higher education systems and a growing appreciation for the strengths of American universities. In short, even as French academics sought to increase French cultural influence in the United States, they engaged in a real cultural exchange between France and the United States, whether they intended it or not.

A persistent theme in French proposals to attract American students is publicizing admission requirements and university course offerings. Paul Boyer, a French professor of Oriental languages, reported to the rector of the University of Paris in 1904 that he found American university presidents very receptive to sending Americans to French universities to study subjects not yet available in the United States. For this actually to occur, he recommended that rectors of French universities send multiple copies of course offerings and admissions requirements to American university presidents for distribution among faculty and students.[68]

Gilbert Chinard, a Frenchman who taught French at the University of California, was well versed in American student life, and in 1916 he recommended the following practices to facilitate American student enrollment in French universities: accept an identification card rather than a birth certificate and end the requirement of an American bachelor's degree; provide French language instruction, as well as translators for courses popular among Americans; organize an information service for foreign students run by French students, and provide updated course listings; and arrange comfortable and welcoming housing accommodations. Chinard, like other French academics who had traveled or lived in the United

States, was convinced that Americans were favorably disposed to France and to the possibility of studying in France and that French universities needed only to accommodate some basic American expectations acquired after several decades of experiences in Germany. However, Chinard, more than some others, recognized how much more engaged students were in university life in the United States, in contrast to France, as well as the importance of nonacademic aspects of education, such as housing. American students, he wrote, were "sentimental, despite their athletic appearance; [French] pensions or rooms that they can find in a hotel repel them. They must know where to go when they arrive in Paris."[69]

In contrast to Chinard's practical suggestions for addressing American students' expectations about higher education as a life experience, not just a course of study, French professors Gustave Lanson and Maurice Caullery presented the national differences in French and American universities as complementary and hence requiring a kind of philosophical as well as practical accommodation. These men based their analyses largely on their experiences teaching at Columbia University and Harvard University, respectively. In a 1912 book Lanson, a professor of French literature at the Sorbonne, claims that American academics were finally realizing the limitations of German erudition at the very moment that they were endowing American universities with a purpose of social unification. That is, because the pursuit of wealth and material well-being was so successful in the United States, intellectual leaders saw a need to divert some of that energy toward the cultivation of ideas and arts. They anticipated that American universities would introduce "more idealism into the strenuous life of this multitude feverishly occupied in earning money or displaying money already earned." And in this project Lanson asserts that American academics perceived an important role for France with its artistic and humanistic traditions.[70]

A different complementarity between French and American higher education was discerned by biology professor Maurice Caullery, who published his views about American universities and scientific life in 1917. In his book he noted that a striking difference between French and American universities was the intense individualism characteristic of France in contrast to the sense of community cultivated in higher education in the United States. Caullery saw much to admire in the American practice of scientific collaboration and in the organization of former students into alumni associations. He, along with French academics who reviewed his book, suggested reforms to improve and modernize

French universities, such as establishing research centers in Paris so that academics could share ideas, integrating applied sciences into university science studies, and forming alumni associations to foster institutional loyalty.[71]

In their efforts to reform French higher education to appeal to American students, Caullery, Lanson, and Chinard found particular features of American higher education well worth imitating, or at least adapting, for French universities. For example, Lanson thought that French academics could learn much from the United States in terms of effective teaching and of establishing a balance between authority and freedom. Thus, as much as Lanson advocated the training of accomplished and effective teachers of French to educate Americans in the United States, he nonetheless cautioned French academics and educators not to delude themselves into thinking that they might "Frenchify" the United States: "It is not a question of establishing the empire of our language, our tastes, and our practices." Rather, Lanson maintained that the task of French higher education is to help Americans define themselves: "We are dealing with a great people that knows and esteems itself; the task is to help it attain its own ideal, to be what it wants to be, according to its own conception of its character and destiny."[72]

Within the French government itself, Charles Petit-Dutaillis, as director of the National Office of French Universities and Schools (Office national des universités et écoles françaises—ONUEF) created by the French parliament in 1910, had the job of promoting French education abroad and the education of foreigners in France. He shared Lanson's belief that spreading French culture and understanding other national education systems went hand in hand. It was obvious to him that "all the procedures that we employ to make France known abroad also help us to understand other countries." According to Petit-Dutaillis, it was in the best interest of French national education to accommodate international students, for, as he asserted in 1917, "the best publicity" for the value of French higher education "is produced by foreigners when they are satisfied with the education they received [in France]."[73] Also in 1917, another commentator, L. Houllevigue, reiterated the need for reforms to attract foreign students when the war ended and ensure that study in France was a positive experience. The ideal Houllevigue presented for the young foreigner who lives and studies in France was that "France became his second country, no less dear because she will not have chased the first one from his heart."[74]

For these French educators and officials, promoting French higher education was vital to French national interest, even if it entailed deviating from traditional French educational practices. In his report Chinard begged the rector's pardon for "wanting to 'Americanize' the Sorbonne" by involving French students in providing an information service for foreign students and in securing suitable housing for them, but the stakes were high. Chinard justified these unorthodox recommendations by arguing that the war against Germany and the possibility of the United States joining the allies had the potential to reverse decades of German domination in American higher education: "We have a unique opportunity to regain in one fell swoop all the ground we have lost in terms of influence in the United States for the past sixty years." However, Chinard took nothing for granted, and he raised the specter that, if changes did not occur, Americans might well return to German universities: "It is to be feared that if these special measures are not taken, [American] good will might dissipate, and as memories of the war fade, Germany might regain its university clientele."[75]

World War I lent urgency to reformers' efforts to accommodate foreign students, and especially Americans, in French universities. Before 1917, French academics, like French government leaders, pressed the case of a Franco-American shared history of liberal republicanism, in contrast to German authoritarianism, militarism, and aggression, hoping to engage the United States in the war on the side of the allies. Once the United States entered the war, reforms were even more necessary to prepare for the anticipated flood of American students after the war ended and to prevent their return to German universities. Additionally, Maurice Caullery wrote in an article in the *Harvard Graduates' Magazine* that after the war, isolationism would no longer be possible for the United States and that "it is, then, very important that the more cultivated part of your [American] youth should be acquainted with intellectual Europe and its tendencies," meaning in particular Britain and France rather than Germany.[76] The first opportunity to install Americans in French universities occurred after the armistice of November 11, 1918, when the vast majority of American soldiers remained in France, awaiting transport home that finally occurred for most in August 1919.[77]

Originally planned by the Department of Education of the Y.M.C.A., and with a professor John Erskine of Columbia University acting as a liaison between the Americans and the faculty of the University of Paris, the educational program shifted in April 1919 to the direct control of the

United States Army.[78] Responding to urgent requests from the minister of Public Education and the rector of the University of Paris, Charles Cestre and Emile Legouis, both of whom had experience teaching in the United States and were members of the Faculty of Letters of the University of Paris, drew up a detailed program of instruction specifically oriented to the needs and abilities of American soldiers in November 1918. Earlier, provincial universities in Nancy, Toulouse, Grenoble, Lyon, and Montpellier had catered to foreign students with special programs that supported their emphases in industrial and commercial fields.[79] The war finally pressured the University of Paris to make changes necessary to accommodate foreign students, especially Americans.[80] Recognizing the importance of housing American students, Cestre and Legouis's report drew on provincial examples of recruiting local families to house foreigners. It noted the need for lodgings that would both satisfy American concerns and provide the means for learning French: "We must help them establish themselves with guarantees of a healthy and comfortable life, surrounded with moral safeguards to which American opinion attaches the highest importance, in a good French atmosphere and with all opportunities to practice conversation in our language." The University of Paris would take responsibility for advertising the need for host families and would process applications. The report also suggested that the volunteer Ladies' Committee should be expanded, and members could help with the recruitment of host families and visit the homes of prospective hosts.[81]

The report also explained that few soldiers, assuming most were in the midst of an American undergraduate education, knew enough French to take regular French university courses. But they would want to take courses that would help them toward the completion of their American BA or BS degrees and that would involve different faculties (schools) of the University (law, sciences, letters, or medicine). The authors anticipated that American professors serving in France could teach courses in English in their own specialties. They also assumed that some American soldiers would be interested in taking special courses intended to teach them French language and civilization. Soldiers would be divided into two groups, reflecting their ability in French—elementary and superior—with appropriate courses for each level of competency. While *lycée* professors could teach courses for the elementary group that would concentrate on grammar, vocabulary, writing, analyzing authors, conversation, and phonics, and would include written exercises, for the latter group Cestre and Legouis proposed courses taught by university faculty in French history; medieval, classical, and contemporary French literature; geography; the history of ideas; phonetics and language; and the history of art. They included additional courses in English on English civilization, literature, and linguistics. Given that Americans were used to paying tuition costs in the United States, the authors had no qualms about charging them for the proposed courses to pay for faculty and other administrative expenses.[82]

From January through June 1919, some 5,000 Americans took courses in French universities in Paris and in the provinces. Accounts of soldiers' experiences in French universities differ, and, not surprisingly, one by French academic Celestin Bouglé recounts only the most positive results, asserting that American soldiers "joyously applied themselves to being students of France." According to Bouglé, the experience of seeing the French overcome great odds in the war led American soldiers to realize that "France of the risqué novels [*des romans demi-mondains*] is not the real France," and they hungered to learn about the "real" France.[83] Stephen Bush, an American from the University of Iowa, was impressed that the combination of two different national education systems in Paris worked as smoothly as it did and quickly accommodated some 2,000 student/soldiers of varying abilities and interests, for which he credited French flexibility and American adaptability. He also noted that many socially prominent Parisian families opened their homes to American students, much against the usual practice of reserving domestic privacy for family and close friends.[84]

Drawing on the cases of Toulouse and Paris, Bouglé noted that a small minority of American students was sufficiently versed in French to undertake serious research and study in their field of specialization. The vast majority concentrated on learning basic French, and a smaller number took courses in general culture, science, law, or letters. To ease the way for students, printed lecture notes were distributed before the large lectures delivered by University of Paris faculty, and an additional question period was added to the weekly lectures. According to Bouglé, these question periods garnered large audiences, beyond just students, and revealed American students to be diligent and curious about their studies. Y.M.C.A. educators monitored students' progress with examinations and provided cultural and educational activities during the Easter holiday. Although conclusions about Americans' reactions to French universities were premature, Bouglé observed that they found material conditions of

French universities impoverished compared to the United States, and missed the playing fields essential to American colleges and universities. He hoped, however, that they appreciated the humanism, artistry, and precision of French pedagogy, and he was optimistic that the courses and organizations established for the American soldiers would persist to accommodate other foreign students and even beginning French students who were finding their way around a university for the first time.[85]

An American view was more skeptical, but nonetheless favorable. In a 1920 article, Robert J. Menner wrote that the majority of men he knew among American soldiers in France knew very little French: "A friend of mine sat through eight classes in law for as many hours a week without understanding a single word except *Jules César*. He is one of many." Nonetheless, he admired the French professors who continued and even resorted to pantomime in order to try to teach American soldiers: "They persisted heroically in their efforts to make us talk and write French, in spite of a general lassitude, not to call it laziness, on the part of soldiers who were tired out physically by the hard knocks of war, and benumbed intellectually by the deadening monotony of the armistice." Menner ventured that French professors were better than those in the United States because they were fewer and selected on the basis of their scholarly accomplishments.[86]

Menner thought that from an educational perspective the effort to teach American soldiers in French universities was limited, but that it was nonetheless worthwhile: "Yet it is certain that a better understanding of French customs and conceptions, and a real friendship for the French people, were the results accomplished, rather than the acquisition of any definite knowledge or the completion of interrupted scholastic careers."[87] Much of this improved understanding occurred outside of the classroom, for American soldiers played games, performed plays, and printed newspapers to communicate aspects of American university life to their French hosts. Menner suggested that French people might wonder if students ever did anything academic at American universities, but the soldiers had an answer for that. They took up a collection to pay for scholarships to French students to study in the United States, "prompted by a genuine desire to maintain friendly relations between the students of the two countries, and also by the proud feeling . . . that there was something which a new country like America might teach an old country like France." Menner was aware that French authorities hoped that this experiment in cross-cultural education would incite more Americans to study in French universities, but he claimed that American universities had developed so much that it was no longer necessary for students to travel to Europe for training that was available in the United States. From his perspective, high academic standards would not draw Americans to France, but, rather, the opportunity to understand French people and culture. Asserting that few soldiers he knew intended to return to France for further education, Menner wrote, "Academic training had been the least important result of their four months at a French university; for through the medium of their universities they had learned to know and to admire the French people."[88]

A July 1919 letter of thanks from Colonel Samuel Lloyd, the American military commander in charge of education, to the vice-rector of the University of Paris expressed the colonel's hope for continued educational exchanges toward mutual cultural appreciation as well as advanced study. Indicating that he was a teacher of medicine and had traveled to medical schools in Europe before the war, Colonel Lloyd wrote: "I am still hoping that out of this short period of association between American students and French teachers, there may grow an international exchange both in faculties and students that will eventually lead to an internationalization of teacher and taught." He went on to assert that a brief visit to Germany revealed an effort already under way there "to try and win back the students who before the war thronged their clinics," and he hoped that the University of Paris "will in the near future so organize work along the lines of medical sciences that there can be no question about the university which we may recommend our students to visit."[89]

Because these special courses ended in the summer of 1919 and only an estimated 1,000 soldiers actually enrolled in them in Paris, historian Martha Hanna interprets the project as less than successful in terms of filling the University of Paris with American men, though it did open the way eventually for more French women to enroll by precipitating reforms in secondary education for girls. Appropriately skeptical of the different sets of statistics on exactly how many American soldiers enrolled in courses at French universities in 1919, Hanna overlooks numbers for all of France; her analysis focuses on Paris only.[90] According to Celestin Bouglé, the total number of American soldiers studying throughout France in 1919 was 5,867, including 1,711 at the Sorbonne in Paris, 1,107 at the University of Toulouse, and a few hundred each at many other provincial universities.[91] A different report counted 1,223 American soldiers at the University of Toulouse, taking a number of courses, including elementary French and more specialized topics in literature, history, and law, especially designed for them in cooperation with their wishes and an American commander.[92] In addition, as Stephen Bush indicated, the project of educating a large and disparate number of Americans in French institutions of higher education was unprecedented and potentially valuable as an educational experiment.

Based on monitoring reports, Bush concluded that ten students of music and eighty-five of art were completely satisfied with their studies, and, in these fields, language was not a serious barrier to learning. The results were mixed with those who flocked to courses at the Alliance Française, as their language abilities and motivations ranged widely and classes were overcrowded. Although some students were disappointed, having expected to pursue their specializations in courses taught in English, Bush concluded that overall the results were good in that the majority of students improved their understanding of spoken and written French. Students who took courses in the social sciences, politics, and business were generally out of their element, though some claimed to have benefited nonetheless from classes at the Ecole interalliée des hautes études sociales. Eighty-three engineers worked hard in their various courses and appreciated the thoroughness of French technical education, especially in mathematics and physics, but they preferred the more practical training of the United States in contrast to the theoretical orientation of France, though such an evaluation suggests a high degree of understanding on the part of these students. The most successful area was law, much to the surprise of Bush, who anticipated that national differences would be insurmountable. He attributed this to exceptionally fine French law professors and dedicated American law students. Courses in French civilization produced mixed results, as the number of students attending was particularly large—375—and difficult to monitor. Overall, Bush evaluated the entire semester as successful, despite an occasional dissenting voice, and found proof in the soldiers' collection for a scholarship fund as a token of thanks: "The vast majority of students were [sic] very enthusiastic and often made extravagant statements on the benefits they gained from their short stay at the University. We find excellent proof of such feelings in the gesture of students from each detachment who took up a collection to give a scholarship to each of the French universities that offered their hospitality." He concluded that, "this effort proved that Americans with only a modest command of the French language can nonetheless take on any type of studies in a French university."[93]

Charles Cestre, who taught English literature at Harvard for a semester after the war and represented the French Minister of Education at other academic functions in the United States, also saw opportunities for women in study abroad in the postwar situation. Noting that France could hardly spare its few remaining men to teach French in the United States, Cestre opined that such work was ideal for educated French women: "A teaching career represents one of the most desirable opportunities for young women of the educated class." Even before the war ended, American colleges and universities offered scholarships to French women to study and to teach French in American universities. According to a communication from the vice-rector of the University of Paris in 1919, some 140 young French women benefited from these scholarships to study and work in the United States in 1918, though he reports that seven or eight had given cause for complaints, mostly because they failed to adapt to American university conditions. This and other documents suggest that officials were concerned about recruitment and selection but that the vast majority of scholarship recipients earned good reports from the American donor institutions.[94] For his part, Cestre assumed that patriotism, along with a shortage of jobs in France after demobilization, would motivate more French women to learn English, earn their degrees, and then pursue permanent teaching careers in the United States. Anticipating that a qualified French graduate could easily become a professor at an American women's college or coed university, Cestre concluded: "There could be no better apostolic work than that of spreading French influence in a country that is already so attached to France."[95] Unfortunately for Cestre, this particular component of French cultural diplomacy would not materialize as he hoped, due in part to gendered practices of the French bourgeoisie and negative views of American women, as we will see in Chapter 4.

Much had changed for American students and in French universities from the 1870s through World War I. Throughout the nineteenth century Americans traveled to Europe, and especially to Germany, for advanced study that was unavailable in the United States and for degrees or certification that would enhance their academic (or artistic) career prospects in the United States. For some, study abroad also entailed a cultural awakening, a sense that in addition to scholarship, Europe offered a more leisured and cultivated lifestyle that might constructively soften the hard edges of American Puritanism and its work ethic. For others, study abroad marked the beginning of a lifetime of transatlantic exchanges and direct or indirect involvement in international affairs. As American higher education became more research oriented, study abroad became less necessary for credentialing and more important for learning about other cultures.

While an influential minority of educated Americans was learning from and about Europe, academic and government leaders in France discussed and implemented measures to expand French cultural influence abroad and to encourage more Americans to study in French universities. University reforms in the 1890s contributed to growth in the numbers of foreign students in French universities, and faculty exchanges in the first decade of the twentieth century helped French academics understand American universities and the expectations of American students. This knowledge motivated a flurry of proposals to attract Americans to French universities, especially after the outbreak of World War I, which French academics saw as a complete discrediting of German values and practices. In anticipation of hordes of American students deserting Germany for France after the war, French officials and university faculty willingly offered courses and accommodation for American soldiers in the spring of 1919. Although this effort affected, at most, some 5,800 men, it provided an enduring framework for an entirely new approach to study abroad that materialized after the war—the junior year abroad.

Dedicated to spreading French cultural influence throughout the world, including in the United States, French educators had to learn something about American higher education in order to appeal successfully to American students. In so doing, they encountered new ideas and practices that some hoped could improve French institutions. A visionary French philanthropist furthered this process of educational cultural exchange by donating money to the University of Paris for student travel scholarships to serve both the national interest and international understanding and cooperation. The complex mingling of nationalism and internationalism in study abroad is evident in the goals and the results of Albert Kahn's Around-the-World Scholarships, a surprisingly little-known predecessor of many private and public efforts to support study abroad for internationalist purposes.

§ 2 Making Internationalists?

The Albert Kahn Around-the-World Scholars' Reports on France and the United States, 1898–1930

Between 1898 and 1930 young French *lycée* professors or students about to earn advanced degrees in preparation for a teaching career might have seen annual announcements from the rector of the University of Paris regarding Around-the-World travel scholarships. In 1920, for example, two scholarships were offered—one for a man at 40,000 francs and one for a woman at 20,000 francs. According to the announcement, the scholarship for men entailed at least fifteen to sixteen months of travel through Europe, the Americas, and Asia, while women's travel would last for one year and include Europe and North America. The scholarships were not intended to fund pleasure trips, but "voyages of observation." The announcement indicated that the donor of the money for the scholarships "thought that the comparison of national habits and institutions with the habits and political, religious, social and economic institutions of foreign countries was of a nature to enlarge and elevate minds, and to make teachers of French youth more able to fulfill their educational function."[1] By 1930 a total of forty-eight French men and twenty-four French women had benefited from Around-the-World Scholarships (bourses autour-du-monde), financed by banker and philanthropist Albert Kahn (1860–1940; see Figure 1).[2] Kahn also provided travel scholarships to an additional seventy-six young Germans, Britons, Japanese, Russians, and Americans, extending his philanthropy beyond French borders.

Like the Americans who pursued postbaccalaureate study in Europe from 1870 to 1914, the Albert Kahn *boursiers* (fellows) were recent graduates at the beginning of their careers in education. Few had ever crossed the Atlantic, and all benefited from the declining cost and improved safety and speed of ocean travel. However, unlike their peers across the

FIGURE 1 Albert Kahn. Photographed by Georges Chevalier, 102 rue de Richelieu, 1914. Courtesy of the Musée départemental Albert Kahn, Boulogne-Billancourt.

Atlantic, when the aspiring *boursiers* responded to the announcements for the Around-the-World Scholarships, they applied for an explicitly nationalist and internationalist mission. At this time private philanthropy assumed a leading role in internationalist initiatives, trying in various ways to construct an alternative to national power politics in the form of transnational cooperation. Scholars are looking again at just how philanthropic organizations implemented cooperation and exchange in an era marked by intense nationalist rivalries and, especially after World War II, extreme national power asymmetries.[3] Thus far American philanthropic organizations have received the most attention, as has the period after 1945. Scholars also tend to focus on organizers' intentions more than on participants' responses.[4]

But before the establishment of the Carnegie and Rockefeller Foundations in the United States, and even before Rhodes Scholarships to Oxford University in England, the beneficiaries of Albert Kahn's largesse enthusiastically embraced and developed Kahn's internationalist vision, amplifying its contribution to what historian Jay Winter recently termed an early twentieth-century "utopian moment."[5] Although *boursiers* traveled to many countries, the focus here will be on their views of France and the United States, accounts that suggest a more complementary and cooperative narrative of Franco-American relations, in contrast to the more familiar studies of Americanization and French anti-Americanism, especially following World War I.[6]

Born in Alsace, Kahn, like many Jews, left for France after Germany annexed Alsace and Lorraine in 1871. At the age of sixteen, he started working at the Goudchaux Bank of Paris, where he became an associate in 1892. He also made a fortune from investments in South African gold and diamond mines. While working at the bank, Kahn earned his baccalaureate in both letters and science, along with a law degree, by 1884. In a letter of 1887 to his friend and former tutor Henri Bergson (1859–1941), Kahn suggested that his successful banking career was only a means to larger, more satisfying occupations. And indeed, the Around-the-World Scholarships that he started in 1898 were only the beginning of several varied, internationalist, philanthropic endeavors, including a Center of Social Documentation to promote the social sciences in France, the Archives of the Planet—a massive photographic collection from some fifty countries around the world—the National Committee for Social and Political Studies, and an offshoot of the scholarships, the Around-the-World Society.[7] These initiatives suggest a fascination with the unbounded possibilities offered by modern technology and science, similar to the fantastic voyages of the novels of Jules Verne (1828–1905), yet grounded in a Bergsonian faith in the positive growth and change inherent in individual experience.

They are distinct from, yet related to, the many different manifestations of internationalism at the turn of the century, including the establishment of transnational organizations to standardize weights, measures, time, transportation, and communication; and other nongovernmental efforts to coordinate shared interests and concerns across national boundaries, like international women's groups, socialism, and peace movements.[8] Other internationalist projects that bear comparison with Kahn's include Pierre de Coubertin's revival of the Olympic Games in 1896, and, after his death in 1902, Cecil Rhodes's bequest of the bulk of his four-million-pound estate for scholarships to enable men of British colonies and former colonies (and of imperial Germany) to study at Oxford University.[9] Both the Olympics and Rhodes Scholarships were simultaneously nationalistic and internationalist, and Albert Kahn stated explicitly that his Around-the-World Scholarships served French national interest as well as internationalism. But as much as he supported France and admired its republican institutions, his philanthropic endeavors manifest a wide-ranging and profound commitment to internationalism in the forms of intellectual and scientific exchange, global awareness, humanitarian reforms, and world peace.

Kahn's original intentions for the Around-the-World Scholarships included the following: They were to provide young *lycée* professors with experiences of the world that they were unlikely to have otherwise, with the expectation that this would make them better teachers, able to communicate more vividly and knowledgeably information about the world to their pupils.[10] Kahn also hoped to further internationalism and the national interest of France at the same time through the cross-cultural experiences of open-minded, educated young French men and, later, women. Suspicious of purely theoretical solutions to the many problems plaguing the world at the turn of the century, Kahn suggested that direct interaction among persons of different cultures might at least offer "solid, vivid, and communicable impressions." Moreover, Kahn hoped this knowledge might contribute to conflict resolution among countries: "We must seek to compile a precise understanding of the role that different nations play in the world, determine their different aspirations, see where these aspirations lead, if they incline nations toward violent shocks or if they can be reconciled with one another." He thought that educated youth would be best suited to learn about other countries and cultures in a relationship of equal exchange: "To enter into friendly communication with the ideas, the feelings, indeed the life of different peoples, who better to do this than young [men] selected from the intellectual and moral elite of the nation, not old enough to have preconceived ideas, but mature enough to know how to observe and understand?" Kahn hoped ultimately that *boursiers* would meet and discuss their findings in order to identify some general trends "capable of usefully influencing the direction of our country's activity."[11]

Kahn assumed that France was a leader in world affairs, but he implied that developments elsewhere were challenging that leadership and that part of the purpose of the scholarships was to analyze the strengths and weaknesses of France and other countries in order to benefit France. Kahn explained:

> The purpose of this travel being to allow these young professors to acquire an accurate idea of the situation of France in the world and a lively sense of the effort necessary to maintain France at a level worthy of her, the essential object of their studies will be to inform themselves directly, outside of any preconceived notion, on the conditions of social life in different countries, on the way that each government endeavors to form public opinion, on the means deployed to develop the genius of each nation, finally on the causes behind any given people, in any given domain acquiring the dominance that is possible.[12]

Kahn enjoined *boursiers* to be open-minded and receptive to other cultures; he expected them to feel "invested with a sense of patriotic and humanitarian mission."[13]

From the beginning Kahn enlisted the institutional support of the University of Paris. Thanks to the university reforms of 1896, he was able to donate the money for the scholarships to the University, and the selection committee consisted of deans, faculty members, former *boursiers*, and other public figures presided over by the rector of the University of Paris. Each year the rector distributed announcements for the scholarships to academics in universities and *lycées* throughout France and Algeria. Applicants submitted proposals of intent and letters of recommendation, and finalists were interviewed and underwent medical examinations in Paris. Kahn required that candidates have a working command of English. A separate, but similar committee selected women candidates from 1905 to 1920. The vast majority of *boursiers* majored in humanistic subjects—literature, languages, philosophy, and history/geography—though proportionately more women were teachers of science and math than were men. In general, the men made their scholarship voyages at a younger age than did the women; most *boursiers* were in their late twenties, but the mean age for *boursières* was thirty to thirty-one.[14] Although Kahn was not a member of the selection committees, he nonetheless took an active interest in the selection process. *Boursiers* were required to submit progress reports of their travels to the rector, and a final report after their return to France.[15]

Although the Around-the-World Scholarships were originally awarded only to men, Kahn included women starting in 1905, a significant departure from the explicit masculinity of Rhodes Scholarships. Kahn said he knew that women teachers did not merely educate girls, but that they were also aware of their "social mission" of shaping the women of the future. Women's influence in the family, according to Kahn, was instrumental in forming the national ideal. "Women destined to instruct other women must be conscious of this ideal, and must work to renew it, if not maintain it."[16] Kahn limited the women's travel to Europe and North America, required that they travel in pairs, and paid them half of what men were awarded, but women soon stretched their scholarship money and ventured beyond these limits.[17]

Although Kahn expected that French *boursiers* should inform themselves of foreign cultures and nations through direct contact and "outside of any preconceived notion," a starting point for many in terms of understanding the United States in the opening years of the twentieth century was *la vie intense*, a translation of the title of Theodore Roosevelt's speech, "The Strenuous Life," delivered before a meeting of the Hamilton Club in Chicago in 1899 and published in the same year. In the speech Roosevelt approvingly asserted that American men were so focused on work and material success and eager to accept a leading role in the world, especially if that entailed empire and war, that they had no time for leisure or culture. The speech opened with Roosevelt's articulation of what "is most American in the American character," that is, "the doctrine of the strenuous life." For Roosevelt, the strenuous life was "the life of toil and effort, of labor and strife"; its practitioners believed that the "highest form of success . . . comes, not to the man who desires mere easy peace, but to the man who does not shrink from danger, from hardship, or from bitter toil, and who out of these wins the splendid ultimate triumph."[18] Historians of the United States have mined this text, along with other writings by Roosevelt, for insights into the construction of masculinity, race, empire, and national identity in the United States.[19] It is also rich with implications for French national identity, because several *boursiers* framed their comparative understanding of the United States and France through "the strenuous life."

Roosevelt suggested that France, along with China, was a model the United States should avoid because the country had become slothful and effete. Citing Alphonse Daudet's concern about declining fertility due to "the haunting terror of the young wife of the present day," Roosevelt continued: "When men fear work or fear righteous war, when women fear motherhood, they tremble on the brink of doom; and well it is that they should vanish from the earth." For Roosevelt, engagement with the world was key to national greatness, and that required preparation for and willingness to fight wars. He wrote of Americans: "If we are to be a really great people, we must strive in good faith to play a great part in the world. We cannot avoid meeting great issues."[20]

French *boursiers* who referred to the strenuous life tended to avoid its gendered and imperial implications and focused on its denotation of the energy and dynamism of the United States. Describing the last part of her trip to Japan and arrival in San Francisco in 1913, *boursière* Jeanne Antoine echoed Roosevelt's contrasting characterizations of China and the United States: "After the awakening of India and China, immobilized for a long time in their dreams or their ritual traditions, after the metamorphosis of feudal Japan into a modern state, . . . it is the rise of a young and strong nation, with no ties to the past, that appeared to me in this brand new country, and from then on I take pleasure in the spectacle of this 'strenuous' civilization."[21] As diplomatic historian Jean-Baptiste Duroselle notes, Theodore Roosevelt was popular in France, and his work, along with Jules Verne's fictional American characters determined to conquer the moon in *From the Earth to the Moon* (1865), contributed to a stereotype of the energetic, can-do, macho American man.[22]

However, in a 1914 essay titled, "Some Reflections on the Strenuous Life of the United States," *boursière* Marguerite Clément challenged Roosevelt's characterizations. Fifteen years before Georges Duhamel's scathing critique of the modern American lifestyle that he feared was the model for future French development, Clément offered similar observations, though framed somewhat differently and in less alarmist fashion.[23] She refused the American characterization of France, and the Old World generally, as mere sites of leisure and cultivation—"the world where one enjoys oneself, or relaxes"—in contrast to the New World, "where one lives." For Clément, the strenuous life of the United States was different only in degree from the life of French people or Europeans and different only because of the lack of obstacles to the development of capitalism and mechanization.[24] The implication was that at the time both Europe and the United States were modern, active societies, but that Europeans were more successful at combining economic growth with philosophical reflection and aesthetic appreciation. Clément regretted that, in the United States, even privileged women, the only group with socially acceptable leisure, eschewed the opportunity for solitude, reflection, and cultivation and instead engaged in the strenuous life themselves, that is, in a flurry of social engagements or frenzied social work. Clément departed completely from the meaning Roosevelt attributed to the strenuous life for American women; for him, it meant childbearing and hard work as wife and mother. Clément also considered the possibility that the intense life was justified because it might contribute to prosperity and happiness in the long term. But ultimately, she decided that it was only an end in itself, perpetuated by those Americans and immigrants who embraced it for its own sake, not for any evident greater good. Her conclusion: "The strenuous life is a mystery."[25]

Clément used Roosevelt's construction of American national identity (or at least, her interpretation of it) as a starting point for addressing Kahn's mandate to *boursiers* to assess France and other countries of the world. Though both admiring and critical of the United States, Clément and other French *boursiers* often tried to extract some kind of lesson from their observations, either for France or for transnational cooperation. For instance, Georges Burghard, a *boursier* who visited the United States in 1899, chastised precisely the imperial aspirations that Roosevelt celebrated, though he did not mention Roosevelt or the strenuous life: [Americans] "call themselves the number one nation in the world in trade, the army, and the navy. Their success in the Spanish war has only increased this pretension, and developed their militarist sentiments."[26] Burghard believed that the United States and the rest of the world conducted their foreign relations on the basis of pure self-interest, and he suggested that France should follow suit.

Similarly, Emile Hovelaque acknowledged that, as an economic power, France was losing ground at the turn of the century, though he believed recovery was possible. In 1904 he contributed a highly critical analysis of French economic practices to a volume of reports by thirteen of the first French *boursiers* who traveled between 1898 and 1900. Hovelaque asserted that France was so well endowed with talent and abundance that it failed adequately to make use of them. Despite the obvious inferiority of the French economy in the modern world, his travels led him to believe that throughout history France contributed ideas and practices to the world that were valuable and that France was capable of learning from mistakes. He viewed France as a modern Athens with the potential to reassert its influence: "it is urgent that France become aware again of her duties and rights, that she remember the lessons of her past, that she address the growing lead of her rivals, and that she cease immobilizing herself at home to shine as before on the larger world."[27]

In the same volume of reports, Georges Weulersse, a *boursier* in 1898, suggested that because the strengths and weaknesses of French and American education systems were exact opposites, then a desirable education would combine strengths of both—that is, the physical exercise, hygiene, and hands-on practicality of the United States with the more bookish, comprehensive, and abstract education of France.[28] Madeleine Mignon, who traveled to the United States in 1911, drew similar conclusions about the respective merits of French and especially American education systems, and she hoped that French educators could adopt certain American practices, like the same scientific education for girls and boys, more attention to physical fitness and hygiene for pupils, and the cultivation of a social conscience among girls in school.[29]

These *boursiers'* reports suggest a pattern of creative and critical thinking about French and American cultural exchanges. They imply and sometimes even state that worthy features of each national culture should be cultivated or adapted for the benefit of both. This pattern appears strongly in reports by French *boursières* on women's education in the United States and how it contrasted with the system in France. Seventeen of twenty-four *boursières* were graduates of the Ecole Normale Supérieure de Sèvres, and a few were outspoken feminists in their applications. Most came from the transitional generation of teachers, identified by Jo Burr Margadant, who sought to expand their own and their pupils' opportunities and identities by rendering women's education more similar to men's education and by advocating that women be more involved in society outside of the home.[30] Successful applicants both reiterated Kahn's intentions and reflected the transition noted by Margadant in that they wanted to study women's education in other countries and social services undertaken by women, notably in the United States. These *boursières* echoed other French travelers' observations about education in the United States before World War I, namely, that it served to unify, even create, a nation of immigrants, in contrast to education in France in order to support the republic. They also noted, along with many others, the high proportion of women teachers in American elementary schools, the lack of rigor in high school curricula, the comparative wealth of American universities manifested in superb facilities, and the emphasis on social life in higher education. However, the *boursières* were more discerning and appreciative of women's higher education in the United States than were most other travelers, and they also found more to admire in American women generally, in contrast to French men travelers who expressed reservations about American women's independence.[31]

The *boursières* all visited some of the women's colleges in the northeastern United States, and most visited at least one coeducational institution, like the University of Michigan in Ann Arbor or the University of Chicago. Interestingly, coeducation versus separate colleges for women was not an issue for the *boursières*. Coming from the Ecole Normale Supérieure de Sèvres, most of the French women had themselves been educated in an intensely female environment. At the same time French universities were admitting women students starting in the 1860s, and coeducational institutions were popular and proliferating in the United States as well, so that observers apparently accepted the coexistence of two different educational environments in the United States and in France.[32] Four related issues were of the greatest interest to the *boursières*, and three of them also aroused considerable ambivalence. These were the extent and implications of social life in higher education; pedagogy and the national purpose of education at all levels in the United States; the independence and freedom of choice of American women students; and the general nature of American women.

In 1908 Marguerite Clément criticized the all-consuming social life of American college women, asserting that "the students organize semi-secret societies, . . . and waste much of their time in useless meetings that engender a mania for clubs that is disastrous for all of America."[33] That same year Annette-Marie Cartan noted that the problem of social life was worse at the coeducational University of Chicago than at some of the women's colleges, because women lacked any supervision at the University, and their practically unfettered freedom led to misbehavior (unnamed). Indiscipline was checked at Wellesley College, Cartan noted with approval, by the policy of self-government, whereby students wrote the rules of the college, decided on punishments, and generally regulated themselves.[34]

By contrast several *boursières* suggested that the importance of sociability and self-governance in American higher education prepared women for life by teaching them self-control, discipline, organization, and order. Jeanne Darlu noted approvingly that a number of women college graduates went on to apply these skills to social work in the form of settlement houses, and she wrote of the combined effects of religion and sociability in college life: "The double religious and social influence forms women capable of usefully serving their country as teachers, doctors, secretaries, [social workers], and mothers of families."[35] Madeleine Mignon was particularly impressed with the orientation toward social work in women's higher education: "In the United States, not only are young people prepared for life in society, but also there is a concern to interest them in social work, and this is another advantage [strong point] of American institutions." She attributed this difference to the larger role of the state in French social services, to the detriment of educated French women. Citing Jane Addams's Hull House as an example of American women's involvement in social work, Mignon wrote, "one regrets that in France, the state, in taking social works into its own hands, leaves women an excuse for disassociating themselves completely from others." She goes on to praise American education for teaching both independence and social concern: "Thus I admire very much this system of education that aspires on the one hand to develop individuality, and on the other to orient activity toward social welfare."[36]

Boursières suggested that the larger social conditions of the United States helped shape a pedagogy of preparing young people for life throughout all levels of education, a preparation that was both socially elitist and democratizing, as well as integrationist with regard to recent immigrants. Mignon wrote, "The American school seems to care more about the education of children than their knowledge, and that especially I found admirable. They believe in education in the United States; they think that school can have an impact on character formation, in other words, that it can prepare [pupils] for life."[37] Lucy Nicole shared that view, indicating that American schools tried to enrich normal life, not just the academic life of children through a practical, social, and character-building education.[38] Although she thought the content of education in American schools was average, Jeanne Renauld was fascinated by the social function of education: "The social significance of schools and universities, their place in general, national life interested me much more than did instruction strictly speaking."[39] Of particular interest to Renauld and others was education as part of a process of assimilating immigrants. Alice Lapotaire wrote, "I admired the rapidity with which little immigrants were Americanized, at least on the outside."[40] According to Darlu, the characteristics fostered in American schools helped to integrate immigrants: "School, like the family, fosters qualities of independence and initiative."

Through this education, she continued, European immigrants assimilate and become a "new race" in the United States. Darlu noted the egalitarian and classist functions of education. On the one hand, she claimed that pupils in the United States worked hard in school, not in order to become part of an elite, but because education was necessary for personal advancement. At the same time, she maintained that educated women took up social work, not out of a sense of Christian charity, but out of a sense of obligation: "the cultivated classes must take masses of ignorant immigrants under their wing to assure the country's future."[41]

In general *boursières* admired the significant role in society that American women assumed, and for which education prepared them from kindergarten to university. They expressed some ambivalence, however, about the autonomy of women students, and school and university curricula. Mignon saw both advantages and disadvantages to the self-government of students at Wellesley, what she called "discipline within autonomy":

> From such practices develops inevitably a sense of honor and of responsibility of inestimable value, though at the same time they produce an almost excessive independence, accustom young minds only to deal with equals, and undoubtedly ruin any last vestiges of respect. American pupils [girls] treat even old professors with a benevolent familiarity that does not seem to me the ideal of this type of relations.[42]

Jeanne Darlu thought that the lack of guidance and almost complete freedom of choice in what courses to take produced an incomplete education, a notion that she said was confirmed by the director of Radcliffe Annex to Harvard College, who acknowledged that literary education was particularly deficient.[43] Disappointed that students in the United States shamelessly admitted to not knowing the dates of the Avignon papacy, the contribution of Louis Pasteur, or the names of contemporary French artists, Clément declared, "If American colleges have convinced me of one thing, it is of the superiority of our teaching [education]."[44]

Nonetheless, *boursières* also noticed that American women students were healthier than French students, in large measure because exercise or sports was important in American education.[45] Cartan wrote of the American college woman: "Sports and physical exercise make her strong and supple and refresh her from her studies."[46] For Mignon the contrast between the physical condition of French and American pupils and students reflected badly on the French practice of excessive study for girls and women to the point of harming their health and causing lassitude: "Seeing all these children and young people radiant with health, whose lives are so happy and sound, I made several sad comparisons with the lot of our young French girls."[47] Although some *boursières* found American women students immature, some also appreciated their enthusiasm and curiosity. Alice Lapotaire described American women students as having a "childish character," but noted, "that is not a criticism when it means an easy good nature and the capacity to delight in little."[48]

If educated American women lacked some basic historical facts, literary appreciation, and scientific theories, they outstripped their French counterparts in independence and initiative, according to the *boursières*. Cartan concluded that women's education in the United States "deserves our admiration." She elaborated:

> clubs and "social life" have, among other benefits, involving the student in other things so that she is not only a historian, a chemist, a philosopher. In her behavior, she always gives evidence of initiative and independence; the instruction she receives develops her faculties of perception to the highest degree. These precious qualities permit her later to make her influence felt around her, whatever position she occupies. She has self-confidence, and is ready for action.[49]

Madeleine Mignon thought that reforming French education for women to include more practical education, exercise, and preparation for social work was possible and "would give good results," but she also acknowledged the difficulty of cultural transfer: "It is unfortunately regrettable that in France so many persons who approve of certain foreign institutions are already so persuaded of the impossibility of their application to us [France] that they refuse even to try."[50]

Overall, French *boursières* concluded that educated American women represented a positive example to French women. Rachel Allard wrote in 1911: "the cultivated American woman seemed to me more developed than ours, by her spirit of initiative and especially by her sense of social life, an example to propose to the French woman."[51] Countering the French stereotype of American women as independent to the point of vulgarity or aggressiveness, Pierrette Sapy claimed that during her travels she met many women who were "distinguished, simple, very far from that tasteless independence often attributed to them from afar. They are very free with that calm decision and reserve natural to Anglo-Saxon character."[52] For Anna Amieux, the empowerment of American women through education, and the achievements of American, as well as Swedish, feminists, were worthy models for French women to emulate.[53]

As historian Rebecca Rogers has shown, American models for women's education were not new in France by the late nineteenth century.[54] Yet, these *boursières*' reports, along with scholarship from both sides of the Atlantic, also suggest different routes to equality of the sexes in the two countries. In the United States it was the social life of higher education, in both women's colleges and coeducational universities, that taught women leadership skills, competitiveness, and the desire for equal access to the same opportunities and resources that men had.[55] The *boursières* noticed that, despite the drawbacks of wasted time and exclusivity, social life in higher education did indeed prepare women for active involvement in American society, whether through teaching, settlement work, or civic reform. By contrast, the French education system emphasized academics, and excelling in academics and demanding equal curricula for women and men were the avenues toward equality for educated French women, as Margadant has shown through the example of secondary school teachers. According to Carole Lécuyer, by 1889–90 *étudiantes* was a category for statistics kept by the Ministry of Education, reflecting the fact that sufficient numbers of women had been admitted into French universities for them to be officially recognized.[56] Although French women students did form their own organizations and support networks, they did not have access to institutionally supported organizations and activities that were prominent in the American system and to which the Albert Kahn *boursières* attributed educated American women's independence and initiative.

True to Kahn's intentions, *boursières* offered thoughtful reflections on what were the distinctive features of women's education in the United States and how they contributed to certain strengths of American society. Though not uncritical, they found more to admire in women's education and in the confident, active women it cultivated than did most other French (men) travelers to the United States at that time. For the most part the *boursières* recognized that cultural and social differences rendered significant changes in the two educational systems unlikely, though some hoped for modest reforms, like more exercise and social activism for French girls, ideas that were not unique to those who had traveled to North America. One *boursière* also suggested a way to convey the strengths of French pedagogy to schools in the United States through a hands-on understanding of American educational practices. Echoing a concern voiced by many French academics before World War I, Annette-Marie Cartan asserted that it would be in the interest of France to prepare French women to become teachers of French in the United States and thereby loosen the hold of German educators: "I dream of a normal school that will accept students when they finish the *lycée*, teach them about things overseas, instruct them rigorously in teaching methods, and help them learn to avoid regrettable errors. Armed with a diploma, they will carry the good word to the United States, and increase the latent sympathy regarding things related to France."[57] Even as Cartan dreamed of a way to convert Americans to appreciation of French culture, she recognized the need for these secular French missionaries to understand the United States.

Although French *boursiers* fulfilled Kahn's charge to understand other countries in order to assess and improve France's position in the world, and *boursières* gathered ideas for improving women's education in France and the United States, some American fellows focused on internationalism itself. After all, in 1911 Kahn established the Kahn Foundation for the Foreign Travel of American Teachers (following similar scholarship programs founded in Japan, Germany, and Great Britain) based on his belief that "the cause of civilization may be greatly encouraged and promoted by travel on the part of teachers, scholars and investigators" and by "the study and comparison of national manners and customs, and of the political, social, religious and economic institutions of foreign countries." Scholarship recipients would thus "become better qualified to teach and to take part in the instruction and education of the people of their own nation."[58] Thus, the fifteen young American [male] professors selected for fellowships by an American board of trustees had a more open mission to promote civilization generally and not so much a national interest.[59]

Walter Williams, a journalism professor at the University of Missouri, concluded from his experience as a Kahn Fellow that international journalism was flourishing. During his travels throughout Europe and Asia from June 1913 to May 1914, he observed almost two thousand newspaper offices and he assessed the characteristics of journalism in four major developed countries—Great Britain, France, Germany, and the United States. He found each to be distinctive, but he also discerned mutual influences of the United States on European journalism, and vice versa. In Williams's opinion, this was positive, because it contributed to a new, "world journalism" that reflected and enhanced democratic tendencies:

> The new world's journalism, which the world-traveler sees, is the outcome of the new world-spirit. It is the outward and visible sign of an inward grace.... It is a new struggle among the people for different relations to the external, a new conviction that they should have more to say concerning their own fortunes. Its manifestations are various. Its attitude is critical everywhere and sometimes openly contemptuous. In some lands it seeks reform, in some it inspires revolt.[60]

Thus, for Williams an internationalist spirit of critical thinking was the essence of a transnational journalism.

Ivan Linforth, an American professor of classics at the University of California at Berkeley who traveled on a Kahn fellowship in 1912, shared Williams's and Kahn's belief that the exchange of ideas and practices benefited both individuals and societies at large. Additionally, Linforth was concerned with issues that hindered cooperation and human well-being, like racism, economic nationalism, imperialism, and rearmament. He was dismayed by the militarism he witnessed in different European countries; for example, he deplored the attitude of a German professor that a war between England and Germany would be fatal: "English victory will lead to its collapse, and from its own defeat Germany will survive to rule the world." Linforth found this statement indicative of a latent tribalism among advanced and civilized Europeans, and this suggested to him that the United States, comprising many European nationalities united in one country, had the opportunity and even obligation to steer clear of the conditions and practices that threatened to lead to war. He proposed that the United States fulfill this mission, in part, by refusing to fight: "To stop thinking of war; to stop planning for it; to stop spending money on army and navy,—these are the steps which will lead most surely to the reign of peace." Linforth believed that if the United States could halt its own "racial prejudice" and other failings, it might serve as a model for a less belligerent patriotism: "a new patriotism must be learned which can glory in the high calling of the country as leader in the salvation of the world."[61] According to Linforth, all countries could (and should) adopt this "true patriotism," serving both national and international interests through tolerance and cooperation.

Like thousands of other internationalists and pacifists at the turn of the nineteenth century, Linforth and Williams saw humanitarian benefits from cross-cultural exchanges and transnational cooperation, though they were well aware of countervailing nationalistic and militaristic tendencies. And although their benefactor Albert Kahn was no pacifist; his views were similar to those of many of his compatriots who were influential in movements for intellectual cooperation, humanitarian relief, and arbitration as means to prevent war.[62] However, when war broke out in 1914, the majority of French people felt compelled to fight a justified, defensive war, and *boursiers* contemplated national differences between the United States and France in this context until the United States entered the fighting in 1917.

Some French *boursiers* were disappointed in the United States' neutrality during the early years of World War I. French economist Emile Hovelaque, who was among the first *boursiers* who traveled in 1898, later criticized the American tendency toward pacifism and avoidance of war, largely, in his opinion, out of economic interests. He charged American idealism with naïveté, a failure to discern the difference between executioner and victim in the European war, but in 1916 he was hopeful that the United States was gradually changing from its pacifist, noninterventionist position. He concluded his article by suggesting that only a long, complex, and troubled history produced beauty and truth and that time was on the side of the United States joining the war.[63] Similarly, Anne Main, who taught French in the United States in 1916 and 1917, attributed American neutrality to a lack of experience, history, and spiritual engagement, though she anticipated that this position would change: "We know things that the United States does not know yet, but that they will perhaps learn."[64]

Nonetheless, Main acknowledged that living the United States changed her attitude toward the country and that its melting pot quality helped explain the absence of hostility toward other nationalities. On her arrival she claimed that, as a French patriot, she found American neutrality "soft." Yet she did enjoy the informality and tolerance of individual difference that she experienced in New York City. She said that Europeans habitually "consider individuals in terms of class or nation. A human being in Europe registers in our imagination as a German, an Italian, a Pole, a bourgeois, a peasant. In America I find myself confronted for the first time with the human species as species." Main also appreciated being in a place of peace and prosperity, in contrast to war-torn Europe, though she was glad that the United States joined the Allies, in spite of a presidential election that favored the noninterventionist candidate and divisions among Americans who were pro-Allies, pro-German, or pacifist.[65]

Both French and American *boursiers* shared Albert Kahn's belief in the merits of travel with educational or internationalist goals. This tendency was even more pronounced following World War I, as internationalist efforts proliferated and expanded generally.[66] Charles Garnier, a *boursier* in 1899, was an ardent supporter of the League of Nations in 1920 and proposed projects for educational and intellectual exchange as part of the new international organization.[67] R. P. Brooks, a dean of the business school at the University of Georgia, Kahn fellow, and member of the Kahn Foundation Commission to select American candidates for scholarships, wrote of the many benefits from the Kahn scholarships in 1931: "Above all else, I feel that the contacts the Fellows make in foreign countries, the sympathetic insight they acquire into the problems and ways of thought of other peoples, is contributing to the creation of the sense of international mindedness, the development of which is so essential to the preservation of peace and furtherance of mutual understanding."[68]

Also in 1931 Félicien Challaye asserted that he and other *boursiers* passed on the new insights gained as a result of their Around-the-World scholarships through their teaching, public presentations, and writing, thereby perpetuating Kahn's goal of universal understanding or sympathy: "By bringing together all the great human races, the creation of the Around-the-World travel scholarships perhaps prepares for the appearance of what [Rabindranath] Tagore calls *the infinite personality of man*."[69]

Altering his original assessment of 1914 about the unique role of the United States in maintaining world peace, Ivan Linforth published another article in 1931 on internationalism, praising the many efforts by private organizations to foster cross-cultural exchange and understanding, of which Kahn's scholarship was an early example. He acknowledged that ordinary citizens felt threatened by internationalism, fearing the loss of the "popular customs of their county, of their institutions and ideals, replaced by universal law, language, religion, and social organization to which they feel no attachment." But he was optimistic that educational and travel scholarships for students and professors could overcome this tendency, for they all shared "the goal of making men of different nations encounter one another and know one another."[70]

Subsequent positions and careers of both French and American *boursiers* indicate that the internationalist perspective gained from the Around-the-World Scholarships was indeed lasting and incorporated into published works and involvement in various activities or causes (in addition to teaching), like journalism and publishing, education administration, the Around-the-World Society, anticolonialism, and the Center for Social Documentation.[71] Indeed, former *boursiers* created the Around-the-World Society in 1906, a social and intellectual organization open to all internationalists that lasted until 1949, specifically for the purpose of "work[ing] to spread, in France, precise knowledge of foreign countries, abroad, knowledge of France, and to understand and foster all that one could call international civilization."[72] In 1931 on the twenty-fifth anniversary of the scholarships, Félicien Challaye noted the value of Kahn's travel project: "All the joys of such voyages center around a superior satisfaction: the joy of intellectual liberation." Speaking of all *boursiers*, he asserted, "Each of us drew from our travel some of the ideas that have subsequently directed our lives."[73] For himself, that idea was the equality of all races: "each race has its value, originality, and charm, such that none is destined to be the eternal slave of another, and one day all the peoples of all races will be equally free and will unite in brotherhood in a peaceful world."[74]

At the very least these reports do suggest some merits of cross-cultural exchange, namely, better understanding of another culture and of one's own, and a capacity to explain strengths and weaknesses of each. As Edmond Eggli concluded from his voyage of 1908: "I have the feeling that these visits in differently structured societies, these ever new relations with people different from us, are inestimably beneficial for a more generous exercise of judgment, for the enrichment of experience in general, and also for the more insightful appreciation of our own nation."[75] Edmée Hitzel, a *boursière* in 1929–30, wrote of the consequences of educational travel: "It is to banish the error of thinking that our way of living and thinking is the measure of all civilization; it is to recognize the variation . . . of forms that life can assume. It is to become very humble and to see in our own civilization only a momentary aspect of human evolution."[76]

Mandated reports by *boursiers* who were grateful for the opportunity to travel around the world were not likely to challenge the beliefs and intentions of their benefactor. But they do reveal how direct contact with other cultures challenges preconceptions and assumptions and results in new understanding. Jeanne Darlu offered this summary of the significance of her travels for a new appreciation of both the United States and of France:

> After these four months in America so full of sensations and new ideas, it seems to me that I understand and prefer the familiar life of our country. I see more clearly than before its faults and weaknesses, its spirit of mediocrity, its inertia to start something new; I am more aware of the reasons that explain the victory of strong competitors on world markets. But I also feel more how the weave of the national soul has delicacy, gentleness, and real humanity.[77]

Although most *boursiers*' reports adhered to a general pattern of describing foreign lands and travel experiences, as well as comparing and contrasting French and foreign characteristics, one *boursière*, Simone Téry in 1928, presented the disorientation of travel in the context of self-transformation, directly addressing the philosophical condition of the traveler. She described the effect of being torn from one's family and from all that is familiar: The traveler "finds himself alone, alone with himself." Being in foreign places causes him to feel like a shadow [*une ombre*], "which causes a kind of uneasiness that sometimes extends to anxiety." According to Téry, the traveler seeks stability in himself, but to no avail, for he himself has changed. She concludes that travel confronts individuals with profound questions of existence: "I think that travel is what allows us to experience metaphysical anguish most acutely, and to feel the weight and the grandeur of these commonplaces—the eternal, insoluble problems."[78] Téry's reflections on the profound personal transformation that travel precipitates suggest the centrality of lived experience to a broader, internationalist view, a position that Kahn obviously shared.

Often reports suggested ways that teacher/travelers from France and the United States could learn from one another and apply those lessons to improve each country and, even, the larger world. Walter Williams, for example, found much to praise in the people of the French countryside, whom he considered to be more representative of France than Parisians. He asserted that France was fundamentally rural, republican, and frugal and concluded: "If the characteristic of the world of tomorrow is the manner of being an individual in daily life, there is much to learn among the serious, friendly, and idealistic rural populations of beautiful France."[79]

Edmée Hitzel, among the last of the Albert Kahn *boursiers* in 1929–30, and perhaps familiar with André Siegfried's (and even Georges Duhamel's) critiques of the United States, mustered a spirited defense of American prosperity as well worth the price of conformity.[80] Arriving in the United States after traveling in Asia, she praised the newer country for its liberation from the hierarchies, servitude, and poverty of old civilizations. Recognizing that imitation of the United States was out of the question, she concluded: "This danger of servile and inopportune imitation must be pushed away, not in awkwardly criticizing American civilization, which is justified and good in itself, as I have tried to show, but in trying to put into place an intelligent and sensitive collaboration between the Old World and the New."[81]

Albert Kahn's philanthropy extended to many other international, educational, scientific, and humanitarian projects, and clearly he contributed to an upsurge of internationalism in Europe and the United States at the end of the nineteenth century and beginning of the twentieth. The reports of the *boursiers* reveal just how the recipients of his philanthropy actually practiced internationalism. Articulating difference is part of the process, something that Kahn recognized even as he aspired to greater, more idealistic goals of transnational understanding and cooperation. Although many *boursiers* reiterated national differences between the United States and France that other travelers noted, the comparisons and contrasts led others to consider how they might be harnessed for a greater good. Equally important was the exchange of ideas, a dialogue among participants to clarify and publicize ideas.[82]

When Kahn founded the scholarships in 1898, France was a great power, and this assumption underlies Kahn's original mandate. World travel provided *boursiers* with new insights into their own national characteristics, including strengths and weaknesses. *Boursiers* juxtaposed these features with the increasingly evident economic and cultural power of the United States, especially after World War I, and advocated complementarity as a means for France to reform itself or to function in the world alongside the United States. Cooperation more than competition was the approach of later *boursiers*. American fellows, grateful to a French benefactor and unburdened by the need to uphold a dominant position in international affairs, responded highly favorably to their travels in France and elsewhere, occasionally indicating a particular feature of French society that might be profitably adopted in the United States (lecturing techniques, earthy rationalism), and noting how the common view of French people as immoral was indeed a myth.

When the economic crisis that started in 1929 wiped out Albert Kahn's fortune, the Around-the-World Scholarships ended. The story of his remarkable vision and actions toward internationalism rarely appears in historical scholarship, overshadowed, perhaps, by the bigger and more influential American foundations that funded educational, scientific, and cultural exchanges for greater human understanding and for practical collaborative achievements, especially following World War II. Yet the success of his efforts is evident in the reports of the young people who benefited from the Around-the-World Scholarships. They testify to the acquisition of a revised sense of patriotism through the articulation of France's strengths and weaknesses with regard to other countries of the world, particularly the United States. Additionally, *boursiers* and especially *boursières* learned to appreciate the culture and society of the United States in a way that differed from the disdainful fear of Georges Duhamel or other French travelers who wrote popular accounts of the United States for the general public in France, suggesting that American materialism, conformity, and uniformity would soon engulf French culture.

The *boursiers'* accounts offer a very different perspective from the Americanization and anti-American models that commonly define Franco-American cultural relations at this time and throughout much of the twentieth century.[83] Without denying the increasing influence of the United States, especially after World War I, many *boursiers* (though by no means all) envisioned constructive exchanges of ideas and practices between the two countries. This particular episode of educational exchange also shows that women participated as eagerly and actively as did men, and benefited from foreign experience to consider reforms of girls' education and alternative models of educated womanhood. Feminist scholars have analyzed the ways that feminists have overcome national boundaries to construct bonds based on shared humanitarian concerns, and others have noted the varying functions of gender in international relations.[84] Yet the evidence here reveals still other ways that women shaped and practiced internationalism.

The *boursiers'* reports suggest an alternative definition of internationalism on an individual level with implications for transnational relations. They testify to the acquisition of a revised sense of patriotism through the articulation of France's strengths and weaknesses with regard to other countries of the world. At the same time, *boursiers* confronted preconceptions or first impressions of another country, often altering them or seeking explanations for cultural difference. Sometimes this resulted in the assertion or perpetuation of national stereotypes, but often the reports express a new tolerance and appreciation for another culture.

As several *boursiers* noted, the United States was a growing economic, cultural, and military power, a fact even more evident at the end of World War I. The American alliance was crucial to French victory in 1918, and despite an inclination toward isolationism on the part of leaders in the U.S. government after 1920, others realized that the United States was very much involved in the larger world. One of these persons was a veteran of the war who had participated in the French universities' programs for American soldiers in 1919. Due to this experience, he returned to the United States with an innovative idea for American higher education—the junior year abroad.

§ 3 Internationalism and the Junior Year Abroad

American Students in France in the 1920s and 1930s

On July 7, 1923, eight students and one professor from the University of Delaware sailed from New York to France aboard the *Rochambeau*. These men were the first participants in the Delaware Foreign Study Plan, a new program whereby undergraduates lived with French families and took classes at French universities under the close supervision of the American professor, for which they earned a full year's academic credit (see Figure 2). Two years later, in 1925, thirty-two students and a professor from Smith College (all women) made a similar journey as part of the pioneering Smith College Junior Year in France (see Figure 3). Although the Smith College program accepted only Smith students, the Delaware Plan admitted and even recruited students, including women, from other colleges and universities after its first year. By 1939 the two programs had sent some twelve hundred undergraduates, from all over the United States, to study in France, until World War II broke out in Europe.[1]

The junior year abroad was a product of World War I and French cultural diplomacy, and it coincided with many private initiatives toward internationalism in the United States after the war.[2] This particular experiment in cultural exchange posed a challenge of simultaneous tasks to American undergraduates: They had to assimilate into French life and culture for one year while retaining and representing American characteristics. Letters and other accounts by the students indicate how they met this challenge by confronting a range of French and American national stereotypes, developing an appreciation for French education and culture, reassessing their American identities, and becoming tolerant of cultural differences in general. But first, just how did the junior year abroad begin?

Internationalism and the Junior Year Abroad

FIGURE 2 First Delaware foreign study group, 1923, in front of the gates of the Place Stanislas, Nancy. Professor Raymond Kirkbride, center. Courtesy of the University of Delaware Archives.

Study abroad is now so common a part of higher education in the United States that it is difficult to appreciate how radical a notion it was in the early 1920s. The idea of a program for American undergraduates to spend one year of college at a foreign university originated with Raymond W. Kirkbride, a young professor in the Modern Languages Department at the University of Delaware and a veteran of World War I who had served in France. After the armistice of November 11, 1918, and before the signing of the peace treaty in June 1919, Kirkbride was one of the several thousand American soldiers who took classes in French language and culture at French universities as part of a joint American-French effort to keep them busy during this long waiting period (see Chapter 1). This "Franco-American University" led the prestigious University of Paris to adopt the Cours de civilisation française, a series of courses for foreigners that became a permanent offering in the fall of 1919.[3] Parisian faculty embraced this new task of instructing American soldiers, for, as Charles Cestre wrote in

FIGURE 3   First junior year in France group from Smith College, 1925, in Paris. "The Juniors in France," *Smith Alumnae Quarterly* 17 (February 1926): 140.

1918, it would "serve powerfully to cement bonds of sympathy and friendship between the two republics; it would enhance the intellectual reputation of our country and the prestige of our higher education in a country that the war has seized from the German hold."[4] Overall, Americans assessed this episode of cross-cultural exchange a success, though Robert J. Menner offered a suggestion about how French universities might continue to accommodate American students: "It is not so much by such radical modifications of academic standards, as by a more adequate supervision and direction of the work of foreign students that the scholarship and the science of France can be made more accessible and more profitable to Americans."[5] Menner was suggesting that the old practice of American postgraduates traveling on their own to Europe to study with renowned scholars should give way to greater monitoring of and assistance to American students. This is precisely what Kirkbride had in mind when he conceived of the junior year abroad.

Kirkbride envisioned a University of Delaware School of Foreign Service similar to that of Georgetown University, but better because it would require the year of living and studying abroad of all its students.[6] University of Delaware President Walter Hullihen supported Kirkbride, and he thought the Foreign Study Plan would "pave the way for formation of a School of Commerce as part of the Delaware University's function."[7] Hullihen assiduously sought publicity and support for the new program, claiming that it would address both foreign relations and economic interests of the United States. He maintained that following the war the United States could no longer assume an isolationist position in world affairs. Indeed, the United States was already deeply involved in expanded trade and financial relations with the European powers. It was clear to Hullihen, and endorsed by trade officials and diplomats, that the United States desperately needed personnel with knowledge and experience of other countries. "We shall always be at a disadvantage in our foreign relations of every kind . . . until there is a much larger number of Americans who know the language and in some measure the customs and methods of the peoples with whom we have to deal." Hullihen believed that prewar study abroad practices, largely limited to graduate students pursuing advanced scholarship, simply could not satisfy the growing demand for personnel with foreign expertise and that programs geared to undergraduates could do so: "If one of our specific aims is to create, eventually, a great reservoir of college trained business men upon whom commerce and government may draw for work that involves a knowledge of the language and customs of other countries, we must reach those who are likely to go into business when they finish the college course."[8]

Although study abroad was a hard sell because of its novelty and implicit challenge to the value of an American institution's four-year undergraduate program, the moment was ripe in terms of a climate favorable to foreign cultural and educational exchanges through private, nongovernmental initiatives in the United States.[9] In 1919 the Carnegie Endowment for International Peace started the Institute of International Education (IIE) in New York City for the promotion of study abroad. Articulating its internationalist objectives following the devastation of Europe in World War I and the rise of American economic and military influence, IIE director Stephen P. Duggan asserted in 1920: "The institute believes that it is as essential for Americans to know of the difficulties and problems of other countries as for the people of other countries to know something about us, in order that international good-will may be realized."[10] With support from the Endowment, and later the Carnegie Corporation and the Laura Spelman Rockefeller Memorial, IIE maintained an information bureau in Paris for American and French students and faculty called the American University Union. It also administered a growing number of study abroad fellowships, most of which involved sending French students to American colleges and universities and Americans to study and do research in France. These included the Franco-American Exchange, whereby some thirty or more American colleges and universities (mostly women's colleges) provided room, board, and tuition for French students to spend a year in the United States, while the French government offered about twenty positions annually for American students in French *lycées* or normal schools. IIE also selected fellows for American Field Service Fellowships for French Universities, which funded 161 Americans and seven Frenchmen (with renewals, a total of 222 fellowships) to do advanced research in the other country between 1919 and 1942.[11]

Duggan noted the importance of France as a leader in establishing educational exchanges with the United States, with French educators and the Ministry of Foreign Affairs responding to American private initiatives.[12] The French also undertook various means to welcome foreign and especially American students to their universities, notably in Paris. For example, in 1922 prominent Parisian women, mostly wives of political leaders and academics, formed the Association to Welcome Students from the United States. In 1921, University of Paris Rector Paul Appel arranged for the construction of the first international residence compound for students in Paris, the Cité Universitaire, and in 1930 money from the Rockefeller Foundation and other American philanthropists funded the construction of the American House (Fondation des Etats-Unis) at the Cité.[13]

Supporters of study abroad in the United States couched its value in terms of an internationalism of free exchange and American involvement in the world. In a speech before the Association of Urban Universities in 1923, Marcus M. Marks declared that "isolation is no longer possible even for 'mind-your-own business' Americans." He called on colleges and universities in the United States and worldwide to cooperate in study abroad. "The ultimate hope for real world peace lies in international education," he asserted, for only through "world-viewing education which enlightens the people of each nation . . . about the affairs of all others" could a new form of citizenship be cultivated. Marks called this "Broad citizenship aiming to elevate one's country, not by the injury of other nations but by policies requiring the highest world-wide enlightenment, is the college ideal."[14]

The new junior year abroad programs added to a growing number of Americans studying in France in the interwar years.[15] According to the director of the American University Union in Paris, there were approximately 400 Americans studying in France in 1920. Increasing continually, this number peaked at 5,584 for the academic year 1928–29. The Great Depression caused a decline in these numbers, but there were still 2,400 American students in France in 1933–34.[16]

The Delaware program grew from the original eight students to ninety-one in 1931–32, mostly from other colleges and universities. The pattern established by Kirkbride became the basic model for subsequent study abroad programs. Students arrived in France in the summer to take intensive language training at a provincial university and live with French families. Then, they went to Paris for the regular French academic year starting in November and lived with new host families. Students took courses at the University of Paris (Sorbonne), usually the Cours de civilisation française, and sometimes at other institutions of higher learning, including the Free School of Political Science. Additionally, American faculty regularly worked with students individually or arranged to have additional French instructors help with their assignments. American faculty and program directors "translated" French grades on written and oral examinations into American equivalents. Close faculty supervision of the students and their work was essential to the credibility of the program, ensuring that the college credit earned was merited. The cost, including travel, excursions, and cultural events, amounted to a thousand dollars, not much more than a regular year at the University of Delaware.[17] The Delaware Foreign Study Plan relied on student fees to pay for the program, though until 1935 Pierre S. du Pont subsidized the effort with an annual check of some five thousand dollars. Money concerns hounded Hullihen and the directors of the program, which is why they recruited heavily in colleges and universities nationwide to persuade students to join the program.

The Smith College Junior Year in France was in several ways a more manageable program, and before World War II the number of students each year ranged from eighteen to forty-seven.[18] In contrast to the business and Foreign Service orientation of the Delaware Foreign Study Plan, the Smith College Junior Year in France that started in 1925 addressed itself to French majors, if not future French teachers. According to Smith College President William Allan Neilson, "The plan was devised to solve the problem of giving the students who major in French a more thorough knowledge of the French language, literature, and culture."[19] He further explained, "The comparative inefficiency of any method of trying to instruct students in a foreign language while they are living in a country where that language is not generally spoken is the primary reason for the experiment which Smith College is trying this year."[20]

Neilson, like Hullihen, emphasized the merits of spending the junior year in France in terms of professional enhancement. Leaders of both programs sought to discourage more frivolous connotations of the project. Kirkbride distinguished the Foreign Study Plan from the "typical" tourist experience: "The American tourist in Europe, being on vacation and out to celebrate, goes the rounds of the 'dens of iniquity' which have been specially prepared for him, and comes home to shock the neighbors with spicy yarns about the wild time he had while 'seeing Paris.'" By contrast, Kirkbride set out the three requirements for a student in the program: "[He] will be expected to conduct himself as a gentleman at all times. . . . He must work, and work hard. . . . He must absolutely avoid speaking English."[21] Similarly, Neilson declared, "The girls who want to go to Paris because they have heard of Montmartre are not going with our group."[22] And co-director Madeleine Guilloton declared in 1927 "that Smith College in Paris was not a sort of 'finishing school.'"[23] Just as colleges and universities in the United States developed more professionally oriented curricula after World War I, and as higher education became important for upward social mobility, both Hullihen and Neilson presented their new programs as serious academic work that would provide students with unique skills that were valuable for later career success.[24] Other advocates of study abroad emphasized less specific, more idealistic goals of cross-cultural understanding that would tend to promote peace while simultaneously advancing American economic and diplomatic interests.

And what of the students themselves? How did they view the prospect of study abroad, and to what extent did their experiences fulfill or fall short of the organizers' intentions? Their on-the-ground perspective was more concrete and also more complicated than the institutional rhetoric. Katherine Bolman, a Smith student, recalled that Neilson expected a lot more of the juniors going to France than merely learning French:

Before the Smith College Junior Group sailed in August, 1927, President Neilson told us clearly what our purpose was. In France we were to do two things: absorb the best of French life and culture, and give in return our interest and our friendship. We were not to criticize what we found there, we were not even to put into words any comparison of French ideas and customs with our own. Instead we were to use our faculties for observation, for study, for the acquisition temporarily of a French viewpoint. Especially we were to remember "to conduct ourselves at all times in such a way as to uphold our own good name and that of the college" and never to forget our own best traditions while we were away from home.[25]

According to Katherine Bolman, students were not to compare French and American ways, yet they were expected to adopt a French viewpoint while still retaining a firm sense of personal and national identity. She wrote, "The responsibility for Franco-American relations seemed to rest upon our shoulders."[26] To do this, they had to learn and understand French cultural values, social practices, ways of thinking, and political views, which necessarily entailed confrontations and comparisons with their American backgrounds.

American students who went to France took with them stereotypes and romantic myths about France and the French that were both affirmed and undermined by the experience of study abroad. For many students the value or myth of France was that it was old, rich in history, and enshrined in literature, in contrast to the United States.[27] Katharine A. Morrison wrote in 1930: "Everything over here is so quaint and different from America. The streets and street noises are entirely different and hard to get used to. In Paris the pavements are made of big stone blocks and remind me of the 'Tale of Two Cities.'"[28] Looking back on her arrival in Paris, Beatrice F. Davis said, "I found Paris just a treasure house of a whole past.... I just found the whole place a living museum."[29] Describing the train ride from Le Havre to Paris, Marian Sage wrote in 1927: "The country of France is so trim and neat-looking ... there were the cutest little farm houses with red roofs, and little towns all huddled together.... everything has been just as I pictured it, and I haven't been disillusioned at all so far."[30]

Although some found comfort in the affirmation of their preconceptions, others acknowledged some disillusionment when France failed to live up to their fantasies. At the end of her junior year in France in 1926, Delia Brown reflected: "First, when I was told I would spend two months in a small provincial town in the Alps, I imagined a cluster of country houses, with peasants wearing costumes, cows, chickens, pigs, a little university where we would be the only foreigners. Instead of that I found myself in Grenoble, an important industrial town, seat of a well-known university where all the great nationalities of the world meet."[31]

Jack Roads revealed a vivid imagination when he wrote to his family about a visit to Versailles and an illusion he had of a historical figure—a healer and organizer of séances who was popular for a short time at the court of Louis XVI: "We visited the Grand and Petit Trianon and continued our dreams of French history and Dumas fiction. Once I was so far gone, I thought I caught a glimpse of Cagliostro lurking behind an arras, but it wasn't he."[32] Florence Elizabeth Bragdon found a way to retain her illusions about Paris as she describes a late afternoon drive on Armistice Day: "And we could not look enough, for everywhere the fountains were playing, there were searchlights on all the buildings and monuments, and the illumination made it look like the Paris you dream about—instead of the everyday, grime-covered, gray city where we walk and shop. It was really beautiful and it gave me the picture to imagine when I want to think about Paris in a sentimental, romantic sort of mood."[33]

Daily life forced students to come to grips with France as a modern, urbanized nation still recovering from the hardship of World War I in the 1920s and struggling with economic depression in the 1930s. It shattered some romantic illusions about France, but it also challenged a popular image of French people and especially Parisians as decadent, immoral, and devoted only to pleasure.[34] Kirkbride was well aware that he needed to address this notion if the Foreign Study Plan were to succeed, and he advised President Hullihen to give wide publicity to the following statement: "The popular expression 'Gay Paree' so often heard in the United States is an utter and absolute misconception." Referring implicitly to brothels, or perhaps to the performance *revues* and the cabarets of Montmartre, Kirkbride asserted that these institutions catered almost exclusively to American tourists: "The average Frenchman doesn't even know where these 'awful places' are. He leaves that to the self-righteous American scandal-monger.[35] Similarly, Hélène Cattanès, the organizer and first director of the Smith College Junior Year in France, had to overcome faculty resistance at Smith College to the idea of American young women studying in France: "Of all places—to send nice young girls to wicked Paris."[36] Beatrice F. Davis, who studied in France in 1931–32, remembered, "my mother had ideas of France as a kind of sinful city of the Western World."[37]

For many American students, Paris initially affirmed the French reputation for sexual immorality, but it also dispelled this preconception. For example, in letters to her family in Michigan, a student with the Delaware Foreign Study Plan, Sarah Johnston, sometimes complained about French immorality after watching sexually explicit French films and viewing Auguste Rodin's sculpture, *The Kiss*. Yet she also offered a good-natured explanation for public displays of affection in Paris: "[I] also stopped to admire a *very* public and prolonged clinch in the middle of the *Boulevard St. Michel*. There's something beguiling about the French frank [sic] and earnestness."[38] For Smith College student Eleanor Daniels, the notion of Paris and especially Montmartre as a center of licentiousness fell apart with actual contact, as she wrote to her parents in 1938: "I made my first (and perhaps only) trip to Montmartre to cash your check. Not really Montmartre, just the outskirts, but anyway I laughed when I thought of what a den of iniquity you were sending your pure daughter to" (for more, see Chapter 7).[39]

In addition to confronting their stereotypes about the French, students also faced French stereotypes about Americans.[40] Many found that French people imagined the United States as the land of cowboys and Indians and of gangsters. "The French haven't any idea what we're like. . . . The majority still think Indians run around at large and that the rest of the population are just a lot of hoodlums! I've given up trying to make them understand and just sit back and smile to myself—and feel quite superior," wrote Dorothy Tebbets to her parents in 1926.[41] After watching a Laurel and Hardy movie in Tours in 1938 and being teased that Americans were just like the film portrayals, Sarah Johnston wrote to her sister: "the movies *do* give the most extraordinary idea of America!"[42] Often during conversations over lunch and dinner, students learned what their hosts thought of Americans, as Florence Elizabeth Bragdon reported from Grenoble in 1929: "We are learning from the Leveau's [sic], however, that all Americans smoke, eat no bread, drink milk, and get divorced, and the young girls lead absolutely free and unhampered existences."[43] Another common notion among the French was that Americans were materialistic, and Mary Louise Cahill picked up on this as she indicates in her account of a visit to a court of appeal: "In the Chambre d'Appel, we saw an exquisite Gobelin [tapestry rug] depicting a hunting scene. It is worth three million francs. I suppose our guide, thinking rightly that we were Americans, thought we were interested only in the material value of things."[44]

Students' experiences were constructed in large measure by confronting French stereotypes of Americans and realizing the limitations of American stereotypes of the French. Although some of the mutual stereotypes persisted over time, others were more historically specific, as is evident in two different letters of Caroline Miller Stabler in which she initially condemned French stereotypes of Americans as rich and insensitive to French suffering coming out of World War I. In 1925 she wrote: "The thing that makes me perfectly furious, is their attitude about Americans. In the first place all Americans are rich." Stabler was frustrated that although she did not have enough money to do all the things she would like in France, she was assumed to be wealthy. In addition, she saw a link between this stereotype and the French view of international relations. "[The French] all think America should cancel their debt. They . . . are forever making remarks about how France suffered more than any other country, lost the most men, gave the most money and had the most territory devastated, and now is weighed down by a terrible debt, while all other countries have drawn an immense profit from the war."[45]

Almost three months later, Stabler reconsidered her exasperation with France and the French, specifically, her impatience with the despair and complaints of her host family:

> That long tirade on the French and their general attitude was much too violent. I'd probably eaten onions for lunch or stayed up too late. It sometimes affects me that way and I shouldn't generalize so quickly. Just because I happen to live with Royalists who are much depressed by the war and hard times doesn't mean that everyone in France is like that. I've met lots of other people now who are gay and happy, and look at the political situation without any great alarm.[46]

Enraged at French stereotypes about Americans, and stung by the French belief that Americans caused France's economic problems, Stabler eventually caught herself doing the same, that is, asserting generalizations about the French based on particular instances. Yet it was also her personal experience that allowed her to see the limits of all stereotypes and to appreciate the particular social and political position of her host family as an explanation for their attitudes about many things, including the United States. Dorothy H. Johnston expressed a similar view in a speech that was broadcast on French radio in 1928: "So many preconceived notions about this country have been destroyed by real contact, so many first impressions have proved false on longer experience that we have learned to condemn nothing on first evidence."[47]

Overcoming stereotypes was a significant component of cultural exchange for American students in France. Another challenge was confronting a different education system as well as a different language. Taking classes in French and from French teachers was a source of immense difficulty for American students, especially at the beginning of the year abroad. Not only did they have to deal with a foreign language, but they confronted different pedagogies and a very different student culture (see Figure 4). All the letters reveal some or a great deal of anxiety over the exams that followed the language instruction in the provinces and, to a lesser extent, the end-of-semester-exams at the Sorbonne and other institutions in Paris. Dorothy Tebbets (an exceptionally gifted student of French, according to the director, Hélène Cattanès) wrote: "I'm a wreck" over the upcoming language exams: "six hours of writtens and if you pass those—a grueling oral."[48] Phebe Adams, a young woman often distracted by shopping, worried about her exams after the first semester in Paris: "I have never been so scared of anything before. When I think of learning all of French art from prehistoric man to Futurism, so that if asked I could give any artist in any period and his works and influences etc., I am ready to curl up and die. I'll try not to though."[49] Henry Kirkpatrick noted in 1929 how much harder he worked at his studies in France in contrast to the United States: "Some of the best [American] students here agree that the work is really too hard. Good Lord—I work my head off—and without too favorable results. Frankly, I do get a bit discouraged now and then. Going to college in America is a comparative snap."[50]

Studying in a foreign language was more difficult than operating in one's first language, but students also learned that the entire French education system was different from that in the United States, despite the fact that most of their classes were specifically intended for foreign students. Dorothy Tebbets noted: "The French certainly had a different idea of education than we have. We diddle through college with a little studying and much 'college life.' Here, they think if anyone comes to study, he comes to do that exclusively. They certainly believe in intensive training."[51] Hilda Donahue, a scholarship student from Smith College, observed that in France students were left much more on their own than in the United States:

FIGURE 4 Students in a French university classroom, no date, probably 1920s. Courtesy of the University of Delaware Archives.

> I, too, noticed that the 'onus is thrown' on the student. I found this at first very discomforting and was very ready to call it 'lack of system' and other names. But since then I have learned that in France it is an honored and time worn tradition that the student worries about and cares for himself—as a result, he is much more capable to handle all difficulties, whether they pertain to his university life or not, very efficiently.[52]

Donahue felt that she had benefited enormously from this realization and from her limited experience as a "French" student, in terms of feeling more self-reliant and capable of handling her own affairs.[53]

Students' observations reflected the different historical traditions and trajectories of higher education in the two countries, including interwar developments. The main purpose of higher education in France since the French Revolution (1789–99) and Napoleon (1799–1814) was to prepare students for, and control access to, liberal professions.[54] By contrast, American colleges and universities fulfilled more diverse and sometimes competing purposes, including moral and intellectual development, training in useful skills, and teaching general culture.[55] Students in the United States and in France were largely from the middle and wealthy classes, but higher education in both countries had to adjust to a growing student population following World War I. David O. Levine contends that the American system underwent significant structural and curricular changes in the 1920s and 1930s, and higher education in general became more broadly acceptable, even necessary for social and occupational success.[56] Reform in French universities, especially in arts and letters where most Americans took courses, was less comprehensive, according to Christophe Charle, largely because of an overwhelming burden on faculty to administer *baccalauréat* examinations to the French equivalent of high school students (*lycéens*) to determine who could progress to higher education.[57] American colleges and universities were flexible and increasingly varied compared to French universities. In addition, social life and peer culture were much more significant in the United States than in France, due to dormitory living, organized athletics, fraternities and sororities, and student government and other student-run activities.[58] American students noted the effects of these differences in a more focused and serious approach to academics in France than in the United States.

For example, American students in France confronted a new way of thinking and different expectations from professors. Several students commented on the French *plan* or system of organizing thoughts, arguments, and written compositions. An anonymous young woman from the Delaware Foreign Study program of 1927–28 wrote this in response to the question of how ideas, opinions, and personalities were changed by the study abroad experience:

> All my habits of thought have been profoundly altered. When I arrived in Nancy I thought the "plan" was a useless and boring tool for homework. Gradually, I submitted to the discipline of the "plan." Now I am in love with it; I look for it everywhere, in readings, in lectures, and even in arguments developed in the course of a conversation. I like order, and I try to arrange all my ideas into a logical system. Through methodical thinking one is able to see, with all questions, aspects whose existence many people have never suspected.[59]

Another student indicated that her thinking changed in a different way: "I begin to believe that I approach, or rather that I have attained, the French spirit, mocking but good-natured [*esprit moqueur mais bon enfant*], that laughs without wounding, and the modern young American girl with her yellow slicker seems to me as amusing as the old French lady dressed in the style of 1890."[60] A Smith student explained the difference between French and American professors' expectations of their students this way:

> The French professors lay a great deal of emphasis on the form in which you give the information you know. At home any signs of intelligence about a question are greeted with shouts of glee by the professor, whereas here an intelligent notion of the subject is taken for granted by the professor beforehand, and your merit lies in giving some individual thought to the question and presenting the result in a clear and interesting fashion."[61]

Of course, not all students accepted new thinking and new expectations with alacrity. In 1937 Mary Louise Cahill wrote, "I am writing this letter during a lecture of phonetics which is very boring. Everyone is either writing letters or sleeping. I am a little disappointed in some of my courses." Yet even Cahill recognized the better study habits derived from taking courses in France while still cherishing the American system: "I can see now why the girls who spent their Junior Year in France get such excellent marks when they get back! I expect we'll all be Phi Bete's when we get back. Boy—give me the good old American system of education any day!"[62]

Through the junior year abroad programs, students discovered strengths and weaknesses of both American and French education systems. National political systems were less salient to American students generally, for as several historians have noted, American students were generally apolitical in the 1920s, and even in the 1930s the politically active on college campuses in the United States were a minority.[63] Nonetheless, students in France in the 1930s could hardly avoid learning something about politics, with antigovernment demonstrations, mass sit-down strikes, and the threat of war so imminent and close at hand. Edith Pardee, for example, was aware that the riots of February 6 and 7, 1934, were serious threats to political stability in France, but her account of earlier demonstrations that she viewed from her apartment window on the Boulevard St. Germain does not suggest much danger. She wrote: "[The demonstrators] were mostly young royalists of the 'Action Française,' and 'Jeunesses Patriotes,' and looked more like a lot of high-school boys after a home-team victory than a mob bent on overthrowing a government. One wondered sometimes, watching them intent on pulling up small trees, if they knew exactly what they did want."[64] By contrast, Sarah Johnston took politics very seriously when she was in France in the fall of 1938. Adolph Hitler's threatened invasion of Czechoslovakia and the Munich agreement that forestalled it resonated with her, especially because she became attached to a young Czech man studying in France at the same time. She presented to her family competing feelings of love for France, pride in the United States, and understanding of European affairs deriving from her study abroad experience: "I adore France—not to the extinction of America, of course and I'm a pretty rampant little patriot when I consider our political system and our ideals as compared with here. There doesn't seem to be a lot of future for anything, but Communism and Fascism, especially the latter, which simply *enslaves* the mind and deliberately distorts Truth for its own ends."[65]

Far more influential than politics on American students was the profound impact of World War I on France and French people, in contrast to its more limited effects in the United States. Almost all student letters reveal a new appreciation for the war, gained from visits to battlefields, annual Armistice Day observances in Paris, views of the damage to cities and buildings, and daily contacts with French people. More than political parties, changes in governments, political demonstrations, the League of Nations, or even the threat of war in the 1930s, the effects of World War I provided American students with a transnational perspective.

With her guidebook in hand and prepared for a lesson in art history in 1930, Florence Elizabeth Bragdon was shocked at the effects of the war on the cathedral in Rheims: "but our interest in Gothic architecture was immediately changed to horror at the mutilation of the whole church."[66] Visits to Rheims, site of a severely war-damaged cathedral, inspired some students, like this one, to reflect on the meaning of war: "The buildings have been restored as they were before the war, but there is something lacking. It is not the fault of Rheims, rather the fault of the war, the despicable thing. Why do men have a passion to kill and to destroy beautiful things? How can human nature be cruel sometimes and so kind at other times?"[67] Similarly, Miriam Allen wrote to her parents about the battlefields of Verdun in 1929: "I can't believe I've actually seen all these things, and how different from an American scene of interest. Perhaps because the war is so sacred to them or something, but none of this was commercialized. Everything just there, and no pop stands alongside."[68] Also in 1929 Frances Hurrey was downright depressed by the battlefields of Verdun: "I can't express the awful feeling they gave me." The "awfulness" continued with the "warlike"

Ossuary and the "sinister" underground forts, so that Hurrey was much relieved to end the trip at the neat, open-air American cemetery brightened with colorful flowers: "I am so thankful that our cemetery is away from the awful stark nakedness of the main battlefield."[69] Even in 1937, nineteen years after the Armistice, a rather skeptical Eleanor Daniels was impressed by the moment of silence on November 11 in Paris: "The 10:59 silence was extremely moving—wedged in that cheap, dirty, noisy crowd, I was amazed at the change after the bugle. The Paris mob became reverent and uplifted for one beautiful moment. It was unbelievable—the Arc de Triomphe, the flags, the motionless guards, the still crowd."[70]

Such comments reflect recent research on World War I battlefield sites that addresses their dual nature as both sacred ground for remembering and honoring the dead and as commercial tourist destinations.[71] Other commemorations of the war, including monuments to the dead, tombs of unknown soldiers, and Armistice Day observances were intended to foster national unity, including between combatants and civilians.[72] Scholars disagree over the extent to which governments and tourist guides manipulated popular emotion or individuals invested pilgrimages or observances with personal meaning. Yet evidence from American students tends to support the position of David W. Lloyd that, for Britons and Commonwealth members, visits to battlefield sites had complex and individual meanings and that visitors were not passive victims of government or commercial manipulation. Moreover, unlike most other American tourists, students came to these sites with an additional kind of preparation from daily life in France and the different meanings the French attached to the war.

In 1929 Laurence Wylie wrote to his mother in Indiana that it was hard to leave his host family in Nancy when the group prepared to move to Paris: "The other night I was talking with Mme Favas when she began to cry. I asked her what was the matter and she said, 'It seems just like my son is back with me again. We're so happy and now you are going to leave.' I certainly felt badly; I told you, I think, of her son my age who was killed during the war."[73] In another example of how living in France brought the war home to students in a new way, Phebe Adams noted in her diary in 1930 an encounter with a bureaucrat who was a wounded veteran: "We had our addresses changed [at the town hall] by a war veteran whose face was horrible scared [sic]. He just didn't have any chin at all & no lower teeth I don't think. We certainly don't know the half about this last war at home."[74]

An anonymous student noted other effects of the war in daily life, as she describes the city of Nancy: "The atmosphere on the streets is so different [from the United States]. People dress in black and seem so serious. The destruction during the war is still plainly visible. The people are smaller, more somber and in general dirtier. You do not find the animation which you find at home."[75] Several of the host families suffered financial and social setbacks from World War I, which is probably why they agreed to lodge and feed American students, as this was a welcome source of income. Frances Hurrey wrote to her family in 1929 about her host in Nancy: "She lost her husband in the war and last night we sat for over an hour listening to stories of the war—what these people have gone through!"[76] And Dorothy Tebbets wrote of the family of the Parisian war widow who hosted two Smith students: "I'm sure they were much better off—financially and otherwise—than they are now. They speak with feeling about the change in classes that the war has brought about. The peasants ride around in autos; the 'haute bourgeoisie' are impoverished."[77]

Some students noted a deep hostility among French persons toward Germans, thus dispelling any notions of an enduring peace. In a long description of an excursion to Verdun, probably in 1929, Katherine M. Pratt wrote: "You know, I think we do not quite appreciate the war. We have forgotten it too soon. I know that I never thought of it at all when I was home, but one can't ever forget it here. The people do not talk about it, and yet, one can sense a rapid undercurrent of feeling. The French still have a violent dislike for everything German."[78] Similarly, Dorothy Tebbets relates how she repeated to her host the inscription she read on the plaque at Compiègne memorializing the signing of the Armistice: "Here on 11 November 1918 the criminal pride of the German Empire surrendered, vanquished by the free people they tried to enslave." On hearing the words, the socially prominent host clapped her hands and said, "Bravo," prompting Tebbets to remark sarcastically: "And some people think we are ready for world peace!"[79] Students learned to appreciate the devastating effects of war in Europe and the challenges that confronted proponents of peace.

French academics and diplomats were less concerned about study abroad's contribution to world peace than they were with cultivating a positive attitude toward France in the United States. And in this regard several expressed satisfaction with the result of many American teachers of French who were imbued with enthusiasm and affection for France from study abroad. The University of Paris archives contain several testimonials from American students like the following. J. T., PhD from Rutherford, New Jersey, wrote on December 17, 1935: "I am teaching French in the high school here in our town; every class I have, I enjoy, because talking about Paris brings memories back to me. I try to instill in my students the love I have for France...." And G. A. asserted, "The students who come here and experience the hospitality and kindness of the French people and those who take so much interest in them carry back to the United States happy memories and gratitude in their hearts. False propaganda and the nonsense that political activities seem to bring to light for the newspapers have no effect on these students, I believe, because they have actually experienced other things."[80]

This effect of study abroad was precisely what Charles Petit-Dutaillis of the National Office of French Universities and Schools had in mind in 1932 when he defended the student scholarship and exchange program between the United States and France; his office had created the program after 1918 as a "very important, very efficacious method" for "creating an atmosphere favorable to France [in the United States]."[81] In a 1931 volume of *Foreign Study Notes*, a publication written and produced by the students of the Delaware Foreign Study Plan, University of Paris Rector Sebastien Charléty, a strong supporter of the junior year abroad, acknowledged how valuable the periodical was for conveying a positive impression of study in France to other Americans: "The publication that you undertake will undoubtedly have useful results. . . . you establish a relationship between the young students and former students who, for the most part, already teach in the United States; it recalls the good memories of a year spent in France, and we are pleasantly touched by it."[82] Additionally, students from both the Delaware and Smith programs formed alumni associations that performed a variety of functions, including organizing reunions, maintaining social contacts, distributing newsletters, keeping up with French politics and cultural events, establishing a placement office, and funding scholarships to help a younger generation of students study in France.[83]

American organizers of the junior year abroad were also satisfied with the experiment, though for slightly different reasons than they originally anticipated. President William Allan Neilson of Smith College found his original goal for the Junior Year in France program—a more effective means of mastering a foreign language—to have been affirmed, but he also noted greater maturity among the young women who studied abroad: "All return with an easy control of French; and their work in college during their senior year is likely to show a greater intellectual independence and a more mature attitude than one finds in the average homebred senior."[84] Walter Hullihen, president of the University of Delaware, who initially touted the benefits of study abroad for American business and foreign relations, acknowledged that students emphasized personal growth, cosmopolitanism, and "a consciousness of release from a stereotyped and restricted point of view in education, a broadening of interests and outlook, contact with an atmosphere of cultural and aesthetic ideals quite new," as their greatest gains.[85] In other words, students valued what Pierre Bourdieu calls "cultural capital" along with a new sense of freedom to think for oneself.[86]

Even before the year abroad was over, students reflected on its meaning in their letters home and in occasional published accounts.[87] Additionally, several questionnaires and studies surveyed alumni of study abroad from both the Delaware Foreign Study Plan and Smith College Junior Year in France. All this evidence is partial in the sense that those students who felt positively about study abroad were more likely than others to write about what it meant to them or to respond to surveys. In addition, the interests of those conducting the surveys also channeled responses to particular purposes and with particular language. And the memory of a junior year abroad no doubt was enhanced over time, especially considering its association with youth and a relatively carefree moment in a middle-class person's life. Indeed, from the beginning, students who elected to and were selected to study in France were favorably disposed toward it. So it comes as no surprise that students' constructions of the meaning of study abroad were overwhelmingly positive. Yet given these and other limitations, the evidence nonetheless indicates that students responded to study abroad in ways not anticipated by program organizers and proponents, that these responses modified the original justifications for study abroad, and that students articulated a distinctive form of internationalism.

Although some students asserted that the junior year abroad programs had enhanced their career opportunities, far more mentioned personal maturation as a positive outcome of the experience. Several students from the Delaware Foreign Study Plan affirmed that the year in France had contributed to career success. For example, R. Wolf, a French teacher, wrote, "I feel that I owe in part my present position to the Delaware Foreign Study Group," and J. Emerson, explaining that he had at last received a foreign service appointment to Japan, asserted, "I believe the Junior Year Abroad experience will be of great help in enabling me to plan my work for the next two years."[88] Others emphasized individual and personal benefits. Students acquired "greater self-confidence and independence," according to Douglas William Alden in response to a 1933 survey of the Delaware Foreign Study Plan and "Greater poise, and ability to cope with different situations," wrote Ruth P. Belew.[89]

Additionally, students identified thinking for themselves, abandoning stereotypes, and learning tolerance as valued gains. Few were as detailed as Ginny Stearns in 1926, but her reflection was not untypical: "I gained, I think, at least the idea of what is a broad and tolerant mind. When I came to France I had already formed opinions about many things, prejudices against Catholicism, horror of easy morals, scorn for people whose habits did not match ours." She acknowledged that one year is not long enough to totally eliminate such a "narrow-minded" orientation, but she articulated the process of change in her own thinking: "I learned that instead of criticizing one must know first how to evaluate [*juger*], and to know how to evaluate one must assimilate all that one sees and try to understand it."[90] Louise Whitney also explained this process of transformation at some length: "In the family with whom I stayed there were many ideas I didn't understand. I tried to see their side of things and to understand the reasons for their ideas. I also have a better idea of the feelings and conditions that exist between France and the U.S. I find it does a lot of good to see with one's own eyes that your own country [can be] wrong. . . . I think I learned to judge a little for myself and not to accept too docilely the ideas of others."[91]

A more thoughtful, even skeptical, nationalism accompanied Whitney's developing tolerance and independence of thought, and this was evident in other students' accounts as well. Louis Blum wrote of his year in France: "One learns to see and to judge for one's self, to have broad ideas and tolerance; one understands his country better in the light of the history and doings of another."[92] Russell Johnson responded to a questionnaire of 1928 by the University of Delaware about study abroad: "It was then that I crept out of my shell and began to realize that other nations require as much attention and study as our own."[93] Althea B. Avery succinctly stated: "such an experience tends to put an end to imperialism in thinking."[94]

Rare was the cynic in voluntary assertions about the value of study abroad, yet one of the original students in the first Delaware Group of 1923 expressed skepticism about the benefits of mutual understanding through study abroad. In a 1970 interview, Herbert H. Lank stated, "all this yakkety yak about traveling and making a better world because you come to know people better and their language and their culture, is just so much hogwash." He thought familiarity could just as easily breed contempt, and he continued, "You may be better off as far as the peace of the world is concerned if you don't understand the other guy and what he's doing."[95] Similarly, Eleanor Daniels was less than idealistic in her account of a reception held by the socialist mayor of Dijon for foreign students in 1937. She characterized the mayor's speech as, "lots of vague phrases like 'Franco-American Friendship' and 'the importance of youth as peace-bearers,' etc.—you know."[96]

Such doubt about the potential of tolerance and understanding to contribute to world peace suggests less global idealism than skeptical realism in students' articulation of internationalism. Their version of internationalism was a way of looking at the world, a questioning of received wisdom, and appreciation for difference. This is evident in results of a 1935 survey of former Smith College juniors who studied in France that posed the question, "How did your Junior Year affect your attitude towards domestic and world affairs?" Summarizing the 232 replies (out of 305 questionnaires sent), Elizabeth Murphy wrote, "With two exceptions the answers state that living intimately for a year in a foreign country has given greater breadth of vision, greater maturity of judgment, more tolerance, and above all, as regards international affairs, 'a greater interest in a subject which until then had been a closed book.'"[97] Students overwhelmingly valued study abroad for a variety of reasons, including internationalism, but not the internationalism of spreading the American free enterprise system or popular culture, and not the internationalism of transnational peace organizations, and not necessarily the internationalism of United States' involvement in foreign affairs. Theirs was a cultural internationalism of exchanging ideas and persons that entailed sufficient intellectual independence to question one's own beliefs and value the beliefs and practices of another culture. It was less an "imagined community," Benedict Anderson's conceptualization of nationalism, than a conscious reevaluation of American nationalism embedded in a larger awareness of a transatlantic framework.[98]

The students' internationalism was a hybrid product, deriving from the union of two different approaches to international relations in the 1920s and 1930s—Americanization and French cultural diplomacy. Unlike these policies, however, the students' experience was not a one-way imposition of one culture on another. Students confronted their own stereotypes of France and French people's stereotypes of the United States to realize their limitations. Adjusting to a completely different educational system, they learned to appreciate the strengths and weaknesses of higher education in France and the United States. Witnessing the effects of World War I on France and on French people led American students to understand a global event they had never before considered, even though some students' fathers had participated in the war. Students were no less patriotic or attached to the United States because of their newfound affection for France or understanding of global affairs. Margaret White's comment about the effect of her junior year in France with the Delaware Foreign Study Plan is quite typical: "While I learned to understand and appreciate another great civilization and found it most stimulating, I appreciate my own country none the less."[99]

During the 1920s and 1930s the junior year abroad established itself as a legitimate option in higher education. Several articles published in American education journals between the wars surveyed students and otherwise assessed the junior year abroad as successful in terms of second language acquisition, courses as rigorous and valuable as those offered in American universities, general cultural enhancement, a greater sense of self-reliance and independence, improved study habits, increased tolerance for cultural difference, and more international-mindedness.[100] Surprisingly, however, no one noticed or commented on the preponderance of women on these programs in France. The Smith College Junior Year in France consisted entirely of women, and women outnumbered men on the Delaware Foreign Study Plan by a ratio of about three to one. In probably the first social scientific survey that compared the views and demographics of students on the Delaware Foreign Study Plan with those of the Sweet Briar College Program after World War II, the author, C. Robert Pace, accounts for income levels, age, marital status, and occupations and careers. Yet the fact that "one-fourth of this prewar group were men; three-fourths were women," warrants no consideration.[101] Gender has hardly figured in any historical or scientific study of study abroad, yet it mattered a great deal to the students themselves, especially to women. As we shall see in the next chapter, women's experiences of the junior year abroad were vastly different from those of men due to contrasting French and American conceptions of femininity.

§ 4 American Girls and French *Jeunes Filles*

Negotiating National Identities in Interwar France

In 1925 Dorothy Tebbets, an American studying in Paris, wrote home to her parents, "The Sorbonne . . . is packed with Americans—girls especially 'abroad studying at the Sorbonne.' To all intents and purposes but really over here to collect a wardrobe for a début and maybe, incidentally, a French count or marquis! Anyway, they don't look as if they had brains enough to come out of the rain but there they sit and represent the American girl."[1] Tebbets noted what various statistical sources reveal—that the overwhelming majority of Americans who studied in France between the wars were women. Additionally, she hints at contestations over the meaning of the "American girl," both among Americans and between French and Americans in the interwar period. Tebbets's comment provides an introduction into the significant differences between American women's and men's experiences studying in France in the 1920s and 1930s and to the salience of gender in comprehending those differences.

As a growing number of historians have recently indicated, women and gender have been highly significant in international relations, though they have been long ignored. Leila Rupp, for example, reveals how feminists in the modern era overcame barriers of distance and especially of national difference to construct an international community devoted to women's rights and cooperation as an alternative to nationalism, power politics, and patriarchy.[2] Focusing on gender in transnational representations, Emily S. Rosenberg, Lynne Frame, Mary Louise Roberts, Miriam Silverberg, and the Modern Girl Group at the University of Washington have examined discourses on the modern girl (or modern woman) in a variety of countries in the early twentieth century.[3] They demonstrate that, through the figure of the modern girl or woman—characterized by independence, education, a career, the pursuit of pleasure, and erotic or sexual indulgence—commentators in Europe and elsewhere articulated their anxieties about modernizing change implicitly or explicitly originating in the United States. The history of American women students in France in the 1920s and 1930s reveals a new form of women's agency in international relations, and it shows how women themselves addressed and overcame the constraints of gendered discourse.

Two gendered national stereotypes—the French *jeune fille* and the American girl—structured the experiences of American women students in France between the wars. These young women engaged in a process of negotiating among the two tropes, and lived experience, to construct new identities for themselves that included an internationalist sensibility of tolerance and appreciation for cultural difference.[4] Paradoxically, by adhering to a restrictive model of feminine behavior in France, some young American women fulfilled the promise of independence and maturity represented in their own ideal of American womanhood. In addition, the resurgence and proliferation of study abroad after World War II and continuing to the present, and the increased recognition of it as a form of cultural diplomacy in the United States, depended, in part, on the positive assessments of study abroad by the majority of participants—women—during the pioneering interwar years of the junior year in France.

Although it was obvious in the interwar years that more American women undergraduates than men were studying in France, no one has explained the rapid feminization of this innovation in American higher education.[5] From 1923 to 1939 close to one thousand women and approximately two hundred men studied in France with either the Smith College Junior Year in France or the Delaware Foreign Study Plan until the outbreak of war caused their suspension (see Figure 5).[6] In addition, French reports on the number of foreign students attending the Cours de civilisation française of the Sorbonne indicate a consistent predominance of women over men. In 1932, for example, there were 139 men and 686 women.[7] Two evaluations of American study abroad programs conducted after World War II noted in passing that women outnumbered men by three to one, but neither regards this as a point of analysis.[8] Evidence from French sources suggests that the preponderance of women students was a bit shameful to French academics and authorities. Historian Martha Hanna notes that when the Cours de civilisation française was first organized at the University of Paris, French officials anticipated

FIGURE 5 The Delaware foreign study group, 1929–30. Note the predominance of women. Courtesy of the University of Delaware Archives.

that American men would replenish the ranks of absent French soldiers.[9] So why was study abroad in France more attractive to American women than to American men?

It is likely that study abroad benefited from the general increase of women in higher education or the growing demand after World War I for French teachers, which was considered an acceptable occupation for women.[10] Additionally, men were probably more invested than women in spending the entire four years of undergraduate education in the United States to prepare for a career in a field other than foreign language, and they were generally more involved in campus activities (sports, fraternities, student government) than were women.[11] Also, France apparently had a special allure for women more than for men, connoting a language of refinement and cultivation, aesthetic domination in the arts, fashion chic, renowned cuisine, and incomparable shopping.[12] Travel to France and familiarity with French culture may have represented elite social status to women especially—a particular form of sociologist Pierre Bourdieu's cultural "capital."[13]

Yet for many Americans France also connoted a place of moral laxness and bohemian decadence, attractive to young men for sexual and erotic adventure but potentially dangerous for women.[14] Beatrice F. Davis, who studied in France in 1931–32 with the Delaware Foreign Study Plan, remembered, "my mother had ideas of France as a kind of sinful city of the Western world."[15] Partly in response to this image, American women studying in France were subject to behavioral restrictions that did not apply to men. These restrictions derived from a particular understanding of traditional, French femininity. This was the French *jeune fille*, the sheltered, virginal, obedient young woman of the middle or upper class.

For more than a century, families of the comfortable classes in France expected marriage to be the destiny of their daughters, and they sought to protect the virginity and preserve the innocence of girls for this purpose.[16] This was not always possible, especially after the economic, demographic, and cultural disruption of World War I. Growing numbers of women seeking higher education and professional careers flouted the ideal of the bourgeois *jeune fille*.[17] Nonetheless, this ideal resonated throughout France in the 1920s and 1930s, and the practices associated with it were common in both provincial and urban settings.[18] American organizers of the junior year in France in the 1920s and 1930s constructed rules for American women students on the basis of this model. Both organizers and students from the United States used the term in the original French, indicating that they understood its cultural and national connotations; a French *jeune fille* was not merely a "young girl," or the French equivalent of an American girl.

The American girl represented another stereotype in French eyes. In both France and the United States, an "American girl" was assertive, independent, and possibly sexually promiscuous. The idea of the American girl often served to focus anxieties about modernity in France in the 1920s and 1930s and to distinguish between alternative constructions of femininity that were regarded as traditionally or at least culturally French.[19] The American girl was also an identity at the heart of controversy in the United States regarding young people generally. Although American commentators deplored an immoral and hedonistic youth in the aftermath of World War I—visually manifested in the androgynous clothing and hairstyles of young women—many college women positively embraced an ideal of the American girl that connoted freedom, self-assurance, sexual maturity, and modernity.[20] For American women studying in France in the 1920s and 1930s, both French and American conceptions of American girls and French *jeunes filles* meant considerably more than just discursive constructs. They were lived identities that contributed to cultural insights and misapprehensions, self-awareness, and, occasionally, the breakdown of stereotypes.

Why did American women study in France in the 1920s and 1930s? Or, what aspirations or objectives animated the programs and the students at the outset? As we saw in Chapter 3, the originally stated purpose of the two junior year abroad programs was professional training. Although Walter Hullihen, president of the University of Delaware, saw Raymond Kirkbride's Foreign Study Plan as creating "a great reservoir of college-trained business men" for careers in international business and the Foreign Service, Kirkbride urged Hullihen to approve the admission of women into the program as early as 1922 and 1923 while he was making preparations.[21] Hullihen did not object to the proposition in principle, and there was interest on the part of the Women's College of the University of Delaware, but it seems to have been expedient to admit only men to the first year of the plan.[22] In addition, faculty members of the Sorbonne had created the series of courses for foreigners with men students in mind, specifically, American soldiers in France awaiting transportation between the armistice of 1918 and the peace treaty of 1919.[23] However, in April 1924 the University of Delaware awarded Helen P. Simon a scholarship to study in France, generating enthusiastic publicity, and she became the first woman student on the plan.[24] The following year seven men and six women studied in France, and thereafter, women outnumbered men in the Foreign Study Plan groups, in some years by as many as four to one.[25]

Smith College also conceived of the Junior Year in France program in professional or at least academically rigorous terms. However, unlike the Delaware Foreign Study Plan, it was limited to French majors, and it did not admit students from other colleges at this time. According to President William Allan Neilson, the Smith College Junior Year in France "was devised to solve the problem of giving the students who major in French a more thorough knowledge of the French language, literature, and culture."[26] Smith College administrators and some students were adamant that the Junior Year in France program was not a mere cultural gloss for upper-class sophisticates. In 1927 one of the co-directors reported to President Neilson that she disabused a few French host families of a misconception about the program: "I even had to explain to two or three of them that Smith College in Paris was not a sort of 'finishing school' offering at a good rate the opportunity to visit fashion houses, tea shops, stores, theater and occasionally the Sorbonne."[27] Student Dorothy Tebbets, as noted above, drew a distinction between what she considered to be the serious Smith College juniors and other, more frivolous American women who only pretended to study in France. Tebbets was obviously concerned about the reputation of the "American girl" in France, and the policies of both study abroad programs regarding women students help to explain why.

In 1926 the Delaware Foreign Study Plan issued a handout entitled "Rules for Girls," that asserted, "it is understood that the female students of the group adapt to French practices for girls during their entire stay in France." It stipulated that young women had to return to their host families for all meals and every evening, unless they obtained special permission from the assistant director (a woman hired to supervise the women students). Such permission would be granted only if a French chaperon, most likely a member of the host family, accompanied the young women. Women students also could not receive visitors without the permission of their host families.[28] Recalling her experience in 1927–28, Mrs. Robert H. Richards asserted: "We never went anyplace without a chaperone—ever." She continued, "French people didn't understand a jeune fille going out without a chaperone."[29] The different requirements for women and men in the group were obvious to all: W. Emerson Wilson remembered, "the girls of the group . . . couldn't go out after 9:00 at night, and so they had it worse than we did."[30] Advice to women regarding appropriate dress while in France was also more extensive than that given to men. Although men were advised that, "All flashy clothing is looked upon with disfavor by the French people," recommendations to women were more pointed: "Stockings, not short socks, should be worn"; "Galoshes are not worn in Paris"; "Sleeveless dresses are not worn."[31]

Similar requirements were part of the Smith College Junior Year in France program. President Neilson of Smith College reported on the first group of juniors after he visited them in Paris in 1926: "The students are submitting to the restrictions as well as accepting the privileges of another civilization, in order to know how it feels to be a jeune fille in a French family. We shall continue to insist that they cannot go to France on any other terms."[32] Hélène Cattanès, a Smith faculty member and first director of the program, required that Smith students go out at night only with a chaperon; they were prohibited from smoking cigarettes in their rooms; they were not allowed to frequent cafés, night clubs, and "hot" spots such as Montmartre; and they had to wear silk stockings, hats, and long-sleeved garments at all times in French cities. Some of these rules remained in force as late as 1936, for Mary Louise Cahill wrote to her parents, "The girls [foreign students at the University of Dijon] don't wear any stockings or hats, but Mlle. Delpit insists that we wear them both, because if we don't we will be taken for 'filles de la rue'—as French girls of the higher classes do not go on the streets of the city without hats or stockings."[33] Similarly, an anonymous student on the Delaware Foreign Study Plan asserted that, in the city, "a *jeune fille bien élevée* [a well-brought-up girl] is supposed to wear a coat."[34] And Marie Holslag wrote in 1931 that even in hot June weather, her host insisted that she wear a long coat or a fur: "But Madame would not let us out of the house without our fur. We usually carry it in our hand."[35] Reassuring her family about her safety in France in 1929, Florence Elizabeth Bragdon wrote of herself and her roommate (also from Smith College), "we are leading much quieter and protected existences here than at home, quite as if we were real French jeunes filles."[36]

Yet, adopting the behavior of French *jeunes filles* could imply that American girls would miss out on some aspects of French life and culture. One student noted the contradiction between Neilson's injunction that they behave like French *jeunes filles* and at the same time take advantage of all opportunities to learn about French culture: "The gist of his talk was that we were supposed to be living the lives of young French girls and not of American tourists, and that we should meanwhile be making the most of our opportunities to see educational things around Paris, which is what French girls rarely do."[37] Similarly, Miriam Putnam Emerson wrote home in 1930 that she and some other Smith College women watched a football match in Grenoble: "we didn't understand it very well but were glad we went to see how different it was. The French boy who comes here for his meal was quite shocked because 'no French girl ever goes to a football game!'"[38] Such contradictions were less bothersome to American students than were the stringent restrictions on their evening activities and other personal freedoms.

Not surprisingly, students chafed at these restrictions. In addition to individual acts of disobedience, such as going out at night unchaperoned with a date and frequenting night clubs, women petitioned for relaxation of the rules. Cattanès reported in the middle of the first year of the Smith College Junior Year in France that "discipline weighs heavily on those [young women] who wish to amuse themselves more and especially in less French ways. They do not understand why the college forbids them from going to places of entertainment [*des lieux de plaisir*] where their parents themselves take them." Students also objected to the rule prohibiting them from smoking cigarettes in their rooms, especially after the rule was removed for students at college in Northampton, Massachusetts. Cattanès held the line, however, on going out at night, and thanks to Neilson's support of her position during his visit to France in 1926, she found that students eventually resigned themselves to the chaperon requirements. And they agreed to a compromise over smoking; students could accept an after-dinner cigarette if their host families offered.[39]

Cattanès justified some strictness on pedagogical grounds and to foster good relations between American students and French hosts. She reported to Neilson in December 1925 that when the group arrived in Paris after their initial stay in the provinces, she prohibited the students from going out at night unless accompanied by a member of the host family (usually the mother): "In this way they can give a little more care and attention to their studies, which is indispensable at the beginning, and moreover they are led to give more consideration to their hosts and to get to know them better."[40]

A woman student on the Delaware program felt grateful in 1927 not to be "subject to some really ridiculous regulations," as she described the situation with Smith College juniors in France.[41] Nonetheless, during the 1928–29 academic year, Delaware women students petitioned the Foreign Study Committee in Newark to relax the chaperonage rules. The students accepted all restrictions while they were in Nancy, a provincial town, but they argued that the cosmopolitanism of Paris rendered them unnecessary. According to the students:

> This international element [a number of foreign students in Paris] has, to a great extent, lessened the former prejudices of the French people. The conventional French attitude concerning the correct conduct of young women to which these rules were made to conform has undergone a rapid change toward the more liberal Anglo-Saxon view-point. The Parisian families in which we live, consider our restrictions surprisingly severe.[42]

The Committee was torn between acknowledging the students' legitimate desire to partake of French culture in its myriad forms and their obligation to parents who had entrusted their children to the care of the University of Delaware Foreign Study Plan. It compromised by allowing women students "to attend lectures, concerts, soirées or the theatre two evenings a week accompanied by friends," subject to parents' written permission.[43]

Naturally, students would enlist their host families' support for their claim that the strict rules limiting women's freedom of movement were outdated. Yet support for this position also appears in a report from the Smith College program director in 1927. Madeleine Guilloton wrote that although the students were submitting to the rules with good grace, their hosts importuned her to let them have a little more fun: "'My girls,' they tell me, 'are all so well-behaved and conscientious that you should make an exception for them. Can't they go to the theater alone, or for supper after a show, etc.?'" Guilloton replied that all the students accepted the strict regulations as a condition of being on the program and that they were necessary to achieve a life for the students "reasonably divided between work and leisure [*les distractions*]."[44]

Restrictions on women students' freedom of movement were common in colleges and universities throughout the United States in the 1920s, and common also were students' demands for their relaxation.[45] In addition, faculty and administrators at Smith College and the University of Delaware felt an obligation to parents for the welfare of their children, especially in a foreign country, and they also wanted to impress the French favorably so that the programs could continue. But a distinctive factor behind the exceptionally strict rules for American women—in contrast to men—in France was the widespread French stereotype of American young women as unrestrained and morally loose. Many years after she organized the Smith program, Hélène Cattanès explained that she had had a hard time convincing respectable French families to house American students because "young American women did not have a good reputation in Paris. 'Girls who spend the night who knows where,' they told me, 'who return home at five o'clock in the morning, like shameless hussies [*des dévergondées*], no thank you.'"[46] This was a rather extreme version of a view, common among French commentators since Alexis de Tocqueville wrote *Democracy in America* in 1833, that unmarried American women were shockingly independent and too free with strangers.[47] Florence Elizabeth Bragdon noted the currency of this stereotype in 1929 when she wrote to her parents that her host family in Grenoble believed that "the young girls [in the United States] lead absolutely free and unhampered existences."[48] Again, in 1939 Sarah (Sally) Johnston recounted to her aunt and uncle the French perception of unrestrained American young women. Describing a "swanky" ball at the Ecole Polytechnique, she wrote: "I went with a *Polytechnicien* [a student of the Ecole Polytechnique] who was very shocked when I asked him his first name, and said, '*Comme les jeunes filles sont libres en Amérique! Mademoiselle, je suis fiancé!* [How free the girls are in America! I am an engaged man!][49] In 1926 Cattanès was so concerned about the reputation of American, and especially of Smith, women in France that she was ready to send home two students who broke the rules and went out dancing in Montmartre without permission: "It seems to me that a young girl could not behave more badly in France, and nothing could give a worse impression of the college and of American habits."[50]

Some American women recognized the difficulty of their position, being simultaneously American girls and French *jeunes filles*. Although they valued the independence and autonomy they associated with "the more liberal Anglo-Saxon view point," they also were concerned about the poor reputation of American girls among French people. This was evident in a report by Mary Louise Cahill to her parents in 1936. Her French host, Madame Rives, told her about a former Smith student boarder, Enid, who went "on a trip for three days with some young men she met on a train. Isn't that the limit? Madame Rives was furious . . . she wrote and told Enid that if such things were done in America, they weren't done in France. On the whole, I guess Enid was pretty obnoxious."[51] Improper behavior took on added, nationalistic connotations in the context of study abroad. President Neilson of Smith College said this of the juniors selected for the program: "they have for the moment to suspend their belief in our self-governing democracy and do what they are told in order that they may see the reason why."[52] Eleanor Daniels thought that it was necessary for the American students to accommodate French norms of feminine behavior. Daniels related to her parents a long story about one of the students who flirted with the male boarders in the house where she lived: "the silly goop couldn't realize that one just doesn't talk to boys in one's pajamas or sit in their laps!" Daniels thought the director, Mademoiselle Saleil, overreacted in wanting to send the young woman home, but she also thought the student was rather insensitive or stupid: "Not that she does anything bad or that she wouldn't do in America, but she can't seem to understand that French standards are different from ours."[53]

These contentions over feminine behavior suggest the pervasiveness of the heavily laden tropes of American girls and French *jeunes filles*, and their inability to contain the new identities American and French women were creating for themselves in the interwar years. American and French women were pursuing higher education in greater numbers than ever before, and more women were working outside of the home. On both sides of the Atlantic, some feared that careers were overtaking family responsibilities as women's primary goal and function in life.[54] Such fears did not appear to affect the American women who studied in France, for there is no indication that they considered their education to be incompatible with marriage, and none had as yet embarked on either a career or marriage. However, they were very sensitive to issues of autonomy and freedom and to a sense of French tradition versus American modernity in the cross-cultural experience.

Certain conditions in France made American women students feel more modern than, and even superior to, French women. One was the persistence of traditional mourning practices. Many American students remarked on the ubiquitous black mourning dress of French women, especially in the provinces. "Four out of every five women you see on the street are in very heavy mourning (including our hostess, whose husband has been dead for three years)," wrote Marian Sage in 1927.[55] Another indicator that France was less "modern" than the United States was that women's clothes in France were still custom-made among the middle- and upper classes. "It is impossible to find anything ready-made here," Eleanor Daniels wrote to her parents in 1937.[56] And finally, there was the matter of suffrage, though students mentioned this less often than they did the mourning clothes and custom tailoring. In 1935 Margaret Goddard wrote of her host father: "He is certainly firm in his belief that woman's place is in the home! And we can see now why French women have never got the vote!"[57]

Yet, were the categories of French tradition and American modernity as absolute or mutually exclusive as women thought? In their descriptions of daily life in France, American students reveal an implicit (sometimes explicit) assumption about the superiority of American values and practices over those of the French. But they also suggest a breakdown of easy distinctions and some attempts to understand cultural differences that could not be explained simply as a dichotomy between tradition and modernity.[58] Women confronted complex cultural differences in their experiences of French heterosocial practices and in their impressions of French women students. These particular encounters of difference, though often misunderstood, contributed to American women students' questioning of certain assumptions and openness to new identity constructions.

In 1925 Dorothy Tebbets discovered how differently sociability between young French women and men was structured, in contrast to the United States. She described in great detail a dance she attended in Grenoble, where the Smith group was taking French language classes, along with other foreigners, at the university. Tebbets explained to her parents that the dance was approved by the director of their program, Mademoiselle Cattanès, and that it was common practice at these affairs for young women to attend without male escorts. She went with three of her Smith friends and had a fine time dancing with men of many nationalities, all students at the university. She drank champagne with some Swedes and Norwegians and was escorted home by an American she met at the dance—a Yale graduate who was studying French and Spanish. Tebbets ended her letter this way: "Imagine! So this is Grenoble—what will Paris be? Not half so much fun, probably. I don't know when I've had a more different time!"[59]

Three weeks later, clearly in response to a horrified or chastising letter from home, Tebbets defended the propriety of the dance. It was sanctioned by Mademoiselle Cattanès, only university students could attend, and "there's always a proper chaperonage of professors and their wives." Tebbets regrets having upset her parents, but she also makes the case that she did nothing wrong. "I'm awfully sorry to have done anything to shock you and mother. I hope I never do again. Perhaps I over emphasize things in my letter to try and make you see how funny and different it was. The drinking in public did not concern me—in the first place it was in the foyer of the university and I only drank one little glass of champagne." She assures her parents that "the college knows about [the dance] and no French girl however well-bred would hesitate to go to one."[60] It is difficult to discern the precise source of her parents' disapproval—dancing with strange men, leaving home without a male escort or returning home with a stranger, or drinking alcohol in public during Prohibition in the United States. Whatever the case, social etiquette in France and the United States was different.

Other American students confirmed this pattern of French sociability. Describing a grand ball for students at the Sorbonne in 1929, W. Emerson Wilson remembered: "And the strange thing was you couldn't take a girl to a dance. The girl came to the dance and met you at the entrance with her chaperone."[61] Marian Sage was initially disconcerted by French manners, as she indicates in this description of a dance at a casino that she attended with her roommate and accompanied by her host in 1927. "There were quite a few students there—men—and one of them came up and asked Molly to dance. She refused, and he couldn't believe it, so he asked me. Mme. was just leaving us to go and play cards, and she insisted that we dance." The two young women did dance, and Sage continues: "so it was perfectly all right and seems to be the thing to do here—although we laughed heartily at the thought of doing it at home!"[62] Elizabeth Brown found this practice amusing rather than strange in 1930: "There is no ceremony about asking a girl to dance, whether you know her or not—except that the young man always asks permission of the chaperone before he asks the girl. Quite a cute idea, n'est ce pas?"[63]

These accounts suggest fundamentally different underlying assumptions about late adolescent sexuality, or about how to regulate it. According to historians Beth L. Bailey and Peter N. Stearns, Americans valued individual privacy and trusted young women to exercise some self-restraint while alone with a member of the opposite sex.[64] Dating in the United States also was predicated on the two individuals knowing one another or at least being of a certain family or class background to justify the association. Beatrice F. Davis remembered that when she was in France in 1931, she and the other American women "were only allowed to go out if we dated American boys. . . . I think their feeling was that we would know what to expect, and how to conduct ourselves with Americans, who would know about us, too."[65] Studies of sexual practices in the United States in the 1920s and 1930s indicate that dating and petting (referring to a wide range of sexual caressing) were common among college-age young people but that the public outcry against sexual immorality was overblown. Scholars find that young people were discovering sexual pleasure and eroticism in anticipation of marriage but that premarital sex, especially among college women was relatively rare, occurring mostly among engaged couples.[66]

By contrast, the solution to the problem of premarital sexuality in France was to keep women away from its temptations, rather than rely on women's self-control in the face of them. According to the young and rebellious Jacques Chevignard, who explained the French system to Eleanor Daniels in 1937, it was a challenge for a "French boy and girl *ever* [to] get to know each other, for it seems they are never allowed alone unless betrothed." He went on to say that the constant chaperonage of young

French women meant that they were "kept in a dish-cover, like cheese, until they become quite rancid!!"[67] This difference may be attributed to the two countries' varying religious heritages regarding sexual pleasure. Sociologist Eric Fassin notes that Catholics traditionally regarded sex as a necessary evil for reproduction in marriage, in contrast to Puritan acknowledgement of sexual pleasure as a benefit to marriage.[68] In any case, historian Mary Lynn Stewart finds that French parents and educators represented premarital sex to young women as dangerous, causing venereal disease or unwanted pregnancy, and then avoided further discussion of sexuality.[69] Other scholars show, however, that young persons privately conducted their own investigations.[70] Dating was not a common practice in interwar France, though petting was making its way into middle-class *surprise parties* for young persons via American movies and novels.[71] Eleanor Daniels describes the "'surprise party' pronounced à la française" as the "best" of three different types of parties for young women and men in Dijon, though it is not clear that she ever attended one. It was also the least supervised (perhaps because it occurred in a private home rather than in public): "there are no chaperons; the crowd just descends at someone's house, the boys armed with a bottle each, the girls with a cake. I guess they are pretty gay—you see the French do get around their strict parents!"[72]

French commentators generally agreed that young women and men enjoyed far more social contact with one another than did pre-World War I generations. Dances were popular in interwar France, as they were in the United States, and French authors asserted that increased heterosocial interactions, particularly among students, contributed to more companionate and egalitarian marriages after World War I.[73] Chaperonage of young women in France was gradually relaxing, but varied from family to family, as Frances Hurrey noted in 1929: "We can't go out at all at night unless *heavily* chaperoned. Our Madame here [in Paris] is much more strict and not nearly so homey as Madame in Nancy."[74] Sally Johnston was shocked in 1938 to find that a young French woman her own age was not allowed to go to cafés. She wrote to her family: "I think French girls are cute and nice but very *protected*—they don't ever *stir* without their families, I don't guess. I asked this girl—Claire is her name—if she didn't ever go walking, to see Paris, and she said no except with her parents. She seemed to feel we were wild, crazy, independent spirits."[75] French author Simone de Beauvoir's account of her student days in Paris in the 1920s records the gradual change in her own socially conservative family. For a time, Beauvoir was prohibited from going out at night unless accompanied by her mother or another appropriate, adult chaperon. Yet as her studies progressed, Beauvoir gained greater independence: "that year my parents gave me permission from time to time to go out to the theatre in the evenings, alone or with a friend."[76] Eleanor Daniels echoed French observers when she asserted in 1938: "At any rate, American customs are taking hold more and more in France and most all the nice girls, Francine says, go out alone now."[77]

Although few students penetrated the underlying assumptions about adolescent sexuality in France and the United States, the recognition of different norms of heterosocial and especially female behavior led some to ponder their meanings. Sally Johnston confronted her host mother's anxiety over her son's relationship with her American roommate, Helen. Sally tried—rather successfully—to explain to her family that where an American saw a casual and normal dating situation, the French mother (Madame Mérel) feared a romantic prelude to marriage. Sally wrote of Madame Mérel: "To her it's inconceivable that any girl should be 20 without matrimonial designs—or along that order! She cannot understand a half-romantic, half-intellectual student friendship of the kind I have been used to all my life... you know, a college romance." Sally went on to note the different attitudes of American and French parents regarding their children's intimate relationships: "Of course Madame can't be blamed for her outlook which is French.... Her attitude in comparison with yours is hilarious—you... have confidence in your daughters but hope that the new interest won't affect school work."[78] One remarkably sensitive young American woman, a scholarship student at Smith College, suggested the possibility for mutual understanding between American and French young women and the breakdown of the stereotypes of both the wanton girl and naïve *jeune fille*. Hilda Donahue wrote of one of the children in her host family in Grenoble: "The youngest envied me my American freedom—and as she wisely remarked, 'Since the American girl knows she has liberty she doesn't abuse it.'" Donahue continued, "young French people... amaze me with their world wisdom, and with the more serious or probably the more saddened outlook on life which they have."[79] Another student, Delia Brown, showed maturity in recognizing stereotypes and their limitations. Disappointed that she never established a warm relationship with her host family in Paris, she wrote: "I saw other French families, and I think there are all kinds, as in America. And it's very possible my Parisian hosts were also disillusioned, that they expected a very different girl who would be more agreeable to them."[80]

American women students encountered social practices in France that sometimes contributed to an understanding of cultural difference and often challenged assumptions or stereotypes. Encounters with French women students similarly disconcerted American women but also led some to glimpse the differences in the respective French and American systems of higher education that underlay different women students' behaviors. American women on study abroad programs in France actually had little opportunity to meet French students, and especially women students. Their main contacts with French people came through the families they lived with or social occasions arranged by the families or other private or public contacts. The few accounts of French women students by American women are usually negative, suggesting an almost insuperable social, economic, or cultural barrier between the two. Mary Louise Cahill stayed in a house with other female student boarders. A French woman, Colette, she described as "a typical 'vieille fille' [old maid]—tortoise-shelled glasses, low-heeled shoes and thick stockings, . . . preparing for her agrégation [competitive examination to be eligible to teach in a secondary school or university] in grammar at the Sorbonne." Cahill also wrote that "she is frightfully bourgeoise—very self-satisfied" and that she and another French student in the house "are perfect bores—we don't like them very well."[81] Eleanor Daniels was slightly more charitable when she described women of student age at a dance party hosted by a French person; in her description she is both dismissive of them and extremely confident about the superiority of American women but also a little aware that she was reinforcing negative French stereotypes of American women:

> These French girls were so unattractive at least compared to the American girls of the same age (17–21 about). So young and inexperienced. It was, I suppose, only natural that we should have a good time—after all everybody wanted to be nice to us, but I did feel *so* badly seeing all the nice, bespectacled Simple Susans holding up the wall. I exaggerate, I know, for there were some nice girls too, but you know what I mean. It being a dance, one had to concentrate on the gentlemen, so we never did speak to many girls. I suppose they thought us horribly forward etc. All I can say is they ought to see a real American flirt![82]

It was obviously difficult for these two privileged American young women to appreciate the material hardships of French people in general in the interwar years, and of women students especially. French feminist Louise Cruppi sketched a depressing picture of women students in France in 1925, most of them living in poverty, lacking self-confidence no matter how brilliant, and desperate for a degree that would enable them to earn a living.[83] Odette Pascaud presented a more positive view of women university students in 1935, though she also asserted that the new educational opportunities were fraught with difficulties for women: "[Women] can, often they must, make a career for themselves, a difficult task. They do not regret, in any case, the times when all was easier."[84] French women students in Paris, although usually the daughters of educated and professional men, were nonetheless plagued by familial and financial concerns.[85] During the 1920s and 1930s, they often sought part-time jobs as tutors, baby-sitters, house cleaners, hair stylists, and home care givers in order to survive and to relieve their families of the burden of their upkeep while at the university.[86] Branded as "brains" (*les cervelines*) and "female intellectuals" (*les intellectuelles*) in the popular press, women students struggled to succeed in the arduous task of earning advanced degrees to qualify for professional advancement and security and to overcome the prejudice that they were therefore destined to be old maids.[87] According to Pascaud and others, French women students had not lost their desire for marriage, but they sought to combine it with the life of the mind. In this they were hardly different from American women students.

Representing a group of French women students in Paris as being clearly feminine, as well as intelligent and committed to higher education and careers, Marguerite d'Escola [the pseudonym of Mrs. Joseph Ageorges] drew attention to their childish gaiety, their brightly decorated rooms, and welcoming manners in a 1926 article: "In truth, none of them has renounced marriage." However, she wrote in her account, deliberately avoiding the term *jeunes filles*, "They consider themselves happy and they frankly rejoice in the new freedoms that contemporary customs grant to young women [*aux jeunes femmes*]."[88] The potential for independence that higher education offered was particularly beneficial in the 1930s because of the great uncertainty facing all students, women and men, as Pascaud noted: "Women rely on themselves more, and they are right to do so, for it is true that the good old days are over."[89]

Even before the Depression, Simone de Beauvoir affirmed the seriousness of the French students she knew: "they were all, like me, grim professionals intent on getting through the competition."[90] She also confirmed Eleanor Daniels's and Mary Louise Cahill's observations about plain clothes and frumpy appearances among French female students, saying that she was usually badly dressed, even when she paid illicit visits to Montparnasse bars and could not hide her bourgeois student status with, "my dingy old frock, my woollen stockings, my sensible shoes and my face ignorant of make-up."[91]

American women students only dimly recognized that the different systems of higher education in the United States and in France presented different modes of obtaining independence for women. Academic achievement and success on competitive examinations were the means by which French women could earn degrees and pursue careers, thus securing financial independence and potentially an active role in public life.[92] By contrast, women's colleges, in particular, and coeducational universities in the United States provided American women with social skills and leadership experience that they might deploy in community service and other public roles—a fact that the Albert Kahn *boursières* had noted with admiration before World War I.[93] Higher education in France was, in general, for both women and men, a more solitary, professionally oriented, and competitive endeavor than in the United States. Dorothy Tebbets explained this difference to her parents in 1925: "The French certainly had a different idea of education than we have. We diddle through college with a little studying and much 'college life.' Here, they think if anyone comes to study, he comes to do that exclusively. They certainly believe in intensive training."[94] Although some gained a glimpse of the academic demands and perhaps the economic hardships that French women students faced, American women students were disinclined to imitate the dour studiousness of their French peers.

Instead, they tended to feel more sympathy for older, bourgeois or upper-class French women than for women students, perhaps because they saw more of them and also because their class backgrounds and social positioning seemed more similar to the majority of students at American women's colleges. American women students were impressed with the social graciousness and cultivation of mature French women, in contrast to what they perceived as the driving, but dull, ambition of French women students. This attitude may also have reflected the greater importance of sociability and social graces in American college life, in contrast to the French university system that lacked dormitories, sports, fraternities, sororities, clubs, and student government—in short, the many sources of peer group sociability. Thus, for many American women students, mature French women, even if they lacked university degrees, were admirable in their manners and intellectual and aesthetic interests.

Caroline Stabler marveled at how her host Madame Bourelly and her friends struggled to retain social graces and cultural pursuits in the face of financial and social decline since World War I: "Lots of Madame's friends have to do embroidery, dressmaking, and other kinds of fancywork twelve or fourteen hours a day the year thru, and yet they continue to have their 'reunions,' and their days 'at home,' and discuss literature and art with their friends as calmly as though they had ten servants waiting on them."[95] Eleanor Daniels described a tea at a Frenchwoman's house: "too, too chic for believing. All the French women seem so flawless and well-groomed—except those like Madame Martin [her host]!"[96] An anonymous former student on the Delaware Foreign Study Plan highly praised the French matron in 1928:

> There is a certain sweet and subtle perfume that exudes from the French woman and her home [*son intérieur*] that makes you forget even your accent; and when people tell me that the French woman is an old game and not interesting, not taking courses at the university, not voting, and not joining lots of clubs, I reply that it is not the instruction but the education and the heart that make the charm of a woman, and that the French woman is the most charming imaginable.[97]

Encounters with French women students and with upper-class mature French women presented American women students with alternatives to the two stereotypes that structured their lives in France. And the socially gracious *femme du monde* (woman of the world) was more compatible with their middle- or upper-class backgrounds and the social orientation of higher education in the United States.

Although the stereotype of the French *jeune fille* yielded to new possibilities for female identity in interwar France for American women, it is difficult to generalize about the responses of French persons to the young American women in their midst. The evidence presented above reveals, not surprisingly, that some French hosts found American women to be headstrong, reckless, and worse (Madame Rives and the "obnoxious" Enid), while others thought their guests so well-behaved and hardworking that they requested exceptions to the rules of chaperonage. Hélène Cattanès believed that the first group of juniors in France had dispelled French prejudices regarding American girls and therefore allowed the program to continue: "Were hostesses satisfied with their guests? They were, for in Grenoble as in Paris their homes remained open to Smith girls in the following years, and more and more of their friends now expressed willingness to receive '*une p'tite Smit.*'"[98]

Nonetheless, the poor reputation of American women persisted, and the subject was debated among men of the French diplomatic corps in the context of sending French women to study in the United States.[99] A 1932 note from the French embassy in the United States to the Council of the Ministry of Foreign Affairs expressed concern about the bad influence of American women students on French women: "In the current climate of customs, American university environments do not seem to me favorable to the development of the French girl [*la jeune fille française*]. She has much more to lose than to gain from contact with her American counterparts." Du Verneuil of the Service des oeuvres françaises à l'étranger acknowledged that, "bourgeois French families of the old school fear the freedom of movement of young American women," and so were apprehensive about allowing their daughters to study in the United States. Charles Petit-Dutaillis of the Office national des universités et écoles françaises took issue with the embassy's position: "If there are some [French women scholarship students] who compromise themselves, it is because they have been badly brought up in France."[100] This discussion did not change French policy of encouraging academic exchanges between the United States and France for both women and men. French academics as well as diplomats were pleased that American students, women and men, usually returned from their year of study in France to teach French or in other ways to promote French language and culture in the United States.[101]

One way that American women students fulfilled this expectation was to approximate the *femme du monde*, for many married, had families, and kept up with French culture and foreign affairs generally, probably more than they would have without the study abroad experience. They bought and read books in French, taught French to their children, participated in the local Alliance Française, formed alumni associations of those who had studied in France, or donated money to scholarship funds for study in France.[102] Yet the results of study abroad were considerably more varied than this. Figures on 305 former Smith College juniors in France indicate that in 1935, 103 of these were married, and of that number, 18 worked full time in jobs outside the home. Of 232 respondents to this Smith College survey, 104 did some kind of advanced study after graduation, and more than 60 taught or had taught French. Other occupations of these 232 women included the following: administrative and commercial jobs in Paris; editor of a travel magazine; secretary to the chair of the Yale French Department while pursuing graduate studies; administrative assistant in a department store; jobs in the art field; personal secretaries; and a translator.[103] Another survey of both Smith College and University of Delaware study abroad alumni emphasized the wide variety of careers, in addition to teaching, that former students pursued. The figures are not divided by sex, and they do not contain raw numbers, only percentages. They show that of the Delaware groups through the class of 1932, 42 percent went into teaching; 20 percent did graduate work; 35 percent were in various careers (including "theatricals, foreign service, the ministry, lecturing, foreign and domestic banking, manufacturing, salesmanship, law, employment work, advertising, newspaper work, life insurance, home-making"); and 2 percent were unwillingly unemployed. For Smith College groups through the class of 1930, 27 percent were in teaching, 7 percent did graduate work; 64 percent were in various careers; and 2 percent were unwillingly unemployed.[104]

The orientation of these surveys, and the figures themselves, affirm at least the broad objective of study abroad for professional training and enhancement.[105] These are consistent with an account by a woman student, Aureta E. Lewis, on the Delaware Foreign Study Plan of 1937–38. Reporting on the career goals of her fellow juniors abroad, Lewis wrote that, "Some wish to spend a year in France in order to master the language as a preparation to returning to America to teach it." She went on to indicate that others were French majors with a secondary interest in business who sought careers that combined the two fields. She claimed that history and political science majors viewed the year abroad as helping their expertise in history and world politics. Lewis specified that some men intended to go to law school and then into the Foreign Service after college; other students planned careers in art, music, and art history; and some had no specific career plans.[106] Not included in the surveys, but relevant in the context of study abroad as preparation for the Foreign Service or international business is the case of former Delaware Foreign Study Plan student Beatrice F. Davis. In a 1970 interview, she stated that her motivation for participating in the program in 1931 was a long-standing desire for a career in the Foreign Service. However, the Depression and a prohibition against hiring married women prevented her from fulfilling this goal.[107]

Equally, if not more, evident in the documentation, however, is the sense of self-awareness, larger understanding, and tolerance that students gained from study abroad. This survey summary by a Smith College Junior Year in France alumna was repeated in Delaware Foreign Study Plan surveys: "Answers state that living intimately for a year in a foreign country has given greater breadth of vision, greater maturity of judgment, more tolerance, and above all, as regards international affairs, 'a greater interest in a subject which until then had been a closed book.'"[108] In 1926 Ginny Stearns asserted that she was "narrow-minded and opinionated" when she came to France, but that she "gained . . . at least the idea of what is a broad and tolerant mind."[109] In contrast to Hullihen's original conception of study abroad to further U.S. foreign relations and trade, students articulated a different sense of internationalism: appreciation of a foreign culture for its interest and value equal to one's own.[110] As Bryn Mawr student Althea B. Avery put it, "such an experience tends to put an end to imperialism in thinking."[111] Responses such as these to study abroad are by no means unique to women, and men have recorded very similar accounts of themselves, as we saw in Chapter 3.[112]

Yet it is worth considering that even in the 1920s and 1930s, foreign travel, with its attributes of self-awareness, education, and maturation, had not entirely lost its masculine connotation. The freedom, dislocation, and reconstitution of identity that had long been the experience of travelers who were, for the most part, men, meant something different and were perhaps more intense for women.[113] Marie Holslag, for instance, took pride in her achievements in French during her year of study abroad, telling her sister that, "Six months ago I was afraid to come [to France] because I thought I was too stupid. Now I see that I have done a lot up to now. From the most stupid I have become one of the most brilliant. I'm very happy."[114] Before returning home, she warned her parents that the year in France had transformed their daughter: "I have been asking everyone if I have changed much since I have been over here. They all start by saying well you have gotten thinner. But they go on to say that I have changed in other ways, too. So, prepare yourselves for a great big surprise. The change is for the better, so don't worry."[115] American women indicate that they felt more confident and self-reliant from the year in France. Caroline Stabler wrote to her parents of her newfound confidence that she could live by herself with a French family: "It's too bad that we didn't realize last June when Mlle [Cattanès] asked us, that we would not mind being by ourselves. I think we were all afraid then. Think how we have improved!"[116] Dorothy Tebbets vaunted her adaptability to the more difficult living conditions in France compared to the

United States, including using oil lamps instead of electric: "But the things I've put up with since I left [the United States]! I would have kicked like a bay steer ordinarily but from now on when I get back you're not going to know me. I won't fuss at anything and will be very easily pleased and made comfortable. You just see!"[117] Even Eleanor Daniels, one of the most voluble on differences between American and French women, and assertive about the independence, and self-assurance of the "American girl," admitted that until she came to France, she really had not been independent and autonomous. "My strength of character must be growing by leaps & bounds for I am trying to make myself do *every*thing frightening that comes along. I hope someday I'll acquire confidence. . . . But I certainly am learning a lot & I ought to be gaining poise gradually."[118] Paradoxically, American women had to travel to France and live the protected life of the *jeune fille* in order to be "real" American girls; that is, independent, autonomous, and self-confident.

Stereotypes such as the American girl and French *jeune fille* served a useful function for the women of the first junior year abroad programs in the 1920s and 1930s. They provided a framework for the administration of the programs and the regulation of the women students. They also helped young American women construct and reconstruct identities for themselves, for observing the limitations of stereotypes allowed them to discover new possibilities for women's identity in the alternatives of the cultivated *femme du monde*, the determined French women students, and in their own resourcefulness in coping with a foreign culture far from home. The breakdown of stereotypes, along with encounters of difference in the form of heterosocial behaviors and the condition of French women students, helped American students develop understanding of and appreciation for cultural difference. Study abroad allowed them to see the world and themselves differently. They were American internationalists who sought new learning from and understanding of another national culture, which they perpetuated and disseminated in various ways after returning to the United States.

When war broke out on September 1, 1939, students on the Delaware Foreign Study Plan immediately left France to return to the United States. The junior year in France programs did not resume until 1948. But when they did, it was with the strong encouragement of the French government. As the French cultural consul in New York reported to the Ministry of Foreign Affairs, these programs had "before the war played an important role in the teaching of French in the United States."[119]

Unstated in this request to support the resumption of the junior year in France with scholarships and travel discounts was the fact that the majority of American students who participated were women. It is reasonable to assume that the positive experiences of women on the interwar junior year abroad programs contributed substantially to the resumption and expansion of study abroad, actively supported by both the French and U.S. governments, following World War II.

§ 5 Warm Relations in a Cold War Atmosphere

Resurgence and Expansion of Study Abroad Following World War II

World War II and the Cold War brought the U.S. government into transatlantic study abroad for the first time. Earlier interventions occurred in 1908 with the use of funds from the Boxer Indemnity to pay for the education of Chinese students in the United States. Then, in 1939 concern about German influence and Nazi propaganda in Latin America led Congress to pass Public Law 355 in support of cultural relations projects with countries of that region, including scholarships for young Latin Americans to study in the United States.[1] These were precedents for the much more extensive state involvement in cultural relations and educational exchanges during the war and after 1945 that accompanied a new realization that cultural diplomacy was vital to American national interest. Aggressive efforts by the U.S. government to combat communism at home and abroad, combined with the political and economic problems of a new postwar French government, reshaped the framework for Franco-American cultural relations generally and study abroad in particular.

The French Fourth Republic began in the midst of war, following the liberation of France from Nazi occupation in August 1944 and before the end of the European theater of World War II on May 8, 1945. The French people hoped for political renewal after military defeat, occupation, and the collaborationist regime of Vichy but were quickly disillusioned when, after two years of Charles de Gaulle's strong executive authority, the constitution of the Fourth Republic in 1946 established a parliamentary system that, given multiple political parties and necessary coalition governments, proved unstable. This instability allowed considerable influence by the United States in French political affairs. In addition, France depended on the United States for aid in economic recovery and rebuilding. Relations between the two governments were fraught in the postwar years as French leaders sought economic assistance and national security in the form of a permanently weakened Germany, while the United States wanted France to cooperate in the rebuilding of Germany and increasingly viewed German economic and military strength as a bulwark against potential Soviet aggression. The Marshall Plan of 1947 resolved the situation by providing substantial aid to France and securing French allegiance to a western alliance, notably the North Atlantic Treaty Organization (NATO). However, tensions remained as the Fourth Republic sought to modernize France while preserving national identity, if not autonomy, and the United States tried to influence French politics by supporting centrist governments and marginalizing the Communist Party through a variety of propaganda efforts. Further aggravations occurred over French military buildup, American assistance, and French conduct of the war in Indochina and colonial policy generally.[2]

The eagerness of the Fourth Republic to maintain good relations with the United States, the zeal of the U.S. government to combat communism, and wariness of the French public toward its powerful ally are all evident in the two countries' cultural relations and, especially, in old and new structures of study abroad. Yet these political and ideological tensions only marginally affected the increasing numbers of students, scholars, and teachers from each country who eagerly embraced a growing array of opportunities for educational travel in the other country (see Table 1). The letters, reports, surveys, and oral interviews of French and Americans who studied abroad during the Cold War era enhance and even correct existing scholarship on Franco-American cultural relations that focuses almost entirely on documentation from governments or organizations working with governments. Frank Costigliola and Brian Angus McKenzie note that overtly propagandistic efforts by the United States Information Service (USIS) and the Marshall Plan were unsuccessful in persuading the French population to embrace American values and practices in the 1950s.[3] By contrast, various programs of the Department of State to bring European students and leaders to the United States in the postwar years enjoyed more success in terms of the students and leaders returning home with a positive attitude toward the United States, despite—indeed because of—their exposure to social problems such as racism, rural poverty, and urban slums. Studies of such individual exchanges by Giles Scott-Smith and Liping Bu emphasize the program

TABLE 1
*Americans studying in France and French
in the United States, 1948–1960*

Year	Americans in France	French in the United States
1948–49	NA	454
1950–51	NA	543
1951–52	NA	588
1953–54	NA	507
1954–55	967	472
1955–56	1,173	548
1956–57	1,252	584
1957–58	1,104	615
1958–59	1,832	627
1959–60	2,420	572

SOURCE: From Institute of International Education, *Open Doors*. Report on International Educational Exchange, 1948–2004 (New York: IIE, 2005).

organizers' underlying assumptions about the superiority and universality of American values and practices and their desire to see them adopted by foreign nationals.[4] They imply that American cultural imperialism overwhelmed or obviated any possibility for mutual understanding, meaningful exchange, and improved international relations.

I argue instead that in the Cold War era study abroad as a form of Franco-American cultural relations served both national interests and internationalism simultaneously because the result was not indoctrination, homogenization, or conversion, but rather an appreciation of difference.[5] Both the French and American governments engaged in cultural diplomacy to cultivate respect and admiration abroad for their respective national cultures.[6] This is evident below in postwar claims and debates surrounding educational exchanges. But the way that study abroad fulfilled these goals went beyond policymakers' notions of national interest. That is, individuals from France or the United States who studied or taught in the other country reassessed their own national identities and learned to understand another national culture with the realization that both were equally valuable. This process was consistent with the experiences of earlier generations of students and teachers, but it also reflects altered material conditions in postwar France, strains and reforms in both American and French higher education systems, and changing social practices of youth. Paradoxically, study abroad in the late 1940s and 1950s served French and American national interests precisely because the political and ideological issues were so marginal to most participants' experiences. Far more salient were social conditions and cultural values, the different characteristics of and reasons for higher education practices in each country, and a broadened understanding from study abroad that benefited individuals, governments, and transnational relations. But first, it is helpful to see how World War II affected the two main junior year in France programs from the 1920s and 1930s, the Franco-American cooperation to educate American soldiers in France at the end of the war, and the French government's support for reviving the junior year abroad.

Although junior year in France programs ceased from 1939 through 1945, many members of the Smith College community felt an obligation to help the French during the war. In 1943 William Allan Neilson, president of Smith College, stated at a banquet of the Association of Former Juniors in France, "You have a reason to help France because your Junior Year was such a high spot that a little part of you is forever French."[7] He offered contact information for various relief organizations to which former juniors might contribute. The Association of Former Juniors in France indeed raised money for French relief organizations and communicated information about France through letters they received from host families still in France. In 1944 Beatrice Howell, an alumna of the Junior Year in France, called on other Former Juniors in France to lead a movement, similar to that of the Women's Christian Temperance Union of earlier times, toward American postwar involvement in Europe. She was explicit that American support for French recovery must be limited to aid—namely, money and materials—so that French people themselves would implement their own reconstruction and thereby avoid resentment.[8] Immediately after the war the Association "adopted" four French orphans, provided them with food and clothing, and sent money to their adult relatives.[9] None of these special efforts to help the French people impeded one of the primary goals of the Association, to fund scholarships for needy Smith College students who might not otherwise be able to study in France. This support, and the Junior Year in France, resumed in 1947.

The war had a different impact on the other major junior year in France program from the 1920s and 1930s—the University of Delaware Foreign Study Plan. Various University of Delaware faculty committees in 1944 and 1945 supported the postwar continuation and expansion of the Foreign Study Plan to other countries. And, in fact, student groups went to Geneva, Switzerland, in 1946–47 and 1947–48 because material conditions were deemed too difficult in France at that time. However, William

S. Carlson, who succeeded Walter Hullihen as president of the University of Delaware, implemented an extensive review of the program, and as part of the review the university trustees decided to suspend the program in 1947. Acknowledging the value for undergraduates—and for the country as a whole—of fluency in foreign languages and understanding of other nations, Carlson was nonetheless concerned about the shaky financial situation of the program since 1935, when Pierre S. du Pont ceased donating to it. Carlson indicated that unless this could be stabilized, he thought the program should be terminated. Neither he nor the university trustees wished to see taxpayer money used to bolster study abroad at a public institution. Additionally, his visit to Paris as part of the program review suggested that American students living in comparative luxury at Reid Hall (a residence and meeting place for academic women) with imported food and heating oil might antagonize French people subject to rationing and penury. He also noted that "a large percentage of the French, especially the Communists, are anti-American," which could lead to "unpleasant occurrences," and he feared that American students "might be infected by the Communist virus."[10] Undeterred by such concerns and buoyed by student demand, President Martha B. Lucas of Sweet Briar College wrote to Carlson on December 19, 1947, indicating that Sweet Briar was interested in "undertaking a plan similar to the Delaware Plan." Carlson replied with enthusiastic support for Lucas's proposal, and in 1948 the University of Delaware approved a request by Lucas that the women's college would take over the program, allowing both men and women students from all over the United States to participate.[11]

But even before Smith College and Sweet Briar College sent juniors back to France, the first Americans to study there after the war were the soldiers who had fought in Europe. From June 15, 1945, to March 31, 1946, some three thousand American GIs became students in Paris, taking special courses for foreigners in French language and civilization; more advanced training for future teachers of French outside of France; and specialized, regular university-level courses at the Sorbonne, the Ecole des Beaux-Arts, the Conservatoire de Musique, and technical schools. Courses for American soldiers were also offered at the universities of Nancy, Dijon, Grenoble, and Besançon. As after the armistice of 1918, French academics and American military personnel cooperated to provide soldiers with educational opportunities. Indeed, Charles Cestre, professor of American literature and civilization at the Sorbonne, and Henri Goy, director of the Cours de civilisation française, also at the Sorbonne, were involved in both postwar programs. Similar to the experience of 1919, Cestre and other French academics and officials were convinced that these programs had value for both American soldiers in France and for Franco-American relations in general. Referring to the soldier/students, Cestre wrote to the rector of the University of Paris in April 1946: "These young Americans who belong to the elite of their country, some of whom will become professors, journalists, or writers, will spread throughout America an atmosphere favorable to France, will thus cement Franco-American friendship. On the other side, our instructors and the French families who hosted the young Americans have known the best of the American spirit and will make this known around them."[12]

Cestre had good reason to hope for such a positive outcome, because by late 1944 and early 1945 both French people and American soldiers were disillusioned and disgusted with each other. Many French found their liberators to be rowdy, drunken, and destructive of property, while a common attitude among GIs was that the French were swindlers, lazy, and ungrateful.[13] In July 1945 French chargé d'affaires Francis Lacoste, writing from the United States, affirmed the importance of establishing courses for American soldiers in France to reverse the negative attitude toward France that he observed: "the GI's who are returning to America have not kept the memory of our country that one would have hoped for."[14] A February 1946 letter from Joseph T. McNarney, U.S. Army Commanding General, to Gustave Roussy, rector of the University of Paris, suggests that the education program did, in fact, succeed in promoting good relations between American soldiers and French academics. McNarney stated: "I appreciate to the fullest extent the value of such a program both from the educational point of view and from the viewpoint of international understanding and amity, and am highly gratified with the results that have been obtained by the program thus far."[15]

Additionally, Major Ian F. Fraser, an organizer of the Training within Civilian Agencies Program of the Information and Education Division of the United States Forces, European Theater, provided a blueprint for how the Servicemen's Readjustment Act of 1944, commonly known as the GI Bill of Rights, should accommodate the veterans who wanted to devote their allotment to studying in France. Fraser recommended that the Veterans Administration establish a permanent staff and structure for ensuring that American GIs were attending classes and learning the material, similar to his practice in Paris of having students "examined periodically by the professors, who reported on the quality of the work accomplished." He also recommended periodic interviews of veterans by advisors "in order that individual problems may be solved quickly and maladjustments corrected." Above all, Fraser wanted to avoid abuses of a program intended to help veterans continue or begin their higher education: "Paris offers amazing opportunities for the young man or woman seeking an exciting continental vacation at government expense."[16] Fraser rightly anticipated the allure of France and especially Paris for thousands of veterans benefiting from the GI Bill, as we will see below.

Just as French university faculty enthusiastically accommodated American soldier/students in 1945–46, French diplomats welcomed the resumption of the junior year in France as contributing to the national interest. In 1948 the French cultural consul in New York City, René de Messières, worked with both Smith College and Sweet Briar College to revive and revamp their programs. Reporting to the minister of Foreign Affairs, Messières asserted that the Smith College Junior Year in France was highly beneficial to France because it sent forty to fifty capable students there each year at practically no cost to the French government. However, given the higher costs of transportation and of living in France since the war, Messières urged his boss to approve some kind of financial assistance, such as waiving Sorbonne fees or a few travel scholarships on French ships so that less wealthy American students could study in France and to acknowledge the regard of the French government for the Smith College Junior Year in France.[17]

A subsequent letter addressing Sweet Briar College's assumption of the University of Delaware's interwar Foreign Study Plan is far more explicit, both about the need for the French government to support the effort and about recommended reforms for the academic content of the program. Messières offered three reasons why the French government should support it: The junior year abroad programs generated more French specialists in the United States; returning junior year abroad students were good propagandists for France during their senior year in American colleges or universities; and an important portion of American social and economic elites was recruited from the undergraduate population. Echoing this sentiment in 1950, Albert Chambon, the French consul general in Boston, asserted to Henri Bonnet, the French ambassador to the United States, that French interests were better served by supporting the travel of American students, rather than tourists, to France. Complaining that tourists often left France with erroneous impressions, Chambon indicated that by living with French families, circulating among a broader spectrum of French society, and "understanding, in general, our language and being interested in our culture," students "become the best artisans of Franco-American friendship, that is the most enlightened," after they returned to the United States.[18]

Along with urging more scholarships and discounts for American juniors studying in France, Messières suggested that these students take more classes with French students at the Sorbonne, the Institut des Sciences Politiques, and the Ecole du Louvre, in addition to special courses for foreign students. He considered the main weakness of the interwar Delaware Foreign Study Plan to be the fact that "the students were too isolated among themselves, taking together courses prepared for their level . . . that did not provide them with a clear idea of real French teaching methods."[19] Accordingly, both the Sweet Briar and Smith postwar programs expanded students' educational options beyond the Cours de civilisation française.[20] Thus, French government support for study abroad between France and the United States continued prewar policies of cultural diplomacy, and officials in the Ministry of Foreign Affairs saw it as an effective means of generating a positive attitude toward and better understanding of France in the United States.

In contrast to the language of French academics and diplomats that justified study abroad as serving the national interest, organizers of the Sweet Briar College Junior Year in France articulated loftier goals of improving international relations for their program. A brochure of 1948–49 stated: "It is our conviction that the colleges have an essential and all-important responsibility to help bring the peoples of the world together in mutual understanding and lasting peace." Invoking the goals of UNESCO [United Nations Educational, Scientific and Cultural Organization] for global understanding through academic exchanges, the brochure continues: "We are confident that the Junior Year in France can do much to implement this purpose by enabling American students to know and work with students of other national backgrounds in a center which has been for many centuries, and continues to be, the meeting place of scholars from all parts of the world." The brochure also identified practical and attainable objectives that earlier programs had achieved, such as fluency in French and a broadened perspective: "One of the principal objectives for all students is that broad outlook and deeper comprehension that come from the mastery of French and intimate contact with France and French culture."[21]

After World War II, French higher education courses for American soldiers, the resumption of junior year in France programs, and official French support for both, all suggest continuity with interwar practices. But a new and influential element in study abroad was the U.S. government. This intervention, primarily through the Department of State, can be credited with expanding and internationalizing educational exchanges on a permanent basis, notably with the Fulbright Act of 1946 and the U.S. Information and Educational Exchange Act (Smith-Mundt Act) of 1948. These new laws also politicized study abroad, because some State Department officials and elected representatives maintained that the only justification for such programs was a national interest to prevail over international communism. Contestation over the purpose of government-sponsored educational exchanges and how to measure their effectiveness characterized the 1950s, but only after a viable and enduring framework for them was established.

The language of mutual understanding and international peace that the Sweet Briar program invoked, and that of national self-interest deployed by the French government, also surrounded U.S. government proposals and resolutions for educational exchanges as soon as the war ended in 1945.[22] Yet arguably the most important program of study abroad backed by the U.S. government originated with hardly any debate over whether educational exchanges should serve primarily internationalist goals or national interest. In 1946 the 79th Congress passed Public Law 584, better known as the Fulbright Act after its sponsor, Democratic Senator J. William Fulbright of Arkansas, which was an amended extension of the Surplus Property Act of 1944. The bill provided a means for war-torn countries to apply foreign currencies or credit from the disposal of surplus American property toward educational exchanges with the United States, because those countries were unable to pay in dollars for landing fields and other facilities built by the United States during the war.[23] Congress passed the bill with little fanfare, for Senator Fulbright asserted that he cannily emphasized its practical benefits, such as avoiding the waste of surplus materials and unpaid debt following World War I.[24] Fulbright later testified to the wisdom of avoiding idealistic justifications for the bill, such as world peace and "mutual understanding," claiming in an interview of 1991 that "In 1945 we [the United States] were a very isolationist country." He also stated that six months after the bill's passage a fellow senator, Democrat Kenneth McKellar of Tennessee, accosted Fulbright and told him: "'that measure you had is a very dangerous bill. If I'd a known about it I would have opposed that.' He said, 'Don't you know it's very dangerous to send our fine young boys and girls abroad, and expose them to those foreign isms?'"[25] The bill authorized the secretary of state to negotiate educational exchange agreements with each participating country, and the first exchanges started in 1948. Subsequently, the U.S. Information and Educational Exchange Act of 1948 (also known as the Smith-Mundt Act) expanded the Fulbright exchange plan to the entire world.

The agreement between the United States and France was signed on October 22, 1948, and its purpose was "to develop a spirit of mutual understanding between the peoples of the United States of America and of the French Republic through the increase of exchanges of scientific, technical, and professional knowledge."[26] Concerned about the extent of American control over the disbursement of funds and the selection of the administering committee in France, French negotiators succeeded in altering the originally proposed group of five Americans and two French, who were appointed by Americans, to a bi-national commission consisting of six French persons selected by the French government and six American members appointed by the American Embassy in Paris.[27] This Franco-American Commission was responsible for publicizing the program in France, soliciting and screening applications and selecting French students, scholars, and teachers for Fulbright awards and travel grants for those who made independent arrangements with American colleges and universities. Additionally, the commission welcomed American grantees to France and arranged for groups and individuals to assist them in Paris and in the provinces. In the United States the main selection body was the Board of Foreign Scholarships, a group of academics and professionals appointed by the president, while the Cultural Section of the Department of State managed administrative details. Given the decentralized nature of higher education in the United States, different agencies handled publicity and the applications of students and scholars—the Institute of International Education and the Council on International Exchange of Scholars—while the U.S. Office of Education dealt with teacher exchanges.[28] For the first fifteen years of its operation, the Franco-American Commission had an annual budget of one million dollars contributed by the United States from the proceeds of sales of surplus goods.

The Fulbright Program started robustly in France, with a total of 292 American students, scholars, and teachers going to France in 1949, while

FIGURE 6 Some of the first Fulbright fellows from France, in Paris, 1949. Photo from Lucien Jambrun, taken by the U.S. Embassy in Paris.

139 French counterparts went to the United States that first year (see Figure 6).[29] It initially met with some skepticism in France, notably an article published in the communist newspaper *L'Humanité,* accusing the program of being an arm of the CIA (Central Intelligence Agency).[30] It is difficult to gauge how widespread this sentiment was in France. And at least one French diplomat thought that French interests were well served by the Fulbright program, because French students in the United States were "making France less distant and more appealing" (to Americans) and "encouraging their American peers to study French."[31] In any case, increasing numbers of French applications and participants reflected the growing popularity of the Fulbright Program in France. By 1951 near parity in the numbers of French and American exchangees was reached, with 283 grants awarded to Americans and 274 to French; thereafter until 1969–70, numbers of grantees from each country usually ranged from

TABLE 2
American and French Fulbright grantees, 1949–1958

Year	Americans in France	French in the United States
1949	292	139
1950	308	237
1951	282	273
1952	270	304
1953	277	288
1954	286	275
1955	298	291
1956	322	319
1957	251	296
1958	295	289

SOURCE: Although figures vary in different sources, the numbers of American and French grantees were close to the above. *Dix années d'échanges Fulbright, 1949–1959*, printed pamphlet by Lucien Jambrun, n.a., n.d., 42.

280 to 300 (see Table 2). Given that the overall population of the United States was roughly four times greater than that of France, these numbers suggest that proportionately more French than Americans participated in the program.

In the 1940s and 1950s Cold War sentiments are apparent in various U.S. Department of State documents related to educational exchanges, as some American officials expressed a sense of mission to disseminate a "truthful" and positive understanding of the American way of life as an alternative to communism. A 1952 published report to the U.S. Congress justified educational exchanges as an important, long-term complement to the Department of State's many immediate-term information (propaganda) programs. Asserting the existence of a global struggle between two different world orders, the report claimed that notions of each system gained from personal and institutional contacts would determine whether people chose "the free or the communistic world" and that "the establishment of such associations and relationships constitutes a large part of the work of the educational exchange program."[32] Evidence in support of this position appears in a semi-annual evaluation report of 1951 sent from the American Embassy in Paris to the Department of State. The report discusses the positive attitude toward the United States among French students, teachers, lecturers, and leaders who traveled across the Atlantic as part of the Exchange of Persons program:

Returning grantees have, almost without exception, been so unanimous and unrestrained in their praise for what they saw, learned, or experienced in the United States, that it is impossible to attribute their statements entirely to politeness. All of them have no doubt talked considerably to their friends, associates, or students about their experiences, and many of them have given lectures or written articles on the subject.[33]

A dispatch of 1952 asserts that one reason for the effectiveness of exchange of persons was that the French were especially resistant to overt propaganda, the purview of the United States Information Service, the overseas successor to the Office of War Information (OWI): "In France, perhaps even more than in most countries, the effect of USIS program [sic] varies directly with its unobtrusiveness. The French pride themselves on having been for centuries of [sic] the world's leaders in the intellectual and cultural fields and any feeling that they are being 'told' anything by others brings strong adverse reactions." It followed, then, that direct experience by French persons in the United States avoided this problem: "Info program has been effective where it has been able unobtrusively to stimulate Fr[ench] interest in, and appreciation for, realities of American life and policy. Exchange of Persons has been particularly valuable in many fields."[34] Further evidence of the success of exchanges, including the Fulbright program, is a quote by a French student, Jean-François Clément, in response to the question, "What aspect of your study in the United States do you consider most valuable to you personally?" He answered: "The disappearance of many prejudices that most of my fellow countrymen have against the Americans."[35] Seeking ever more ways to challenge communism in France, the USIS semi-annual evaluation report for the period ending November 30, 1950, recommended recruiting French social workers and elementary school teachers for Smith-Mundt scholarships "for the purpose of achieving the aims of the Campaign of Truth," because these professionals could reach working-class families and school children who might not continue their education beyond elementary grades.[36]

Not everyone within the Department of State agreed that educational exchanges should be part of an explicit anticommunist campaign, and this debate permeated the administration of the Fulbright Program. In 1953 the Fulbright Board of Foreign Scholarships that set Fulbright policy, especially with regard to the selection of American candidates, suggested reforms to improve its applicant screening process. Objectives were, "a. that foreign grantees in the U.S. be provided an opportunity better to understand the elements of U.S. democratic strength and obtain the maximum value from their stay in this country; and b. Insuring that American grantees be given an opportunity to assist more effectively in fulfilling U.S. objectives."[37] According to Walter Johnson and Francis J. Colligan, both of whom were involved in the Fulbright Program, the Board believed that it was remaining true to the purpose of the Fulbright Program as educational rather than propagandistic. Yet critics accused it of both blatantly serving American national interests and of insufficiently attending to the task of persuading others of the merits of American policies. An attempt to separate clearly the informational or propagandistic from the educational aspects of U.S. international cultural relations occurred in 1953 with a congressional decision to retain educational exchanges within the Department of State while creating a new and separate United States Information Agency (USIA) outside of the State Department.[38]

The separation of information services and educational exchanges in 1953 reduced the fever of anticommunist rhetoric in connection with the Fulbright Program, although it did not entirely eliminate confusion over or overlapping of information and educational objectives. For example, in 1955 Public Affairs Officer Leslie S. Brady suggested that American students in France were less mindful of their ideological responsibilities than were lecturers: "The American professors and lecturers, perhaps because of their maturity and backgrounds, are considered to have contributed more than the students, many of whom, all too often, tend to ignore the concepts of the program under which they were enabled to study abroad."[39]

French diplomats were also concerned about the way that French students represented France and French policies while in the United States. In 1952 Henri Bonnet, French ambassador to the United States, recommended to his superior at the Ministry of Foreign Affairs that more effort should be made to inform Americans of French prowess in science and technology, and not just culture:

> It is in our interest to show consistently that France is not only a fine museum, a sparkling hotbed of artistic and literary life, of refinement in thought and in manners, a place where the art of living develops, but also a nation of workers, technicians, scientists, soldiers, a lively country, integrated into the movement of the modern world, and capable of offering a valuable contribution to the solution of contemporary problems.[40]

Additionally, the French Ministry of Foreign Affairs sought ways to counter American public opinion that was unfavorable to French colonial affairs. In a communication to Henri Bonnet of April 4, 1952, Minister Robert Schuman (member of the Christian Democratic Party [MRP] and architect of what became European economic integration) acknowledged Bonnet's efforts to develop the cultural and press services of France in the United States at that particular moment, "when the defense of French interests in Africa and Asia, which involve that of Atlantic civilization, do not always seem to be exactly appreciated by political circles and the American public." Nonetheless, he stoutly asserted that informational and educational functions by the Ministry must be separate: "I wish however that the Section of Education and Scholarships within Cultural Services preserve a certain autonomy and that no confusion be allowed to establish itself in American intellectual communities between the services charged with relations with universities and foundations, and those that due to their purpose, must conduct a political activity susceptible of assuming the guise of propaganda."[41]

As historian Irwin Wall demonstrates, diplomatic relations between France and the United States following World War II were complex; the United States exercised pervasive influence in France, particularly through economics, but failed to achieve certain goals of anticommunism and political influence. Yves-Henri Nouailhat asserts that American cultural policy from 1945–50 succeeded in terms of maintaining France's alliance with the West and fostering a generally positive attitude in France toward the United States, though he does not venture to say what specific parts of the policy contributed to this.[42] What is striking about the evidence from participants, as opposed to policymakers, regarding study abroad is how minimally these tensions at the state level of Franco-American relations registered among the scholars, teachers, and especially students who crossed the Atlantic in the immediate postwar years. That is, American and French exchangees generally came to appreciate the other country and culture, even to admire them or love them, while retaining loyalty to and identification with their individual nationality, regardless of whether officials expected them to espouse anticommunism or defend national policies. A cultural internationalism of toleration and appreciation for difference based on lived experience was sometimes what program organizers desired (along with world peace or cultural imperialism), but it was almost always a response from students or other academics involved in Franco-American educational exchanges. In the immediate postwar years, sympathetic understanding for the other nationality rested substantially on sharing the material circumstances of the host country, notably the devastation of war in France in contrast to the prosperity of the United States in the late 1940s.

For Americans studying in France after World War II, the effects of the war and occupation were ubiquitous. Students could not ignore the scarcity of food, heat, and electricity that persisted in France long after the war's end. Reid Hall, a former residence for American women that housed the Ecole Normale Supérieure de Jeunes filles de Sèvres from 1941 to the end of the war, reopened in 1947 to accommodate sixty-five American women students, importing tons of powdered milk and eggs, jam, and canned butter from the United States to feed them.[43] Living at the Fondation des Etats-Unis in the Cité Universitaire in 1947–48, Miriam Halbert, a recent graduate of the University of Miami in Ohio with a scholarship from the Institute of International Education to study in France, became used to food substitutes (corn starch to thicken the breakfast hot chocolate), ate a lot of macaroni that she cooked on a hot plate in her room, and relied heavily on food packages from home (cans of condensed milk, Nescafé, marmalade, sugar). Describing the hard, dark bread served with meals at the "Cité U," she wrote: "We have to eat quite a bit of it since we can't get full on the meager allotment of meat and vegetables." Hot water was available only once a week, and she wore a sweater and jacket at all times because the rooms were so cold, but she also recognized that the French generally had even less than she: "You can't imagine how little some of these people live on."[44] Invited to dinner at the apartment of a French family in 1948, Martha Churchill with the Smith College program wrote, "The place where they lived was quite shabby, on the verge of being a tenement and I felt quite embarrassed at dinner because there was hardly enough food to go around."[45]

Laura Sherman, another student with the Smith College Junior Year in France, recalled the divergent war experiences as an obstacle to understanding between Americans and French in 1949, which she strived to overcome: "When we visited sites that were still just rubble, and when I realized that these people had experienced things that we knew nothing about, and there was no way even to empathize because we couldn't experience it. So, there was a terrible barrier for us to hurdle, and I think some of us worked really hard at it."[46] Richard T. Arndt, a Fulbright fellow from the United States in 1949–50, got a new perspective on the war when the director of a student hostel in Dijon, France, where Arndt stayed, asserted without rancor, "We had *two* Occupations, theirs and yours," referring to the Nazi German occupiers and the liberating American army. According to Arndt, from the Frenchman's perspective, "armies are armies, war is war, no one including the victim behaves very well." In a recent account of the impact that this year in France had on him, Arndt wrote: "the War and its memories marked the beginning of my political education." In addition, he also discerned the extent of French pride in overcoming or evading the humiliation and the deprivation left by the war, writing, in hindsight, of the "heroic and touchingly vain French effort in the forties to keep up appearances at all costs—above all, it seemed to me, with us Americans, casually unaware of the troubling cultural threat we posed."[47]

The experience of living in France in the late 1940s gave American students a new perspective on World War II, on the French, and on their own relative good fortune to have lived in the United States during the hostilities. As late as 1964, Sister Anne Louise Westerburg, an American nun studying musicology in Paris as a Fulbright student, reported that living in France helped her understand the long-term impact of World War II: "After seeing for myself the philosophy of the French since the War and gaining a much deeper understanding of the psychological impact it had on the minds of the people, I have begun to comprehend the underlying meaning in the works of such writers as Mauriac, Anouilh, Camus, etc."[48]

For some French students in the United States right after the war, the security and prosperity of their hosts affirmed a commitment to rebuild their own country. Cécile Rabut, a French lawyer on an International Study Grant from the American Association of University Women in 1945–46, was relieved to forget the war and appreciated the United States where she "met a normal and unknown life, where you have time to learn and to live in the real meaning of the word." She reported that she learned much about the laws and treatment of juvenile delinquency in the United States and that she also gained a new perspective on France. "But now after those interesting months, . . . I can have a better and clearer judgment. I love my country more and feel an obligation to go back and do something—something to help the children and people in need, and there is a lot to do about it."[49] Three French women who studied at Smith College in 1945–46 indicated that they, too, were glad to leave behind the anxiety and hardship of war, "agreed upon their liking for America, its people, and Smith College," and were "grateful to be here." But they also expressed concerns about the black market and inflation in France and the "growing hostility between France and the United States," due to "the adverse effects in France of American policies, the friction between some of our GI's and some of the French people, their distrust of the policy of fraternization between American troops and the German people, and the withholding of American help which France needs so badly." The author of the article concluded by writing, "disturbed as they are about France, these French girls expressed unswerving faith in her [France's] future."[50]

The Cold War and anti-Americanism did appear but were not prominent in accounts by American students in postwar France, for as Richard Kuisel argues in his study of French political and popular responses to Americanization since World War II, real anti-Americanism was generally limited to leftist political and cultural elites at this point.[51] However, some students noticed a certain amount of resentment among French people toward Americans, primarily due to their respective economic positions and to the presence of foreign troops on their soil, including the U.S. military. Laura Sherman recalled the effects of the war on Franco-American relations: "I think an awful lot went on during our occupation in France that the media didn't cover for us . . . my impression was that we did not leave behind a country who thought highly of Americans."[52] Also in 1949–50, her classmate Mary Coan encountered communist ideology and a Marxist professor at the University of Grenoble. "The whole working class and communist thing became real to her in France," she conveyed, and she remembered that, as an American, she was "blamed for the war in Korea, for being imperialistic." Coan claims that she and others experienced "having the Marshall Plan thrown in their faces by French people."[53]

American students in France at this time responded in two different ways to encounters with anti-Americanism. Some became more patriotic and understood the value of being American in new and concrete ways. At the same time, they recognized the legitimacy of other national experiences and views of the world. For example, Barbara Nosanow initially felt flattered when French people said she didn't seem "American," but she became "indignant" because she felt no less American even if she failed to conform to a particular French stereotype; "it made me aware of the heritage of my own country and pride in my own country."[54] Mary Ann Hoberman echoed her sentiments:

we met all kinds of young people who were very left wing and very anti-American often, and so I sort of was a lethal combination of being anti-American, and seeing everything that was wrong with my country, and at the same time, when other people criticized it, and when they talked about it as if they knew what it was like, never having been there and obviously off the wall in some of their conclusions, I would defend it, and could see that there were good things about it.[55]

Smith College student Anne Rittershofer was an ardent supporter of Republican President Dwight D. Eisenhower and an avowed anticommunist, but in 1956 she wrote from Paris to her family in Cincinnati, Ohio, that she was gaining a new perspective on American presidential elections and the Suez crisis from reading French newspapers:

I'll probably be sending home a few caustic remarks about the U.S. as I read *Le Monde*! [smiley face] However, I love my country very much. I think I'll have to travel all over it when I get home so I'll *really* know what is America. Right now I am in love with Europe. France—its beauty of countryside, its civilized mind, its knowledge & wisdom. I'm ready to learn.[56]

Anticommunism and anti-Americanism were peripheral in accounts by both American and French persons studying in the other country, in contrast to a broader common narrative of gaining a new and more thoughtful understanding of one's own culture and pride in one's national identity, along with a simultaneous recognition of the merits and value of other cultural norms and practices. An obvious focus for assessing these differences was higher education itself. After the war, higher education in both countries confronted issues of student diversity, overcrowding, and, especially in France, the contemporary relevance of the university curriculum and the effectiveness of university pedagogy. Educational exchanges brought these issues to the fore as French and American educators and students tried to make sense of two very different higher education systems.

Significant political and social changes occurred in American universities as a result of World War II. Whereas universities in France had always been centralized under the government, after World War II the U.S. government became much more involved in funding research and supporting education than it had ever been before, spurred in large measure by the Cold War and with serious implications for academic freedom and curriculum development.[57] Helen Lefkowitz Horowitz notes other social and cultural changes on American college campuses after the war. Whereas fraternity and sorority members had effectively dominated university life throughout most of the twentieth century, the GI presence lent influence to a group that she calls "outsiders." And in the 1950s the civil rights movement contributed to the eventual ascendancy of those she terms "rebels," political activists who challenged the status quo.[58] While administrators, faculty, and students in the United States grappled more or less successfully with these changes, in the sense that higher education continued to flourish along with its fundamental objectives of professional formation and social advancement, the situation in France was more critical as educators and students addressed the fundamental question of the function of the university in modern society.[59]

According to Didier Fischer faculty and students in France agreed that major reforms in higher education were necessary, but they differed on what they should be and for what reasons. Faculty members were concerned about modernizing the university in the sense of preparing students for a job market that increasingly favored scientific and technical skills. Some advocated opening up the university to the growing number of educated young people from increasingly diverse social backgrounds, while others thought that admissions must be tightened so that graduates would be guaranteed of a job. French students also supported reform, including democratization of the university through increased admissions. They also called for improvements in student living conditions, which had been inadequate for at least a century, but were aggravated by the war.[60] In the 1950s several commentators suggested that France might benefit from the adoption or adaptation of American university practices.

In 1952 the progressive Catholic periodical *Esprit* devoted a special issue to French students, presenting a gloomy assessment of higher education in France. Common complaints of the approximately two hundred students who responded to the nationwide survey included the increasing numbers of students, professors who were distant and who failed adequately to prepare students for their professions, a lack of a sense of vocation among students who were destined to be teachers, and a decline in job prospects. *Esprit*'s editor, Jean-Marie Domenach, was pessimistic about the future of French students: "the situation of French students is without solution and without end."[61] He thought the example of universities in the United States and other Western European countries suggested obvious reforms—decentralization of the university, clearer distinction between and articulation of research and teaching, relaxation of the tyranny of competitive exams in favor of a selection that required more personal and team work, and, of course, more money—though he did not expect such changes to occur any time soon.[62]

The situation was deemed somewhat better in 1957 when the mass-circulation periodical *Arts, Spectacles* published two special issues, one on youth with an emphasis on students (according to UNESCO figures, one of every three hundred inhabitants in France was a student, a proportion surpassed only by the United States with one student out of fifty-nine inhabitants), and another on the question of Americanization in France, including higher education. Students continued to complain about overcrowding, boring teachers, impractical teaching, poor university conditions, and they indicated that they had no time for leisure.[63] However, the authors of the survey were optimistic about the future of French youth. They concluded that young people were serious about their careers and saw them as vocations for doing something worthwhile; that students in the sciences and technology wanted to spread French expertise throughout the world; that youth were proud of being French and of Western civilization and they rejected the Soviet model; and that a large majority of youth were religious or had traditional moral values, such as marital fidelity.[64]

The editors/authors of this special issue on youth and Americanization, Voldemar Lestienne and Philippe Labro (who was a Fulbright student in the United States in 1953–54), drew stark, even exaggerated, contrasts between French and American students in 1957 as part of an examination of American influence in France. Asserting that, "the French student is definitely very cultivated and well educated, but he is a beast of competitive exams, a drudge for work, a *diplomaniaque* [maniac for a diploma]," while the "American student is a fool for [sports] records," the authors implied that Americanization had not yet affected the French education system. But they also thought that some American influence would be beneficial to France. They encouraged educational reforms that were in progress, such as the availability of new courses with a more practical orientation and professors who were less distant from students and more interactive in the American manner. And they applauded the Fulbright program of student exchanges, noting that three hundred French students experienced American campuses each year, while three hundred Americans enjoyed the benefits of the Sorbonne and provincial French universities: "Here, perhaps is the only opportunity for understanding between the two countries; young people living with young people for twelve months. The French [man] takes the pulse of America and the young American assimilates the customs of France. They return to their respective homes. They know the real problems. It is possible for them to combat false prejudices and gossip."[65]

Labro and Lestienne's optimism about improved understanding of France and the United States through student exchanges and, specifically, the Fulbright program is borne out by accounts from French and American students who left their home countries to study in the other country. Their writings reveal perceptive insights into the merits and weaknesses of each educational system, along with appreciation for differences. Occasionally exchangees support the transfer of a particular practice in one country to the other, but most often students, researchers, and teachers, especially from France, articulate an understanding of the different national cultures and societies that engendered educational structures appropriate to those conditions.

Surveys of French and American students in the 1950s, as well as students' own accounts, reveal the persistence of some basic differences in the two countries' systems of higher education. According to a 1956 survey of French and American Fulbright students, the American system prepared a student for social and civic life, rather than cultivating intellectual acumen. Another difference in higher education was the accumulation of course credits in the United States, as opposed to the required courses necessary for a certificate in France, which reflected the fact that American students gained their general knowledge in the university, whereas French students had acquired that broad culture in the *lycée*, so that the university was for specialization. Survey respondents agreed that the French required more original work from students than did Americans, because style, organization, and analysis mattered more in France. However, traditional French exercises, namely, *la dissertation* (original, reasoned scholarship) and *l'explication de texte* (critical analysis of literature), found favor with both American and French students who had studied abroad as useful and distinctive intellectual practices. American graduate student Pauline Newman said this about French education in 1950: "I very much like French teaching, which is well constructed, logical, classical, and develops the intellect. . . . To be sure I very much like France, and I will make others love it when I return home."[66] Students of both nationalities described the different purposes of exams in each country similarly; that is, American exams tested the progressive accumulation of knowledge, while French exams evaluated assimilation or mastery of a subject. All of these methods reflect fundamentally different American and French views of culture—the former a mass culture accessible to all, and the latter an elite culture pursued by those with the proven ability.[67]

French students and teachers studying or working in the United States also noticed a considerable difference between undergraduate and graduate student life, a distinction that did not apply in France. Micheline Jammes, a Fulbright fellow, noted the gaiety and sociability of undergraduate life at a Catholic women's college in the United States: "Student life is a joyous adventure," she wrote in 1956, with parties occurring on all sorts of occasions, including the introduction of future floor mates, pajama parties at Christmas, St. Patrick's Day celebrations, ice skating parties, picnics, and marshmallow toasting on the first warm day of spring. Heterosocialibility was even more exciting to the college women, according to Jammes. She described the different forms of social interactions between college women and men, including drinking a Coke, "mixers" that "mixed" men and women from different institutions for dancing, formal dances, and blind dates.[68] Bernard Poll, another French Fulbright fellow, observed that American graduate students regarded fondly their happy undergraduate days: "dating, dances, and alcohol consumed in large quantities belonged to the happy days of college that [the American graduate student] evokes with nostalgia after one or two beers."[69]

This comparatively leisured existence of undergraduates in the United States more often made its way across the Atlantic following World War II than it had in the interwar period. Juniors in France in the 1920s and 1930s often commented on how hard the academic work was in France and how much easier college and university were in the United States. But the postwar accounts suggest that while some American students worked hard in France, others took greater advantage of extracurricular opportunities. Accounts also differ by the age and maturity of students. That is, Fulbright and other scholarship students tended to be older and more mature than traditional undergraduates, and generally took their studies more seriously both at home and abroad.

A new type of American student, the GI, was the butt of a number of comments on how little he worked. Journalist Stanley Karnow remembers that while traveling in France after the war, his relationship with a young French woman precipitated his decision to remain there and study on the GI Bill: "As a veteran, I was entitled under the GI Bill to seventy-five dollars a month—on condition that I enroll in school. It was a decent sum in francs, and I promptly signed up for La Cours de civilisation française, a curriculum for foreigners at the Sorbonne." However, he also claims that, "I was to learn more about France from Claude [his girlfriend and later wife] than from attending classes."[70] In an article on American students in Paris published in 1950, French reporter Henriette Nizan described the academic obligations of GIs, as well as their way of dealing with them: "25 hours in class per week in selected courses, two reports per year on the subject that interests them. They do not have the right to fail any exams, or they risk the withdrawal of their scholarship. That is why, a few months ago, one of them asked a French friend this extraordinary question: 'Tell me which is the easiest course I can take in Paris?'"[71]

No doubt some worked hard, as historian Keith Olson found was true of the majority of veterans who studied on the GI Bill in the United States and outperformed traditional undergraduates.[72] Also, a 1949 article in the *Saturday Evening Post* chronicled the student life of James Robert Hewitt, a graduate of the University of Pennsylvania who was studying in Paris on the GI Bill along with thirteen hundred other American veterans. According to the article, Jim Hewitt, who was preparing to become a teacher of French, "carries a heavy program at the Sorbonne," and, "there is nothing Bohemian, nothing Flaming Youth about him. And the same can be said for the great majority of his fellow veterans now studying in Paris." The article continues: "This is an amazingly mature crowd, which knows where it is going."[73]

Young American students discovered a wide array of possibilities awaiting them in France both outside and inside of the classroom. Martha Churchill, a Smith College student in France in 1948–49, noted several times in letters to her parents that she was not working very hard on her studies. She attributed this in part to the greater independence enjoyed by students in France, including juniors abroad, and the many alternative activities available in Paris that arguably had some academic or at least, experiential value. In answer to her family's question about her studies, she wrote: "I must admit I am working much less than at Smith, . . . Choir takes up one night a week, and there are always things like plays, or lectures on the Marshall plan or some other vital subject which you don't feel you should sacrifice to the altar of studies."[74] A French observer, who had taught in the United States, noted that American students in Paris, though "the most numerous of all nationalities, the friendliest to others, the most lively and also the least disciplined," were not the most assiduous. She wrote: "American students in Paris, outside of a few brilliant exceptions, are not, taken together, very convinced intellectuals."[75] Junior year in France program organizers recognized the challenge that American students confronted in regular courses taken with French students, because "the small number of class hours and limited assignments [put] much of the responsibility for educating oneself on the individual," and "the analytical thinking that is expected of the student implies a personal initiative and an effort that is not generally expected in America."[76]

Nonetheless, many students worked hard and benefited personally from the French system. Miriam Halbert, who studied in France in 1947–48 on an IIE scholarship, took enormous pride in the "*mention bien*" (good) that she earned on her exams for the certificate at the end of the Cours de civilisation française. Halbert certainly took advantage of many social and cultural opportunities in Paris during her stay, but she felt an obligation to fulfill the expectations associated with her scholarship. She also claimed that in France, "even the American students are fired by an inspiration they never had in the states."[77] Laura Sherman, who went with the Smith College Junior Year in France in 1949–50, would probably have agreed. She said in an interview that the education in France made her a better student: "I used my mind so extensively in France that when I came back, my senior year at Mills [College] was really easy." She noted that American students "had to work awfully hard in order to get good grades" in France because, in some cases, they were competing with French students who were specializing in the particular subject, in this case, an art course at the Ecole du Louvre.[78] For her classmate Mary Ann Horenstein, the year in France led to her receptivity to experiential learning methods when she became a teacher. Horenstein claimed that by taking several different courses (art, philosophy, literature, and history) that all addressed nineteenth-century France, she "learned how to learn." She continued: "I learned how to see relationships in a way I never did before. . . . I'm [sic] always looking for ways, when I was a teacher, of relating things to kids, you know, having relationships with other subjects, for them to see beyond the subject that we were doing."[79]

Several features of Franco-American educational exchanges in the 1950s were different from what participants noticed in previous decades. Both French and Americans acknowledged and usually admired the greater rigor of French higher education compared to undergraduate curricula in the United States. However, respect for certain American university practices (such as more teacher/student interaction, more practical or hands-on courses, more balance between work and leisure) was growing in France and extending beyond reformers within the academy to students and the general public. The impetus for change toward some of these practices in French higher education mounted and came to a head in the late 1960s (as we will see in Chapter 6). Other factors distinguished the experience of Americans studying in France in the 1950s from that of earlier generations, including more diversity of academic majors (most interwar juniors in France were French majors), a wider range of course offerings in France to accommodate this diversity and to integrate Americans with French students, and an expectation that studying in France represented a kind of liberation from moral and social restrictions. Many Americans claimed that they learned to appreciate a different lifestyle in France. And from the French perspective, educational travel in the United States in the 1950s dispelled stereotypes of American superpower hubris and uncultivated eating habits by revealing American people to be friendly and provincial and successful in improving daily life through modern technology.

Evidence from American students abroad in the 1950s reveals a different orientation from those who went to France in the 1920s and 1930s, due largely to greater freedom for American women and a sense of escape and adventure that life in France represented (see Figure 7). Young American women who studied in France after World War II no longer adhered to the strict regulations that governed their prewar antecedents, such as being chaperoned at night and avoiding certain "hot spots" in Paris. According to Mary Coan, "In France Smith students could date three or four boys in one day, which was a great liberation from Smith."[80] In letters from France, her classmate Elizabeth Simmons regaled her family with accounts of her social activities, including outings to cafés, "Arab bars," dances, dinners, the theater, concerts, opera, "a terrific show with lots of naked women," jazz clubs, and a *chansonnier*, an intimate night club [sic] where "many songs are sung—usually naughty or satires on the state of the world." She wrote that she dated many men of different nationalities and often violated the 11:00 P.M. curfew.[81] Simmons and her roommate, also with the Smith group, went to Belgium, where they spent a weekend traveling with two young Belgian men by motorcycle; during Easter break, she visited Spain in the company of two other women from the Smith group and two French men.[82] At the end of her stay, she became enamored of a young Frenchman, whom she described to her family: "I met the most darling French boy two weeks ago & we've been out

FIGURE 7   Class of 1951, junior year abroad in France. Photographer/creator: Wide World Photo. © Wide World Photo. Smith College Archives.

practically every other night since."[83] Romances with Frenchmen and men of other nationalities were common, sometimes even resulting in international marriages.[84]

Students' accounts reveal an appreciation for new ways of being, new possibilities for identity that they learned from being in France. In her letters to her mother, Miriam Halbert commented repeatedly on the French emphasis on pleasures of the mind, in contrast to American materialism, as well as on the capacity simply to enjoy life: "I can remember the time when I would have thought it a waste of time to spend two hours just walking. Some people don't take time out to live. I think I've learned it over here."[85] The father of a Smith College student visited the juniors in Paris and wrote this open letter to all parents of juniors in France in 1949, suggesting how the experience affected their daughters:

"Today she is the 'foreigner' who has to make her way with people who don't know her language and customs. She is meeting foreigners not only who sell fruit but who paint pictures, study in famous schools and are perhaps a little better educated than she is. It is both an exhilarating and somewhat humbling experience. She will return to America with a much broader tolerance and a better understanding of the human race and its problems. She'll no longer be a snob."[86] According to French reporter Henriette Nizan in 1950, American students came to France precisely to experience a different way of being: "They all seem to have understood that there is more than one way to be happy on this earth, that neither comfort, money, or technical progress are sufficient to assure happiness, . . . that what counts, for man, is not so much the conditions of his well being as his capacity to be happy. And that, they learned in France."[87]

French students and teachers who studied or worked in the United States often remarked on the warm welcome they received, an immediate friendliness and hospitality that was unusual in French culture. A French intern wrote in 1956 of his experience working in the University hospitals in Madison, Wisconsin: "what struck me the most upon my arrival at the hospital is the great friendliness with which I was welcomed. All the doctors, whatever their rank, put themselves out to facilitate my adaptation to social life as well as to medical activities."[88] In 1958 forty-five students and two professors from the National Electrotechnical, Electronics and Hydraulics College of Toulouse, traveled to the United States and Canada. In a report of the visit, the travelers professed to initial apprehensions about the language barrier and the awkwardness of being strangers in private homes. But the hospitality of the families surprised the engineers and allowed them to share comfortably in daily life: "It was this spirit of cordiality and good will, completely natural and unforced, which allowed us to adapt ourselves to situations which, in France, would generally have required hours in order to become acquainted. The fact was, there, that we were adopted and we really participated in all the activities with people we had just met."[89] The engineers dwelled at length on American food and cooking. They were taken aback by how quickly lunch was consumed, though they learned that, in contrast to the French, Americans consumed their main meal in the evening and started with a copious breakfast. They were dubious about eating corn until they tried it, were amazed to see frozen bread slices ("hard as a rock") toasted to perfection in ten minutes, and even suggested to their hosts that fresh meat rather than frozen and/or sterilized meat might be more flavorful.

However, they all agreed "that they always ate plenty, and often tasty dishes" and that fresh-squeezed "orange juice, along with air conditioning, must be placed among America's greatest achievements."[90]

The engineers were keen analysts of social life, labor, and national values in the United States. They found Americans eager to meet them, talk with them, and learn about France and Europe, but they "were surprised by the ignorance the Americans show about Europe and the great problems of the world in general." This they attributed to the narrow domestic focus of the American press and radio. Americans, they noted, were eminently sociable, and significant gulfs of geographic distance and ethnic diversity were bridged by a shared ideology of unshakable confidence in capitalism, progress, and technology and the satisfaction of knowing that this faith is confirmed in the United States' global economic dominance. In addition, work was the avenue toward social and economic improvement for everyone in the United States: "On every rung of the social scale there is the same desire for change, the same desire for advancement," and any American "can hope to make progress through his labor." Clearly, the group enjoyed and valued the visit, calling it "a complete success" and "an unforgettable memory" and framing it in the language of cultural diplomacy: "We hope that such projects will be encouraged and that other, later classes may have, as we did, the privilege of serving abroad as ambassadors of the enthusiasm and seriousness of French youth."[91]

Several surveys conducted in the 1950s show how students personally benefited from study abroad and how these programs served national interests and promoted internationalism. A 1954–55 study by sociologist John T. Gullahorn and psychologist Jeanne E. Gullahorn identified and ranked four main reasons why young Americans studied in France: first, to further a professional or academic objective; second, to learn more about French culture; third, to assimilate this culture through total immersion; and finally, to indulge a spirit of adventure.[92] The Gullahorns noted a significant difference between the goals of students (foreign students who came to the United States also put a priority on professional and academic development) and those of institutions, for whom improved international relations or a better understanding abroad of the United States were the main objectives. Yet the Gullahorns also concluded that student motivations for professional advancement were not incompatible with an outcome of greater international awareness and an improved attitude among French people toward Americans. They quoted a student response: "'Improving international good will is all well and good, but just what in hell does it mean?' 'For myself, I hope I've gained a bit of understanding of French civilization; and perhaps I may have helped a few French friends understand a little better what Americans are really like.'"[93] Still another study positively assessed Americans studying abroad in terms of improved language skills; an increased interest in intellectual and cultural matters, as well as international affairs, which enriches campus life after students return; and a reassessment of American values and policies, along with increased patriotism.[94]

In the late 1950s, the Gullahorns, who were concerned that the U.S. Congress might reduce funding for the Fulbright Program, conducted more research to try to find concrete answers to questions of the effectiveness of student exchanges, namely, the impact on American students of studying in France and how American students affected attitudes of French persons toward the United States and Americans. Their survey findings revealed an overwhelmingly positive response to study in France on the part of American students, who found that the experience resulted in "a broadened perspective on their own values, those of their country, and those of Europeans." Despite difficulties of adjusting to a foreign culture, frustrations, and loneliness, this student's evaluation of living and studying in France was typical, according to the Gullahorns: "I've taken a good look at some of my own smug assumptions about life, and I guess I used to be somewhat of a conceited bore. I've also looked at the United States with fresh eyes, and I've hated some of our superficial qualities while learning to feel a deeper love for the things we really stand for."[95]

All studies found that French attitudes toward Americans improved through contact with students, in contrast to negative impressions from American soldiers and tourists.[96] The Gullahorns' findings were more ambiguous than these but also more detailed. Although French students reported that American students were less serious than the French, less philosophical, and more materialistic, they appreciated Americans' enthusiasm, "their simplicity, their practicality, their honesty, their good sense and good humor."[97] Thirty-seven percent of French students surveyed believed that Americans studying abroad in France improved French attitudes toward Americans because through them, "American life presents itself to the French in a more agreeable light."[98] And the majority of French adults interviewed claimed that American students "succeeded in their role as ambassadors of American culture."[99] In a later study, French comments on American students in their country were also mixed, suggesting that the French admired American students' friendliness, energy, and enthusiasm but deplored other features of American politics and society, such as a hysterical anticommunism that threatened freedom and toleration and a rampant materialism. Nonetheless, the Gullahorns cited one French student as representative in commending educational exchanges between the two countries: "Exchanges between French and American students are very important because they show that the United States is not just about power, but that Americans need culture and other values that they lack. Additionally, they combat in France a part of the false image that one gets from tourists who are rather detestable."[100]

In 1955 Sweet Briar College commissioned C. Robert Pace to evaluate the interwar University of Delaware Foreign Study Plan and the postwar Sweet Briar Junior Year in France program. Pace distinguished between cultural enhancement and internationalism as results of study abroad, noting that respondents who had studied in France considered appreciation for another culture, tolerance for diversity, and greater maturity and self-awareness, in that order, to be the most important benefits of study abroad.[101] He identified internationalism as follows: "What reduces barriers of communication or exchange among nations and peoples, whatever brings more nations together in common association, whatever involves the United States more wholly and cooperatively with other groups is regarded as reflecting, very broadly, an internationally-minded attitude."[102] He found that students rated internationalism lower than cultural, interpersonal, or personal results based on responses to statements such as the following: reading books about international relations, talking with friends about other countries, verbally defending other countries, and listening to United Nations programs. Attitudes toward the United Nations figured prominently in this study as a measure of internationalism.[103] For Pace, culture and internationalism were separate aspects, with internationalism being explicitly political.

But this is not the only possible interpretation. I take appreciation of another culture and tolerance for diversity to be a form of internationalism. As Anne Dyer Murphy wrote when thanking the Smith College Association of Former Juniors in France for the scholarship that allowed her to study abroad in 1952–53, "The whole process of being in an almost completely French milieu, . . . living in a French family, studying with French teachers, . . . is the most liberalizing and broadening process an American student can go through. It is bound to change some ideas, and to suggest many new ones. And it makes you think, and in a very vital and practical context."[104] Indeed, Pace's overall conclusion was that study abroad significantly affected students in several aspects of their lives: "alumni themselves believe strongly that their experience influenced them in many ways—culturally, vocationally, in personal maturity, in understanding other people, and in political and international interests."[105]

As Pace's conclusion and the findings of other surveys in the 1950s affirm, national interests and internationalism were not incompatible results of study abroad during the Cold War era. While American policymakers were divided as to whether educational exchanges should promote American values or contribute to mutual understanding, the students, teachers, and scholars who crossed the Atlantic achieved both. French visitors to the United States found much to admire, and they often abandoned pre-travel stereotypes about Americans as materialistic and focused on power. Americans in France reassessed their notion of American national identity and learned to value French culture. Policymakers' fears that Americans in France might be tainted by communism, or that educational exchange programs were not doing enough to persuade the French at home or in the United States of the superiority of American democracy and free enterprise, were unfounded. Even as individuals ignored either government's concerns about improving their national images in the other country, they actually fulfilled those state objectives. They also contributed to an internationalism of difference, rather than conversion, homogenization, or competitive ranking.[106]

Study abroad between France and the United States changed in other ways in the late 1940s and 1950s. Educational opportunities increased, participants became more diverse, and numbers of students, scholars, and teachers crossing the Atlantic rose substantially from prewar levels. At a time when airplane travel was just beginning to become affordable for middle-class Americans and television was still a new and limited communication medium, especially in France, study abroad was an important means of acquiring, disseminating, and even correcting information about the other country. This continued to be the case in the 1960s, when an educational crisis in France and the dual issues of race and the Vietnam War homefront in the United States, converged and reshaped the contours of study abroad.

§ 6 American National Identity and French Student Life

Politicization and Educational Reform in the 1960s

Paul Benhamou was teaching English in a *lycée* in Algeria when he applied for a Fulbright scholarship to study American literature in the United States. He had completed a degree in English at the University of Dijon that included a two-year stint teaching in England, and he had already been awarded a Fulbright scholarship in 1960 to study at the State University of Iowa in Iowa City. He declined this award because he had never heard of Iowa. In 1961 he reapplied and went to Iowa City on a Fulbright, indicating in an interview that "when I was teaching in Algeria, there was a revolution going on and the atmosphere was not terribly propitious to studying." He never went back. Algeria became independent in 1962, and Benhamou chose not to go to France because "France considered me *pied noir* and not a full-fledged French citizen.... so I decided to stay in the States and become a citizen."[1]

Throughout the many decades of students crossing the Atlantic, politics figured in a number of accounts of study abroad experiences, but it gained resonance in the 1960s, even before the global events of 1968. Not all those who studied abroad were as personally and directly influenced by politics as was Benhamou, but politics or social issues provided a significant backdrop for many, especially Americans, either in terms of affecting a decision to study abroad, or, more often, as part of the experience itself. Despite widely publicized conflicts between the governments of France and the United States during the early French Fifth Republic, the numbers of students crossing the Atlantic continued to increase. For Americans, study in France often entailed a new interest in politics generally and in U.S. policies in particular. French students, teachers, and scholars in the United States tended to notice more cultural and educational differences, and reforms in French higher education following the events of 1968 incorporated several practices common in American universities. Additionally, both French and American students and teachers increasingly described their study abroad experiences in terms of personal transformation and identity exploration, joining appreciation for cultural difference with introspection. I am not claiming that study in France caused the politicization of American students in the 1960s, or that French experience of American higher education influenced the liberalizing reforms of French universities in 1968. However, impressive increases in the numbers of young people studying abroad, both between France and the United States and globally, along with students' own interpretations of the personal, national, and international benefits of study abroad, suggest that study abroad and youthful optimism for positive change in the world mutually reinforced each other in the 1960s.

Recent global perspectives on the 1960s locate the United States within a context of transnational change, rather than as a superpower exerting dominance. Historian Elizabeth Cobbs Hoffman argues that the Peace Corps represented an alternative American identity to that of Cold War aggression—a manifestation of global idealism and humanitarianism to address problems of poverty and racism in the world.[2] And Jeremi Suri claims that the global popular protests of the late 1960s actually ended a Cold War stalemate and propelled the governments of the United States, France, Germany, China, and the Soviet Union into détente.[3] Both studies suggest the important role of ordinary people, and especially of students and young people, in influencing international relations and modifying (or at least complicating) a Cold War, mass consumer image of the United States. Similarly, this chapter views French and American developments, such as growing university populations, student activism, political engagement, and higher education reform, as linked to international relations through students, teachers, and scholars from one country working and living in the other country.[4] Such persons often experienced these changes on a deeply personal level, and rarely did they echo or reinforce often antagonistic government relations between France and the United States. To the contrary, students of one country who were living abroad gained understanding and appreciation of the other country's culture and politics, even when they disagreed about particular national policies, such as French President Charles de Gaulle's pursuit of national greatness, racial discrimination in the United States and in France, and the American involvement in Vietnam.

The French Fourth Republic fell in the midst of the Algerian War, replaced in 1958 by the Fifth Republic led by Charles de Gaulle. Under his leadership and against considerable opposition, French troops finally left Algeria, and the former colony became independent in 1962. De Gaulle also presided over a period of tense relations between his government and that of the United States over nuclear weapons capabilities, a European defense community, NATO, the respective roles of France and the United States in global affairs, and the American war in Vietnam, among other things. According to diplomatic historians, including Frank Costigliola and Charles Cogan, de Gaulle inspired a certain amount of respect among Americans as an authoritative and patriarchal leader, in contrast to the short-lived governments of the Fourth Republic. These historians also indicate that the young American president John F. Kennedy respected—some would say that he even admired—the elder statesman. Nonetheless, keenly aware of the enormous disparity between the United States and France in terms of military and economic power, de Gaulle resorted to a language of defiance and acts of uncooperativeness as a means of asserting both French independence in relation to the United States and French dominance in European affairs. Americans thought that a series of actions by de Gaulle in the 1960s were provocative gestures of disdain for an Atlantic alliance that Americans presumed to control.[5]

In 1963 de Gaulle declined to participate in a multilateral force that was intended to unify Western Europe in a nuclear alliance dominated by the United States, and he vetoed Great Britain's membership in the European Common Market. For many in the United States these actions represented a threat to allied security, whereas de Gaulle's intentions were to secure an independent French nuclear weapons capability and dominance in Western Europe. American frustration increased in 1966 with de Gaulle's withdrawal of French forces from NATO; his ordering of American troops off French soil; and his public criticism of U.S. policy in Vietnam, which he expressed periodically from 1963 to 1968. Although Presidents Kennedy and Lyndon B. Johnson more or less understood de Gaulle's position and avoided direct confrontation with him while still exercising a controlling influence in the Atlantic alliance, public opinion in the United States regarding de Gaulle was often negative.[6] News media found his actions deliberately hostile to American interests, and calls for boycotting French wine and other products were rife in the 1960s.[7] For their part, French people agreed with de Gaulle's criticism of U.S.

TABLE 3
Americans studying in France and French in the United States, 1959–1971

Year	Americans in France	French in the United States
1959–60	2,420	572
1960–61	2,906	564
1961–62	2,077	587
1962–63	1,633	663
1963–64	2,742	751
1964–65	2,112	833
1965–66	4,223	940
1966–67	2,347	1,239
1967–68	4,013	1,391
1968–69	2,064	1,625
1969–70	6,219	1,977
1970–71	6,072	1,994

SOURCE: From Institute of International Education, *Open Doors*. Report on International Educational Exchange, 1948–2004 (New York: IIE, 2005).

policy in Vietnam, and popular protests against it increased in the late 1960s.[8]

Against this backdrop of Franco-American disagreement at the highest level of policy making, young people and, especially, students in both France and the United States began protesting policies and conditions that they considered imperialistic, racist, and unjust. Although only a minority of university students in the two countries were actively involved in political organizations and public demonstrations, the causes of anti-imperialism, racial equality, and social justice gained sympathizers among a far larger young and not-so-young population. In addition, student agitation for university and larger social reforms spanned the entire decade of the 1960s, peaking with demonstrations, occupations, and violence in 1968 and the years immediately following.[9] French and American students, teachers, and researchers who lived and worked abroad felt the influence of all these developments, even if they were not actively involved in political or social movements. Nonetheless, contentions over the conditions of higher education, racial attitudes and practices, and foreign policies hardly deterred the transatlantic flow of educated youth. Indeed, study abroad flourished in the decade of the 1960s.

Numbers of American students living in France and French students living in the United States continued to increase (see Table 3), as did numbers of students abroad on a global scale. Aggregate statistics from

TABLE 4

Leading host countries for all foreign students, 1962 and 1968

Numbers of Foreign Students Hosted in 1962	
USA	64,705
Federal Republic of Germany	24,177
France	23, 089
USSR	14,400
United Kingdom	14,020
Numbers of Foreign Students Hosted in 1968	
USA	121,362
France	36,500
Federal Republic of Germany	26,783
Lebanon	18,811
United Kingdom	16,154
USSR	16,100

SOURCE: UNESCO, *Statistics of Students Abroad, 1962–1968/ Statistiques des étudiants à l'étranger* (Paris: UNESCO, 1972), 19–20, 24–25, 27, 43.

UNESCO reveal a global trend of increasing numbers of students abroad in the 1950s and 1960s, reaching a total of 429,000 in 1968, which represented an increase of 300 percent over nineteen years. The UNESCO report also noted an increase in the number and proportion of women students ("girls") in the 1960s, and a shift toward more students from developing countries than from developed countries seeking education abroad. Throughout the 1950s Europe was the destination of close to half of all foreign students, but although that proportion declined in the 1960s, the proportion of students going to North America, and especially the United States, increased (see Table 4).[10] There is no doubt that efforts by the U.S. government to wage Cold War against communism through cultural relations contributed to this phenomenon. For example, starting in 1961, President Kennedy increased funding for Fulbright exchanges and created a new position within the Department of State—an assistant secretary of state for Educational and Cultural Affairs. Yet these initiatives were limited and short-lived.[11] More significantly, following World War II, the United States was a superpower, and it had replaced Germany as the global center for scientific research, modern technology, and higher education.

The United States was clearly a magnet for foreign students, but where, then, did American students go? According to statistics gathered by the Institute of International Education (IIE), during the 1960s three countries alternated as the top destination for American students: France, Canada, and Mexico. Close behind in either fourth or fifth place were West Germany and the United Kingdom.[12] Thus, outside of North America, France consistently drew the greatest number of American students for the entire decade of the 1960s. Why was this so? The same myths and imaginings attracted students in the early 1960s as had appealed to young people of earlier generations, but new experiences of political awakening and self-actualization, especially in the later 1960s and 1970s, also figured among the results and satisfactions that students attributed to living and studying in France, as we will see below.[13]

As study abroad programs proliferated in the 1960s (and into the 1970s), concerns about their effectiveness and about continued public support for educational exchanges arose. Many studies tested the presumed benefits of study abroad, such as vocational enhancement, internationalism, national interest, increased circulation of knowledge, and personal growth. They also distinguished between two main groups of study abroad participants: older, more advanced students and teachers; and American undergraduates. On balance, researchers found that the benefits of study abroad outweighed the drawbacks, but they also clarified what the benefits were and exactly who benefited. In addition, they generated recommendations for improvement.

While some American educators sought to expand study abroad opportunities to students outside of humanities fields, others saw dangers in sending students abroad with poor preparation in the history, culture, and language of another country.[14] Edward J. Durnall affirmed this concern in an examination of fifty-six American study abroad programs in 1967. He discerned that the self-regulation practice of a few, select, small junior year abroad programs was no longer effective among so many new and larger initiatives. The latter tended to be open to almost all American students, regardless of language skills and, in Durnall's opinion, were neither academically rigorous nor sufficiently planned and organized. Durnall wrote: "The basic principles of a worthwhile study-abroad experience have been fairly well accepted for several years. However, the survey leaves the impression that many U.S. institutions have embarked on such ventures without the careful planning, administrative and faculty support, and continuing evaluation which are necessary to achieve academic excellence." The remedy for guaranteeing high academic quality, according to Durnall, included rigorous admissions standards, well-qualified administrators, and a system of accreditation through visitation committees.[15]

In addition to inadequate preparation of American undergraduates and poor administration, other studies noted problems such as the reluctance of French educators to admit American students to already overcrowded French universities[16] and American students' difficulty in readjusting to American university life and to American life in general after study abroad. In 1976, Dennison Nash, a professor of anthropology and sociology, tested the claim that American undergraduates gained autonomy, self-confidence, and greater individuation from study abroad. Nash surveyed students who had studied in France and a control group that stayed in the United States, and he concluded that study abroad did increase students' autonomy and "expanded or differentiated sense of self." However, the results did not confirm that increased self-confidence, tolerance, and flexibility were an outcome of study abroad. Nash called for more research and suggested that his results might have been strongly affected by the large number of students who had left boyfriends or girlfriends behind and who experienced a loss of self-esteem for this reason.[17]

If study abroad programs in private and public universities were subjected to scrutiny, it should come as no surprise that the Fulbright program, partially administered by the Department of State, also was questioned. In 1966 psychologist Jeanne E. Gullahorn and sociologist John T. Gullahorn analyzed survey data from a pool of four hundred American students in France and more than five thousand Americans who were Fulbright grantees all over the world between 1947 and 1957. The Gullahorns were looking to discern whether or not the following goals of American institutions for study abroad were being met: "the promotion of 'international understanding'; the development of friends and supporters for the United States; assistance in economic, social, or political development of other countries; educational development of outstanding individuals; and the advancement of knowledge." They found that advanced graduate students and teachers gained the most in terms of professional development and prestige. By contrast, younger students cited personal maturity and a broader perspective as most salient, and, less burdened by academic or professional ambitions, these students also engaged more with people in the host country than did researchers and teachers.

The Gullahorns evaluated these results as mixed in terms of fulfilling institutional objectives. They asserted that the older professionals benefited most vocationally from their experience abroad, and the professionals furthered knowledge and communication between Americans and foreign nationals. Although young students left both favorable and unfavorable impressions on their hosts, advanced students and teachers favorably impressed their hosts with their dedication to learning, thereby improving foreigners' impressions of Americans and the United States. Nonetheless, some, though not all, younger students seeking resolution to internal identity conflicts through study abroad fulfilled the goal of "international understanding" (if we accept, as the Gullahorns did, the following statement as constituting "international understanding"): "The true value of the Fulbright grant is . . . to be found in the maturity of the individual. He is, I think, a more thoughtful person, more tolerant, he knows the value of fluent foreign language. . . . He has been able to study the culture of other countries; he has learned to understand and accept national traits which formerly seemed peculiar and unreasonable."

Because the Gullahorns attributed the failure of many young students to "acculturate" and achieve such a point of "international understanding" to lack of structure and clear objectives for their study abroad experience, they ultimately recommended that the Fulbright program give preference to older students with focused research agendas.[18] Similarly, the Franco-American Commission's annual report of 1966 noted that achievement was easier to measure among advanced graduate students. Also like the Gullahorns, this report recognized benefits as well as shortcomings of study abroad for young students: It "would not want these circumstances to appear to reduce the importance it attaches to the younger students whose year in France, although devoted to much less specific aims, is nevertheless of substantial value and often a determining factor in their future academic careers."[19]

In 1976 Michael J. Flack reviewed research on foreign students in the United States, namely, the effects of study abroad on individuals, the American university and immediate society, the students' home society, and international relations. He found that competence in English language, greater expertise in a field of study, personal contacts in the United States, and familiarity with a wider range of professional information and possibilities usually enhanced foreign students' personal and professional stature after their return. Additionally, they gained a more sophisticated, less stereotyped understanding of American society and politics. Flack found that developing countries often benefited from students' return from the United States in terms of technological and social changes but that American universities and host communities were little affected by the presence of foreign students.

Acknowledging the difficulty of assessing the impact of study abroad on international relations, Flack noted that in general, foreign study furthered the development of globalization and cooperative international relations through fundamental international training and the personal transformation in understanding. Flack described an almost forced internationalism of circumstances in the 1970s:

> The infusion into almost all societies of internationally trained modern professionals, technicians, teachers, analysts, managers, and public servants who speak one of the international languages makes it practicable for the first time in human history to engage on a worldwide scale in coordinate, rather than superior-inferior, cooperative ventures; ... and to make feasible the many bi-, multi-, and international programs by the growing availability of counterpart personnel and leaderships, from almost all nations in our radically transformed world.[20]

Flack concluded, "If—beyond the personal and human growth of the ex-foreign students involved, ... study abroad has facilitated the achievements sketched in the preceding paragraph, then it would seem to have justified in good part both the investment and the effort."[21]

Like foreign students in the United States generally, French students also emphasized professional enhancement as a major motivating factor and a result of studying in the United States. The author of a 1964 study, Jeanne Mars, found that the main motivations for young French people to study in the United States were the excellent instruction—notably in nuclear physics, biology, and psychology—and the value of the experience for professional success and advancement. An economics student noted that a year in the United States set him back one year before exercising his profession, a problem that all French students confronted because study in the United States did not directly advance their degrees. In terms of professional experience, however, he claimed to have gained five, maybe ten years: "since my return, because of the internship I did, I was offered a position clearly better than what I would have obtained one year earlier." Study in the United States was no cakewalk for French students who had to adjust to constant evaluation through testing in courses, a high cost of living, and intense competitiveness among graduate students, because most French students went to study or work at the graduate level. Yet students overwhelmingly valued learning about the complexity and diversity of the United States, in contrast to the stereotypes with which they arrived, and overall,

Mars concluded that study in the United States for French students "is positive."[22]

Surveys and personal accounts by French Fulbright students affirm Mars's findings. The Association amicale universitaire France-Amérique (alumni association of former Fulbrighters from France; AAUFA) surveyed its membership in 1962 regarding their American experience and professional careers. With 592 responses to 1,373 questionnaires sent, the results indicated clearly that former Fulbrighters were successful in obtaining positions after their return from the United States.[23] In recent interviews, former French Fulbrighters identified immediate professional benefits from studying in the United States. Marie-José Taube, a Fulbright student at the University of California at Berkeley in 1961–62, attributed her satisfying job working at a research center on Asian business in Paris to her year of study in the United States; Rosine Lorotte, who studied at Harvard University Law School in 1964–65, said the same of her position working in the Paris branch of an American law firm.[24] Jean-Michel Roche, an exchange student at Harvard University in 1969–70, continues to specialize in the subject of the history of American foreign relations, for which he credits his experience in the United States.[25]

Overall, surveys and studies conducted from the 1950s through the 1970s indicate that study abroad's merits outweighed any drawbacks. Academic achievements and professional success were more easily measured than personal growth or international understanding, yet individual accounts consistently convey the latter in rich and detailed language, notably in oral interviews of alumni of various junior year abroad programs and reports by Fulbright students, scholars, and teachers. To be sure, these sources are limited in several regards. Subjects who made themselves available for interviews recalled their study abroad experience with fondness. Additionally, oral interview questions and standardized form questions guided individuals' accounts of their education abroad experience. For example, American Fulbright grantees were required to complete standardized forms addressing questions such as the following: to what extent they had achieved their academic goals, what stereotypes of France were challenged and what stereotypes of the United States they encountered, what recommendations they had for future grantees to prepare for study in France, and whether or not they felt that study abroad contributed to international understanding.[26] Fulbright grantees tended to look favorably on the agency that funded their study abroad, but criticism of the Fulbright program and suggestions for improvement were common; occasionally, a grantee expressed disillusionment with a particular aspect of French higher education, culture, or society. Many who responded to the question about international understanding raised doubts about the meaning of the term and offered their own interpretations. Yet the grantees' own accounts, and those of Americans who studied in France on other programs, closely match the hope Senator J. W. Fulbright expressed in 1967 regarding international education as a distinct alternative to foreign relations among states:

> We must seek through education to develop *empathy*, that rare and wonderful ability to perceive the world as others see it. Or, as Charles Frankel has put it, "A primary purpose of education and cultural exchange is to become aware of others' cultural codes and of our own—to bring to the surface the context of unspoken facts and assumptions within which their words and actions, and ours, can be correctly interpreted."[27]

Accounts by students and teachers from France or the United States who studied and worked in the other country in the 1960s highlight a range of characteristics that distinguish them from earlier generations. These include a wider range of motivations reflecting more diverse ethnic and social class backgrounds, greater esteem for American higher education as a result of study abroad, challenges and rewards of social interactions with the host population, and a new awareness of politics and race relations from study abroad, especially among Americans. The issues of national foreign policies and race relations often shaded into national stereotypes that became focal points for visitors and hosts' interactions. Students and teachers of the 1960s and the 1970s—irrespective of the demonstrations and events of 1968—found that the foreign and domestic policies of France and the United States were much more salient as entry points for understanding one's own nation, the other nation, and oneself than students and teachers earlier in the century did.

Sarah Price, who studied in Paris on the Tulane/Newcomb Junior Year in France program in 1963–64, was originally drawn to study in France because of her European family background; she was born in Germany, and her parents were Polish Jewish refugees in the early 1940s. She also professed to having "had romantic ideas about France, from movies, books, and history," and she wanted to study in France because "her mother had studied French and France was appealing because it was welcoming to Jews and it was cultured and refined." But she claimed she was also motivated to try "to understand the Holocaust."[28] Her classmate,

Steve Whitfield, had more vocational goals in mind when he signed on for the program. Older by one year than the other juniors, he had decided to pursue an academic career in European intellectual history, for which he knew he needed language skills. Nonetheless, the appeal of Europe for him, both professionally and personally, derived from a similar European heritage: "my parents were both refugees from Europe, Jews who had fled in the late 1930s. So I always had . . . a kind of consciousness of Europe, as an alternative to the U.S."[29]

By contrast, Herbert Larson at Tulane University wound up studying in France in 1972–73 quite by chance and practically against his family background. Having decided in the middle of his sophomore year that he no longer wished to continue in premed, he said, "I was sort of floundering. And one of my friends who was going to go JYA [Junior Year Abroad] to England said, well, you should go JYA next year, to England." On inquiry, however, Larson found that the program for England was full, but an advisor suggested that, because he had studied French, he might try the program in France. "And so I did." This was a considerable leap for a young man from Missouri, who claims he was "considered unusual" for attending college out of state, "And then to go away from school to a foreign country was a little bit odder." In addition, Larson's father, a military man and veteran of World War II, was not fond of France. Larson recalled, "there was no love lost for the French from my father, I think frankly as a result of his combat experiences in France."[30] A larger and more diverse population in American higher education in the 1960s is evident in this small sample of students who went to France, and this probably also explains the varieties of motivations for study abroad.

Americans who studied in France in the 1960s learned to esteem American higher education more than did previous generations while still valuing their study abroad. Many American students arrived in France with the assumption that French higher education was superior to that in the United States and then revised that view. In 1962 Karen Stedtfeld wrote in her final report to the Fulbright Commission: "One of the most striking misconceptions that I have encountered and been subsequently enlightened about is the misconception of the superiority of the European education in relation to the American. A positive result of the exchange experience was learning not to generalize about such and such a country in any respect—that the good goes along with the bad."[31] Paul Simon, a music student from New York University, arrived in Paris in 1963 "aware of the 'snob appeal' of having studied in a European university or conservatory." However, he wrote in a report of his Fulbright year: "I have found no good reason for this now, and have been pleasantly surprised with how the quality of my own educational background measures up."[32] Another Fulbright student, Samuel Rutherford, expressed similar sentiments reporting on his year at the University of Lyon in 1962–63: "Before leaving the U.S. I thought that the European system was fundamentally better than ours and therefore we should remodel ours. Now I realize that it is not a case of being 'better' but just of being different."[33] The reputation of French universities for rigor and quality was gradually declining in the face of modern and successful American institutions of higher learning, though most students still found something to appreciate about their educational experiences in France.

French students who studied in the United States with Fulbright grants and other scholarships or exchanges expressed high regard for the reputation of American higher education, both before and after their experience abroad. Jean-Michel Roche, an exchange student at Harvard University from the Paris Ecole Normale Supérieure in 1969–70, recalled his motivations for studying in the United States: "The United States represented a power that nonetheless fascinated [me] by its modernity and equally by the prestige of its universities." He was not disappointed in these expectations. He extolled the professors and the teaching methods he encountered at Harvard. Although he saw merit in the French method of taking notes and learning to write, he noted that in France students "did not learn to question." Roche greatly appreciated the American approach and said that he had trouble readjusting to France because he found that "students had difficulty, I recall, when they were asked, 'well, do you have any questions?'"[34] Similarly, Paul Benhamou found that American teaching methods in the early 1960s contrasted favorably with the "dogmatic, authoritarian" approach in France: "in the States I discovered that students were allowed to question the instructor, to interrupt the instructor, and I really grooved on that." He recalled that several years later, when he was a professor of French at Purdue University in Indiana, he could experiment with innovative teaching methods: He taught "a course on songs and poetry, using Brassens and people like this, and this would never be accepted in the '70s in France."[35] As will be seen below, the reforms of 1968 would relax the rigid hierarchy and structure of French higher education, though not to the point of complete "Americanization."

An issue of notable difference in American and French encounters with the other society was the level of interaction with the host population. Many Americans noted the difficulty of meeting French people, a problem that study abroad program organizers tirelessly addressed. Housing Americans with French families was one solution to the problem, but young people still wanted to associate with French persons nearer their own age. The difficulty was probably more structural than due to hostility or unfriendliness, because in both France and the United States students had their own personal, social, and cultural connections.[36] American Steve Whitfield recalls that when he studied in Paris in 1963–64, "the biggest disappointment" was that he did not meet more French people, though he highly valued the experience as a whole. He attributed this in part to his lack of spending money, but also to the impenetrability of French society: "there was just no way that I could figure out how to penetrate the French society that I was so eager to join, if they'd only let me, for those few months."[37] Jeffrey Coatsworth, a Fulbright scholar who worked toward a master's degree in international relations in Paris in 1965–66, wrote in his final report about social relations with French people: "Socially I learned more about their ways than I participated in them. The camaraderie of the French student or worker is not easily broken into."[38] Even a student who associated almost exclusively with French people while she earned a master's degree at Middlebury College in 1968–69 thought that her experience was exceptional. Karla Taudin lodged in a boardinghouse with other French students—all men—who became her friends and one of whom became her husband: "I didn't live the way a lot of Americans did, who came over and kept among themselves a lot. . . . I didn't really see the Americans on my program that much. I spent more time with these people at the boarding house basically."[39]

By contrast, several French students in the United States found Americans very friendly and sociable. Paul Benhamou had not been enthusiastic about attending the University of Iowa, but, with hindsight, he claims that "it was a great opportunity for me to discover American culture, to meet lots of students because the Midwest is extremely hospitable."[40] Similarly, Rosine Lorotte, who earned a master's degree in international law at Harvard University in 1964–65, worked hard at her studies but also enjoyed an active social life with other foreign students and with Americans. She had two American roommates who helped her "enormously," and she was also struck by the institutional ease of student sociability in the United States in contrast to France: "One could, for example, reserve the hall of the dormitory to invite friends and have a party. It was incredibly, incredibly easy."[41]

Nonetheless, some students had difficulty meeting American students. One example, Gérard François, a French student from the University of Nancy, studied at Ball State University in Indiana in 1975. According to François, many students left campus for the weekends and holidays to go home; they were mostly from Indiana, and they had cars. That left the foreign students together, with no means of transportation to leave the university. François also found that American students just were not very interested in foreign students, "because I guess they can't relate and they don't really know a whole lot about our country." He made more American friends during the second year of his stay at Ball State, "because I decided to go and look for Americans." Additionally, he met the woman who became his wife, and that also helped him to socialize more with Americans.[42]

Socializing with peers in the host country was problematic, especially for American students in France, but it was not necessarily an insurmountable difficulty. For a while the AAUFA in Paris provided a "godparent" service, whereby former French Fulbrighters took an American Fulbright student or scholar under his or her wing, inviting the American for a meal and introducing him or her to French professionals. Individual students found other ways to interact with their French peers. As a Fulbright student in Nancy, Karen Stedtfeld had little difficulty in adjusting to the group socialization practices of French students, recounting that she often participated in mixed-group activities "to go to the movies, do this, do that, meet for a beer—whatever."[43] Leslie Roberts, a member of the first Tufts University in Paris program in 1965–66, found that her roommate's dietary practices led them to socialize with a particular population. In a recent interview Roberts explained that her roommate (also from Tufts) was an Orthodox Jew who "wanted to eat kosher food, so we ate in kosher student restaurants, and we were about the only people there that weren't North African. So we got to know a fascinating community of Jewish North Africans.... They were mostly Tunisians, and we ended up going to their homes, seeing celebrations that they had, eating food."[44] For some American students in France, sociability shaded into political awareness, for contact with French people, including racial and ethnic minorities, precipitated questions about political and social policies in both countries.

Sociability and political awareness coincided for Sarah Price, who in a recent interview indicated, perhaps with hindsight, that she was looking for an identity for herself, and that ultimately, her experience in France helped in that quest. In Price's corrected version of my notes from our conversation, she said that "she felt alienation (too strong a term) at [Sophie Newcomb] college. She didn't like being in a sorority, drinking parties. She found refreshing that European students were not like that; they were involved in politics." Living and studying in France heightened Price's awareness of politics, including in the United States. She noted that, "1963 was the year of the bombing of the black church in Birmingham, Alabama" (where she had once lived before attending college in New Orleans). "There were lots of Africans from the former French colonies in student restaurants in Paris," she continued. "They wanted to discuss race with American students. In the orientation program her professors told her not to criticize the United States. She found it hard not to criticize. It was not nice to feel your country was accused of racism, even though segregation was racist." After she returned, she found a new niche for herself in college with more politically aware and active students, an outcome of study abroad that she values, along with "her continuing interest in France and European affairs."[45]

In interviews and documents, Americans on the Fulbright program in the early 1960s repeatedly mentioned that French acquaintances queried them on racial inequality and civil rights in the United States. A typical example of this appears in Illinois-native Nancy Hires's final report to the Franco-American Commission, submitted at the end of her stay in Aix in 1963, regarding French misconceptions of the United States: "[Racial] prejudice is their greatest preoccupation and the subject that most frequently arises in conversation. Though the racial problem is not a misconception on their part, I find my French classmates without equipment to even understand the problem—their historical, social, and geographical understanding of America is, in fact, quite vague—and on this point simple narration of the fact seems to be the most effective and helpful means of increasing their understanding of the situation."[46] Similarly, Joy Sellers of Minneapolis noted four common misconceptions she found in France in 1963, starting with "the Negro problem in the United States. In view of the coverage given to integration difficulties in the United States, I was constantly asked about this problem. Without falsifying the grim reality of this situation, I think my answers in discussion on this topic helped to further an understanding of the complexities involved. My contact with some of the African students, which I did not intentionally force, was a living witness to the fact that not all Americans are completely hostile to the colored race."[47] The experience of living and studying in France precipitated reflection on race issues in the United States and in France in other ways as well. Leslie Roberts recalled that in 1965, "One of the first things I was very surprised at [in Paris] was to see signs in cafés that said, 'No Turkish people allowed.'" She continued: "I hadn't yet traveled through the United States; I'd only been in the North, so I hadn't actually seen bathrooms, where 'Negro' had been crossed out, so this was an absolute shock to me, and there was a lot more of it, 'No North Africans here.'"[48] Learning about the Algerian War and the racial tensions that it aggravated in France was an essential part of Roberts's study abroad experience.

Countless American students commented on how often they explained American social conditions or foreign policies to French acquaintances, and many confessed to feeling somewhat ignorant about their own country when confronted with questions by French hosts. As Anita Maier of Arizona wrote in her final report in 1963, "it is extremely necessary for students to know something about their *own* country before coming abroad—politics, literature, music, etc. They will be continually confronted with questions from students who no doubt know more about the subject than the American himself."[49] Many also claimed that learning about race relations and politics in France also led them to learn more about the United States or become involved in activism after their return. Lucy Carr, a student in the Sweet Briar program in 1960–61, claims that part of her introduction to leftist politics occurred in the theater course she took: "The TNP [Théâtre National de Paris] was deeply influenced by communist or certainly socialist theorizing . . . so I was being introduced to a very left wing view of the world through that avenue." According to Carr, this exposure to new ways of thinking combined with a more general spirit of the age and with her personal struggle with race issues in the United States: "I was 20–21; it was a stage in life where you feel empowered and you have to change the world. . . . It was very easy to look critically from France at my own country. I don't think that I was yet deeply critical of the politics of my own country, but I was already deeply concerned about the racial problems in our country."[50] Leslie Roberts, a participant in the first Tufts University in Paris program in 1965–66, recounts how she "learned" about the United States' involvement in Vietnam through study abroad: "I'd be asked by various people [in Paris], 'Why are *you* in Vietnam?' And I did not know. So I learned; I had to read books in French about Vietnam; I learned about it and I realized that I had truly wished we weren't there. Remember this is 1965, so this is early, but when I got back, a lot of other people had figured out the same thing, so I became part of the antiwar movement."[51]

Politics infused American students' experiences of living and studying in France in the 1960s, enhancing their questioning and reassessments of national identities and American identity in particular. Historian Rusty Monhollon found in his research on students and residents of Lawrence, Kansas, during the 1960s that civil rights and antiwar demonstrations provoked debate in Lawrence about Americanness and the meaning of the "American way of life." He claims that these debates also "personalized" politics, as individuals drew on history, faith, and experience to verbalize their conceptualizations of freedom, equality, and justice.[52] Similarly, study abroad had always challenged American students to explain the United States to others and to understand their country in more deliberate and often new ways. Issues of race and imperialism were publicly prominent in both the United States and France in the 1960s and often served as a lens for comprehending oneself, one's own country, and another nation.

One Fulbright student wrote about how politics as a topic of conversation between himself and French persons improved mutual understanding during his year in France (1965–66): "I've had to discuss openly and honestly everything from segregation to Viet Nam. We have agreed and we have differed, but nobody lost from having talked about it. I don't, for instance see how anyone could begin to understand General de Gaulle, right or wrong, as he withdraws from the NATO structure, unless you have spent some time talking to Frenchmen."[53] As a student at the University of Besançon in 1966–67, Fulbright scholar Alison Bennett studied realism and naturalism in Emile Zola's novels, but she also valued what she learned about France and the United States: "Today I consider much more seriously my country's role in the world situation than I did one year ago and I can also appreciate more what the United States offers me."[54] Reflecting on the effects of study abroad in the early 1970s on his political views, Herbert Larson indicated: "I think if France did anything it made me aware that the foreign policy of the United States is frequently quite misguided."[55]

In the late 1960s American involvement in Vietnam precipitated heated discussions and efforts to explain and understand French and American perspectives.[56] One student, Barbara Boonstopple, conveyed the frustration of discussing "the problem of the U.S. in S.E. Asia" with limited language skills at the beginning of her year in France. Writing to her family in 1966, she asserted, "What is really a problem is that the French seem to think that just because we talk like morons we can't think and reason like normal human beings." What frustrated Boonstopple was that Madeline, a woman whose father was French and mother was North Vietnamese, "kept explaining things over and over, simpler and simpler, because she couldn't realize that just because we couldn't answer well we didn't understand the problem."[57] Precisely because of tensions at the level of policy between France and the United States in 1966–67, Frederick Berman believed Fulbright exchanges were vitally important because they provided him "the opportunity . . . to express my views, NOT as an official representative of the United States government, but as a private citizen," which he thought "had considerable value in terms of international understanding."[58] Vivian Scanlon, who studied French literature at Aix-en-Provence in 1967–68, explained at length in her Fulbright report how much she learned about transnational understanding and American identity during her year abroad. In conversation with French persons, she:

> was forced to articulate what up until this year had been an intuitive but unanalytical comprehension of American problems. I must admit that it is very difficult to convince people . . . that one can be opposed to U.S. policies in Vietnam, that one can believe in integration, and at the same time still believe in America. . . . a sincere mutual effort on my part and on the part of my foreign friends to understand America has brought me to a new realization of what it means to be an American youth.[59]

Personal interactions were vital to the exchange of ideas and acquisition of new knowledge, and several accounts suggest that these still mattered even in an age of modern, mass communication. Just as Americans sometimes felt obligated to disabuse their French hosts of a superficial or incomplete understanding of race relations in the United States, French Fulbrighters also tried to counter stereotypes and misconceptions that Americans held regarding the French. Yves Legras, a Fulbright exchange teacher at a high school in New York State in 1963–64, blamed American mass media for "each day skillfully distilling in American opinion half truths that are not made to bring us together," though he acknowledged that the French were not blameless either. Thus, he concluded that his role of teaching the young was important because they were receptive to dialogue; he considered the value of his experience to be the extent to which he participated in a true exchange of ideas between France and the United States.⁶⁰

Debates and demonstrations at home and questions from foreign hosts abroad challenged American students to assess or reassess their identity as Americans and articulate their views on American foreign and domestic policies. In providing a new vantage point for such considerations, study abroad also introduced them to a deeper understanding of French policies and practices. Although French students, scholars, and teachers in the United States no doubt enhanced their knowledge of American politics, French identity was less salient in the study abroad experience. It is likely that French political culture had led most to form their national identities and political positions before traveling abroad, and they may have encountered less questioning about French policies from American hosts. Throughout the 1960s, young people in both France and the United States grappled with political issues, especially in academic settings, a phenomenon that peaked in 1968. This was especially true in France with the protests and demonstrations that happened in May of that year. The greatest impact of these events on study abroad occurred in terms of reforming French higher education.

Student revolts and movements culminating in 1968 shared common characteristics and themes in France and the United States as well as worldwide. Many scholars have identified global conditions and factors behind youth revolt, including generational conflict and anti-authoritarian sentiment on the part of a demographically powerful group seeking a modern social identity; anti-imperialism crystallized around the United States' war in Vietnam; idealism for a more racially and socially inclusive university and society; and frustration with a Cold War political and global order.⁶¹ In the context of study abroad, however, a long-term effect of the 1968 student protests was to strengthen the appeal of transatlantic education. Higher education reform in France made it easier for French students to transfer credits from the United States toward completion of their French degree. American students and, increasingly, French students, found study abroad valuable for consolidating personal identities as well as broadening an understanding of national identities. Thus, the process of seeing the United States from a new, global perspective and assessing one's American identity, which students had experienced for several decades from study abroad, was enhanced by the general politicization of the 1960s worldwide. And practices common in American higher education were embraced by French students and embodied in permanent reforms, a form of "Americanization" not addressed by most historians of this phenomenon. For the most part, students, scholars, and teachers took the disruptions of 1968 in stride and added their voices in support of academic exchanges, notably when cuts in funding by the U.S. government threatened the continuation of the Fulbright program.

Throughout the post-World War II years, French university students had suffered from overcrowding, inadequate housing, poor job prospects, elitism, a sexually repressed atmosphere, and outmoded courses and teaching methods. Neither student organizations nor university administrators had succeeded in transforming this situation, though they wrote manifestos and implemented reforms in the early 1960s. The revolution of May 1968 was unexpected, but the crisis that precipitated it was clear.[62] David Alcan, a professor of American literature who taught at the University of Pau in 1967–68, was not alone in suggesting a need for pedagogical reform in French universities on the eve of 1968. In his final report to the Fulbright Commission, he wrote: "I hesitate to be critical, but I believe that French education would do well with a lot more American style informality"; he specifically wished that French students could overcome their "diffidence" and "ask questions, engage in discussion."[63] That same year, another Fulbright visiting lecturer, Joseph Bender, claimed of his experience teaching at the University of Strasbourg: "In the current explosive state of ferment in France I am at least a living exemplar of the American system which many French students and professors say they would like to see imitated to an extent in the forthcoming reforms of French universities."[64]

Reform followed 1968 in terms of immediate structural changes in the universities and more liberal policies in student residences. Reforms under the minister of National Education, Edgar Faure, included the participation of student and junior faculty representatives in university decisions and the breakup of the old academic divisions into more flexible Units of Teaching and Research (UERs). Curricula became more flexible and multidisciplinary, and although state examinations were not eliminated, students were eligible to take them after accumulating a certain number of course credits (*unités de valeur*), replacing the previous standard list of requirements. Universities themselves became more independent and showed greater tolerance for students' freedom of movement and sexuality.[65] Exchange student Jean-Michel Roche characterized this transformation as "a form of university Americanization."[66]

Historians Michael Seidman and Didier Fischer caution against interpreting the events of May 1968 in France as revolutionary. Significant liberalization of higher education did result from the crisis, but both scholars interpret this as reformist rather than revolutionary.[67] Indeed, the events of May 1968 in France had little effect on American study abroad programs in France, though the reforms that followed may have increased interest in study abroad on both sides of the Atlantic and spurred further cooperation among institutions of higher learning. Reports by directors of the study abroad program in Aix-en-Provence sponsored jointly by the University of Michigan and the University of Wisconsin suggest that in 1968 uncertainty about course offerings and class meetings was the biggest concern. Director Guy Mermier noted in December 1968 that "classes were slow in starting," that a French professor "assured [him] that order would certainly be achieved by January, and that classes which had not yet met (psychology and sociology) would probably do so without delay after Christmas. Nevertheless there remained among students (French students) an air of uncertainty, but mostly (and as usual) of 'laissez-faire.'"[68] Lucien Jambrun, former head of the Service for French Exchanges at the Franco-American Commission in Paris from 1949 to 1984, recalled that he did not think the events of May 1968 in France constituted "a very important revolution."[69] Several different American programs centered at Reid Hall in Paris noted an increase in enrollments despite "the volatile situation and the uncertainty of the date of the fall reopening of the Paris faculties."[70]

Franco-American Commission reports for academic years 1967–68 and 1968–69 were cautiously optimistic about the implications of the changes in higher education in France following the 1968 events. First, the report for 1967–68 evaluated the entire Fulbright program since 1949 as a success in terms of increasing the number of "French professors teaching American subjects in French universities. When the Commission was created, only one full professor for American literature was teaching throughout the entire French university system, whereas there are now approximately 60 professors of American subjects in French universities, practically all of them alumni of this program." The report speculates "that probably the same can be said of French subjects taught in the U.S. but the decentralized American system renders precise figures difficult." Having noted this measure of success of the program overall, the report also registers a cautious expectation of increased interest in France for the exchanges precisely because of anticipated changes in French universities: "the Commission feels, however, that it is reasonable to hope for an even more receptive atmosphere for its projects within French universities and even more pronounced eagerness on the part of French students and scholars to spend a year in American universities."[71] Indeed, the annual report of the following year noted that "the number of French student candidates applying for grants in the United States was higher than ever in 1969–70."[72] Although the commission expressed concern for the disruption caused by drastic changes in French universities, it identified more serious problems for the exchange. Namely, the report noted changes in procedures of the U.S. Selective Service (military draft) that pulled accepted American candidates from the exchange at the last minute.[73] And withdrawal of American financial support after 1968 also threatened the program, as will be seen below.

For students and teachers, the eruptions and disruptions of 1968 heightened the intensity of the study abroad experience. Steven Sadler, a recent graduate of Northwestern University and a Fulbright student in 1967–68, recalled the events of May 1968 as a memorable part of his year at the University of Aix but not because of any revolutionary change. "There were *manifestations* [demonstrations] throughout the city," he explained in a recent interview. "The university was, of course, occupied, and the day would be divided up between individual sessions where people would talk about the problems of Aix, the university, the problems of the educational system in France; in another room [they discussed] the problems of French politics and [in] a further room, the problems of the universe." He noted that because of the general strike, he was actually out of touch with developments in the capital and elsewhere; "aside from a transistor radio there was no access to information really, just word of mouth." He knew he was in the midst of something extraordinary but could not understand what the outcome would be: "when everything, practically everything is shut down, and people are walking around with radios all the time listening to events, and this sense of immediacy that some of the things were going to break, but exactly where it was going to go and how it was going to affect me as an American wasn't quite clear." In addition, Sadler's French girlfriend was in the hospital with a curable ailment during the events, and he divided his time between the sessions at the university "and the hospital which in some ways actually was a greater personal concern." Sadler followed the shifting moods of the French people around him with de Gaulle's brief disappearance and the possibility that Pierre Mendès-France and François Mitterand might form a provisional government. But for him the turning point was the settlement with the refinery workers, which restored the flow of gasoline: "I mean once the

French could drive, those who had automobiles could drive again, they felt the spell was over. There was a return to normalcy, and I sensed that when I was there, and this is one of the few things that I really have remembered very strongly, is a clear sense of a break after that occurred."[74]

The nonrevolutionary nature of May 1968 in France was echoed in a recent interview with Jean-Michel Roche, a French student who spent the academic year 1969–70 at Harvard University as part of the Fulbright exchange. Roche recalled the intense atmosphere of that time at Harvard as both optimistic for the future and rent by the war in Vietnam: "There was a strong contrast between a feeling that the world was there, ready for the taking, . . . that life promised to be happy, and at the same time the anguish created by Vietnam. I experienced at Harvard . . . the intensity of protest, for example the invasion of Cambodia, a very striking event." He acknowledged that a similar sense of the possibility of a renewed world existed in France, but not to the same extent as in the United States: "One had a little bit the same thing in France in '68, but there . . . it was very impressionistic, more institutionalized, more, how shall I say, rooted in our customs."[75] Historical scholarship and accounts by students and academics abroad suggest that whereas 1968 in the United States was a high point in a longer crisis of American national identity, its effects for young people in France centered more on student life and the position of students in the larger society.

American students and scholars in France during and immediately after the events of May 1968 found education disrupted and some notable changes in the universities. Student recitations became more important than professors' lectures, a situation that displeased Eleanor Allard, a student of French literature and a Fulbright fellow at the University of Grenoble in 1968–69. In her final report she advised the Fulbright program that "students should be warned also that as a result of recent reforms, lecture courses have—unfortunately, in most cases—been replaced by 'semi-magistral' courses in which students share the burden with the professor by delivering exposés. Even though I had been well-versed in giving exposés in small classes at home [Wellesley College], I found it difficult to adjust to these massive lecture courses with 300 people, in which students were asked at random to address the group with a literary analysis."[76] Monica Billings found her medieval art history studies seriously disrupted at the University of Poitiers: "courses were begun then cancelled, then begun again as students and professors took part in endless discussions on the content of courses and the way they were to be conducted. This atmosphere of chaos lasted in a lesser degree almost the whole year."[77]

Vivian Scanlon found much to criticize about the French higher education system as a Fulbright student in 1967–68, including the formality of student-professor relations and course requirements that did not necessarily interest students. "This causes for [sic] a general atmosphere of indifference, if not resentment," she wrote in her Fulbright report, "and students and professors were mutually uninspired and uninspiring." Nonetheless, the events of May 1968 provided her with a new perspective: "I must say that my admiration for both French students and professors has soared during the past few weeks, as I would not have thought them capable of such courage, lucidity, and total commitment in the face of a system which is in great need of total reform." She wrote that her studies at Aix "helped me to appreciate all that I have taken for granted in the American University System, as I see the French struggling to obtain what I have always considered basic, as, for example, student-faculty boards to choose courses."[78] Although Geoffrey Aikins, a Fulbright student in 1968–69, declared after his year in Paris that he understood "better the superiority of the American system," he also urged continued funding for the program, not only because he personally gained much from his experience, but also "to preserve the good will that USA reaps from the relatively small amount invested each year in it."[79]

As Aikins's comment reveals, the major effect on the Fulbright academic exchanges was less the student protests of 1968 than a significant cut in funding by the U.S. government. A new accord of May 7, 1965, established binational funding of Fulbright in France by both the United States and French governments. In 1968 France's contribution rose from about 25 percent to close to 50 percent, a time when the entire Fulbright budget in France dropped from $950,000 in 1968–69 to $391,100 for 1969–70.[80] Commission members had dealt with smaller cuts in previous years and managed to reduce administrative expenses so that scholarship funding could continue at the same level, but the drastic cut from the U.S. government in 1968 incited fear that the program might not continue. The program report for 1969–70 indicated that "the funds from American sources, which in 1968–69 amounted to $700,000, were reduced in 1969–70 to $136,000."[81] The French government maintained its level of about $250,000, so the number of awards to French citizens persisted, while those to Americans fell substantially from 210 in 1968–69 to 12 in 1969–70.[82]

At a time when U.S. foreign policy interest was shifting away from Europe and toward underdeveloped parts of the world, and the war in Vietnam and student protests roiled societies in the West and beyond, the budget cut created considerable anxiety among those who worked for Fulbright about the future viability of the program. Lucien Jambrun, retired head of the Service for French Exchangees at the Franco-American Commission in Paris, remembered that after the 80 percent budget cut of 1968, he feared that the Fulbright program "might no longer be credible in France."[83] However, supporters of the Fulbright program vigorously protested the funding reduction. Dr. James R. Roach, chairman of the Board of Foreign Scholarships, wrote a letter to Secretary of State William P. Rogers on March 6, 1969, to make a case for an increase in funding for the program as a whole. His main argument was that such abrupt and drastic cuts in cultural programs threatened American credibility worldwide. He asserted that Americans affiliated with the Fulbright program are distinctively well-regarded in other countries: "the 'credibility' of 'Fulbright scholars' has remained remarkably high, in part because of the binational character of the program. It is 'clean' and is widely so regarded. Its decline, given the present climate in some countries, would do irreparable damage, and would be impossible to replace."[84]

American grantees also supported the restoration of funding for the Fulbright exchange. After a year studying Renaissance poetry at the University of Strasbourg, Cynthia Seymour made an impassioned plea for continued U.S. funding of Fulbright. "It is with the deepest regret," she wrote in her final report of 1969, "that I have learned of the recent congressional decision to curtail the program so severely." Her first concern was for poor students who would be deprived of an opportunity to study abroad: "Obviously, for many young Americans who do not happen to have come from wealthy families or to have gone to the 'right' schools, the ideal of a year's study abroad will become much more difficult to realize." Second, Seymour really believed that educational exchange was an effective means of combating national stereotypes and increasing transnational understanding: "The character and the extent of some of the misconceptions which some of these people [the French] have concerning America are truly startling, but no more startling than the lack of comprehension, the gratuitous hostility, and the unwarranted assumption of being universally resented which so many Americans seem to have with regard to the Europeans." The solution, she wrote, was better communication: "it is at this point that the student, proficient in the foreign language, is able to accomplish what the average tourist or soldier is incapable of doing."[85] Other students echoed this sentiment, such as Elizabeth Saltzman, who acknowledged that a "broadening of understanding, an increasing elasticity of spirit" that characterized academic exchanges were difficult to measure, and therefore persuading Congress to support such a nebulous project was also difficult, "but as I see it, it is just this real wisdom and largeness of spirit that can save American politics and society, and the tragedy is that there isn't half enough of it in our educational system. I think every effort should be made to re-establish the Fulbright program, in fact to enlarge it."[86]

The crisis passed, and Fulbright funding was soon restored. An article in *Newsweek* credited "intensive salesmanship by members of the academic community both in the U.S. and in other countries, by key State Department and Congressional officials and by former Fulbright scholars," for a Fulbright "renaissance," along with contributions by other countries. Nonetheless, a greater focus on developing countries, as opposed to Europe, remained.[87]

Students of different ages and levels generally described their study abroad experience in the 1960s as both professionally and personally rewarding. Americans in particular valued a new sense of identity and a better understanding of themselves as individuals and as Americans. Vivian Scanlon described in detail the process of her growing appreciation for another culture:

> In the beginning of the year, I found myself making constant comparisons between French and American students to justify my disillusionment with what I considered the superficiality of the French.... When I grew out of the defensive critical stage after the first few months, and became more analytical, asking myself what it was in the structures of the two societies which made their youth so different, I was led to some very interesting conclusions concerning the unstable nature of a relatively new society in America, as compared with that of France, which is so rooted in the past. I ceased making value judgments, made more of an effort to understand and to see through French eyes, and at that point all unhappiness vanished.[88]

Steven Sadler specifically noted the personal identity issues he confronted as an American studying in France for a year:

> Although this year has enabled me to learn a great deal about myself and my capabilities, it has produced something of an identity crisis in that I am not sure how to fully combine those elements of the American and European

worlds which most appeal to me. Life in France has enabled me to realize what I miss in America and what I wish to continue missing in America. At the same time, many old illusions about what Europe is all about have long ago been dispelled. What this year has produced, then, is an uprooting of many old values and expectations.[89]

Students struggled with the question about "international understanding," often finding it excessively idealistic or, as one put it, "a grandiloquent mouthful." But some considered its meaning on a small scale, as did, for example, Shelly Reardon of Arkansas:

I'm not sure my experience can be discussed in terms of anything so large and ephemeral as 'international understanding.' I certainly haven't convinced anyone of the justness of American foreign policy or that everything is rosey [sic] in the United States' domestic scene. I did, however, take part in an exchange of cultures and made some close, I feel, lasting friendships. So perhaps my experience did contribute to international understanding if it is defined, as I think it should be, as the sense of multitudes of individual personal relationships.[90]

Another American Fulbright grantee, who spent a year at the University of Caen in 1964–65, wrote: "If I have grown to love France, it is because it is so unlike America, and yet it is through France that I have come to appreciate my own country." He went on to say that the personal development that derives from a year well spent abroad extends beyond one's "appreciation of France. It is at once a new way of seeing himself in relation to another world and to his own. It is the beginning of an education and a way of life."[91]

Even French students, usually more focused on professional advantages from study abroad, recorded elements of personal transformation, as a 1963 survey by the AAUFA reveals. One respondent indicated that the way for a French student to benefit most from the study abroad experience was to "unlearn" the European education:

A year of study in the United States represents a traumatism that must be lived and that is very enriching on condition that the French student not try to find traces of Europe and its values in the United States; otherwise, he would not be able to absorb anything of the United States and would be very unhappy. It is necessary to forget Europe for at least six months to reappropriate it later without risk of losing the American assets or of being incapable of assimilating it.[92]

For some French Fulbrighters, coming to the United States was the beginning of independence: "For me, my stay in the United States was the open door to freedom, to responsibility ... I could guide my life, find my way [*me débrouiller*], and do a good job of it."[93] Some found the traumatism of living in the United States equaled by that of returning to France. Several described French reactions to them after resuming their lives in France as "suspicious," "a kind of jealousy," and "skeptical."[94] Nonetheless, the respondents found both immense professional and personal gains from studying in the United States.

By the late 1960s both Americans and French greatly valued the resources and methods of higher education in the United States. Although study abroad increasingly connoted personal growth and self-understanding for young Americans, French persons acknowledged how their personal identity developed as a result of studying in the United States. Politics impinged in different ways on both French and American students' experiences abroad, mostly as a focal point for exchanging ideas and information, challenging stereotypes, and acquiring understanding. The main effect of the May events of 1968 on study abroad was to increase interest and participation on both sides of the Atlantic, in part because French higher education became more accommodating of educational exchanges.

Both the limits and extent of mass global communications are evident in Franco-American exchanges during this period. Transatlantic travel was on the rise, but travelers to another country still represented a unique authority in their own countries. In some ways, information about the rest of the world was supplanting this eyewitness authority, but for individuals who had studied abroad, nothing could replace the particular understanding gained from lived experience. In 1962 two French teachers of English who had taught or studied in the United States surveyed their secondary school pupils in France regarding attitudes toward or interest in the United States. They found that young French people, especially between the ages of seventeen and twenty, were fairly well informed about American politics, social issues (especially race relations), and student life. A professor in a girls' *lycée* in Toulon noted of her pupils: "In the heart of more than one [girl] awoke the obsession of a pleasure trip to this marvelous country, which appeared at the same time a country so welcoming to youth. Yes, but America is so far away!"[95] Other French teachers, like this one, who cherished the opportunity to travel, learn, and teach in the United States, noted how important it was for young French people to have such an experience, despite the difficulties and expense. Not only would such a trip disabuse French youth of Hollywood stereotypes, but also it matured them and developed their self-possession. Noting that American students were more independent than French students because they often attended institutions far from home, one French teacher said of studying in the United States: "The trip represents a unique opportunity to enrich one's understanding of a foreign country, of one's own [country] seen from a new perspective, and of oneself, since in these circumstances one has no other guide than the elements of a character more or less formed."[96]

Much has been made of a global youth culture that developed in the 1960s, because young people, especially in the West, enjoyed similar material comforts, educational opportunities, distance from and even rebelliousness against an older generation, and high expectations for the future. Transatlantic flights became more common, and news coverage, recorded music, and fashion crossed borders with ease. Nonetheless, mass communications and transportation still had limitations. National cultural differences persisted that were best comprehended through individual experience. This was acutely apparent in social and sexual relations, as will be evident in the next chapter.

§ 7 Sexuality, Gender, and National Identities in Twentieth-century Franco-American Exchanges

In 1962 a story by French author Robert Mengin, titled "For Helen," appeared in the *Revue des deux mondes*. The first-person narrator, Anthony, a young American man with French family relations, looks back to 1935, when he took summer courses for foreigners in Paris after completing his undergraduate studies. At that time he fell in love with another American, Helen, who was in Paris studying art. But Helen was in love with a French *polytechnicien*, Paul, for whom she suffered the loss of her scholarship, her room at the Fondation des Etats-Unis in the Cité Universitaire, and, eventually, her virginity.

This story reveals common French and American notions of the other's sexual and social behaviors that were evident in the 1930s but were more explicit in the 1960s. According to the fictional Helen, her mother had warned her, "with the French, if you are not careful, you will wind up in bed!" And sure enough, Helen claimed that the French do not engage in flirtation, as was her custom in the United States; instead, her French boyfriend Paul took love seriously—so seriously that he wanted Helen to sleep with him. His reasoning was that marriage was even more serious, and hence required certainty. She quoted Paul on marriage: "it must not be entered into lightly, to end in divorce two or three years later, as you do in America. One needs *solid guarantees*!" By refusing to sleep with him, Helen failed to provide "solid guarantees."[1] Anthony, the American, offered to marry Helen, but she refused, even though Paul's insistence that she be his mistress filled Helen, a woman of the American "aristocracy," with horror. Nonetheless, she eventually succumbed to Paul.

Distraught over Paul's continued hesitation regarding marriage, Helen discussed with Anthony the French stereotype of American women: "is it

171

true that American women are . . . 'vulgar women, neurotic, incapable of housekeeping, who raise their children to be savages, and whose relationships go so badly that they all divorce, or make their husbands die of heart attack, ulcer, or nervous breakdown'?"[2] With hindsight, Anthony thinks Helen might have succeeded in marrying Paul, but World War II intervened. When the war broke out, she joined the WAVES, and Anthony served in the U.S. Navy. In 1943, after she learned from the Red Cross that Paul was in good health, had never replied to her letters, and had married someone else, Helen married an American veteran. Anthony married also and stayed in contact with Helen. They had one last meeting after the war was over, and then Helen drowned in a boating accident, much to Anthony's regret.

The gendered national stereotypes in this story were a persistent theme in study abroad between France and the United States from the 1920s through the 1960s. However, the characters' difficulties with contrasting French and American heterosocial and sexual practices were more typical of the 1960s than the 1930s, because young people on both sides of the Atlantic engaged in more unsupervised peer sociability and they were more open about describing social and sexual matters. Students' accounts and studies published following World War II reveal in considerable detail how young people grappled with and came to understand sociability and sexuality in the other country. I wish to suggest that sexual imaginings of each country about the other in popular culture were influential in motivating and constructing the experiences of French and American students and that both the pre-travel fantasies and narratives of experience became more elaborate and explicit in the post–World War II decades.

It is not surprising that sexuality figures prominently in various types of documentation regarding study abroad; students are of an age to be highly sexually aware and even sexually active and the experience of living abroad elicits commentary about differing norms of behavior and social and sexual practices that are usually assumed about one's own country. Unlike travelers and tourists from one country who had less contact with communities and institutions of higher education in the other country, students were more likely to engage in social and sexual relations during their long periods of stay in one location. Negotiating sexual stereotypes of the opposite country and the different national norms of social and sexual behavior constituted an important process of misunderstanding and discovery for students abroad. This chapter addresses how students interpreted dating, sociability, and sexuality from the 1920s and into the 1970s through the lenses of particular preconceptions or stereotypes, primarily, American views of France as a site of immorality and of French men as sexually dangerous and French views of American women as sexually promiscuous. It also notes how American responses to mixed-race relations in France evolved over this period.

Recent histories have analyzed particular discourses of sexuality as part of the construction of national or regional identities, but cross-cultural comparisons among Western countries are few, as are studies of the interaction between such discourses and lived experience.[3] Even though historians, including Harvey Levenstein and William Keylor, have noted the pervasive stereotype of French sexual immorality in the United States since the nineteenth century, and its attraction for American tourists, they address how these stereotypes played out in cross-cultural social or sexual encounters in very limited ways. For example, Levenstein asserts that in the late nineteenth and early twentieth centuries American tourists found confirmation of French sexual decadence by going to Montmartre clubs and cafés to watch prostitutes. And Keylor notes that American servicemen returning from France at the end of World War I recounted stories of their encounters with prostitutes, contributing new expressions to the American lexicon, such as "French kiss, French way, and French tickler."[4] Addressing the other side of the Atlantic, studies of French ideas about the United States usually end with World War II, or they address responses to Americanization, that is, efforts by U.S. enterprises and the U.S. government to impose American tastes, values, and practices on French consumers and citizens and say little about sexuality.[5] But study abroad represents a different mode of cultural exchange, person-to-person encounters that confront stereotypes or imaginings and usually result in better understanding of one's own culture and of another culture. It shows how sexuality participates in international relations, not just as discourse but in precipitating and framing transnational interactions.

Histories of sexuality in the United States and in France chart roughly parallel developments toward more open and more varied sexual expressions among young people over the course of the twentieth century. But in each country the social frameworks for these practices were distinctive. For example, dating couples were the norm in American high schools and universities, whereas group sociability was more common in France.[6] And restrictions on middle-class young women were more stringent in France than in the United States. In her history of flirtation in

France, Fabienne Casta-Rosaz suggests that flirting was an Anglo-Saxon, but primarily American, import, and that it was a means for a limited number of privileged French women to explore erotic and sexual possibilities over several generations.[7] Despite numerous indications that educated American youth, and notably young American women, were engaging in socially acceptable sexual caressing earlier than were their French counterparts, Americans tended to imagine French people as sexually immoral. This was due in large measure to realist French literature's portrayal of prostitutes and courtesans, popular American fiction's reinforcement of this image, and World War I veterans' tales of sexually available French women.[8]

When Raymond W. Kirkbride, an American veteran of World War I who had served in France and who was a young professor of modern languages at the University of Delaware in the 1920s, first conceived of the project of the junior year in France, he set out immediately to disabuse potential students and their parents of the notion of France as a site of moral decadence. In a 1923 letter to Walter Hullihen, president of the University of Delaware and a supporter of Kirkbride's scheme, Kirkbride recommended wide publicity for the following clarification about France's reputation for immorality among Americans: "The popular expression 'Gay Paree' so often heard in the United States is an utter and absolute misconception. . . . True, there are 'dens of iniquity' in Paris, catering expressly to the American tourist, . . . The average Frenchman doesn't even know where these 'awful places' are. He leaves that to the self-righteous American scandal-monger."[9] Some students admitted to harboring such notions. For example, Beatrice F. Davis remembered in 1970 that before she went to France in 1931 she viewed the French "as a very profligate and free and easy kind of people with few morals."[10]

Despite the wide currency among Americans of French immorality, students were nonetheless shocked by public displays of affection in France. W. Emerson Wilson reflected upon this discovery when he studied in France in 1929: "at home we never saw a girl and a boy kissing on a street."[11] And a year later Phebe Adams made a similar observation in a letter describing a drive through the Bois de Boulogne in Paris: "we saw . . . people embracing publicly in the middle of the path. The French people are very excitable."[12] One student, J. Edward Davidson, offered an explanation for this difference in acceptable public behavior. In 1937 he wrote, "Although we often take walks here in imitation of our French 'confrères,' we don't go completely native by adopting their habit of making love in public. . . . The French conception that any trait which is natural, should not be inhibited by any prudishness and their explanation undoubtedly accounts for what an American would consider promiscuity." Davidson concluded, "We believe we understand [the philosophy of romance] of the French, but we don't exactly share it."[13] Similarly, an anonymous woman student wrote in 1928 regarding public displays of affection, "What I found almost indecent and vulgar in the manners and conversation of the French, now seems to me a natural and charming honesty. I can no longer be scandalized by small signs of affection that one sees exchanged from time to time in the corners of the Luxembourg or in the middle of the street."[14]

During the interwar years, these and other American students came to accept public expressions of affection between men and women and no longer considered such behavior promiscuous or immoral. After all, American students indulged in similar behavior, but in private rather than in public.[15] As J. Edward Davidson indicated about American men students: "We still think that our own shady-arbored campuses are more 'sympathique' for kissing one's best girl than a public park which is the haunt of all types of French from infants to decrepit old men, or a busy boulevard, or a crowded café."[16] Class distinctions of which students were perhaps not aware were probably at play here; that is, the French bourgeoisie, like the American middle class, could afford to maintain a public façade of propriety because it had access to private and comfortable locations for indulging in sexual behavior. By contrast, persons of lesser means had fewer choices regarding where they might kiss and embrace. In any case, some students tried to understand different public behaviors as a result of different cultural norms.

Another surprise to American students in France was the public toleration of mixed-race couples. This portion of a letter from an anonymous student on the University of Delaware Foreign Study Plan, probably in 1929, is typical: "The Negros [sic] here seem to think that they are just the same as the whites. I see a couple—one white and the other colored, rather often. The first day I walked down the street here a colored man was flirting with a white girl."[17] And in 1926 Dorothy Tebbetts and her chaperone, a visiting parent from the United States, took some offense at an interaction between a black man and a white woman in a performance at the Folies Bergères: "I enjoyed every minute—except one scene between a colored man and a French woman. Mrs. Foley—from Tennessee—was disgusted at the equality basis."[18] For Tebbets and Mrs. Foley the "equality" between races was more problematic than the nudity of the performers, but such incidents inspired no further reflection by American students at this time about race relations in either France or the United States, a situation that would change following World War II.

According to some Americans, French men in particular were dangerous to American women. John Lee Clarke, father of a Smith student who fell in love with a young man in her host family in France, berated President William Allan Neilson of Smith College for putting his daughter in such a vulnerable position. In a 1928 letter he asserted of "Latin" men: "They are the most wonderful pleaders in the world; they can make any girl or woman believe almost anything they want to tell her; and yet they have a vastly different moral code from ours, even the best of them. While they are courting a woman nothing is too good for her; yet in a year after marriage they will be living with another woman, and nobody except the poor American wife thinks it anything out of the way. This is common knowledge."[19] The pervasiveness of this stereotype is evident in a statement of 1928 by an anonymous woman student who challenged it: "I am happy to report that there are faithful husbands in France, and that all married women are not slaves."[20] Delia Brown, a Smith College student in France in 1925–26, also acknowledged how contact with French people belied the image of the dangerous French male. She claimed she had been told that French men were "*méchants*" (badly behaved), but instead she found "that a young French man knows better than a young American how to respect a well-brought up girl, that he has more taste, that he never takes her to places where she should not go."[21]

Although Americans feared the seductive powers and infidelity of French men, French people believed young American women were immoral. As Hélène Cattanès noted in 1965 regarding the first Smith College Junior Year in France program in 1925, "American women, it was clear, were no better in the eyes of Parisians than were the French in the eyes of Americans."[22] In 1935 Charles Petit-Dutaillis of the National Office of French Universities and Schools within the Ministry of Foreign Affairs acknowledged that French bourgeois families were reluctant to allow their daughters to study in the United States because they "fear the freedom of movement of young American women."[23] As we saw in Chapter 4, confronting French stereotypes about young, sexually liberated American women helped some American students appreciate the limits of stereotypes in general. Sarah (Sally) Johnston revealed a painful awareness of the negative images of Americans in France, especially women, in

1938: "American girls have very bad reputations! Lots of them live in the 'divey' places down in the Ve *arrondissement* [district] and believe in free love and stuff and it's weird." Her response was to show by her own example that "Americans *can* have fun and behave themselves, too!"[24]

In the interwar years the imaginings of the French about American sexuality and Americans about French sexuality affected study abroad between the two countries in a variety of ways. It may have drawn young American men in particular to France with the promise of erotic or sexual adventure and given parents pause about exposing their daughters to the charms of French men. Certainly French parents were apprehensive about the bad influence American women students might have on young French women. Young Americans who succumbed to this enticement or overcame this barrier sometimes learned that social practices and their cultural underpinnings were more complex than they originally thought. The experience of living in France made some students aware of both the power and limitations of national stereotypes and even led them to try to alter those stereotypes, whether by presenting a different view of France to Americans or by setting an alternative example of American identity to the French. American students were relatively restrained in the 1920s and 1930s about what they conveyed to parents and program organizers regarding their heterosocial or sexual encounters, but this changed after World War II. Although each country's sexual and gendered imaginings of the other country persisted, changing sexual mores in both countries allowed for greater openness regarding these matters.

An image of personal and sexual freedom—what writer Henriette Nizan called the "air of Paris"—motivated thousands of young Americans to study in France following World War II.[25] Author James Baldwin noted that what drew Americans to France in the early 1950s was a "legend" of Paris: "For Paris is, according to its legend, the city where everyone loses his head, and his morals, lives through at least one *histoire d'amour*, ceases, quite, to arrive anywhere on time, and thumbs his nose at the Puritans—the city, in brief, where all become drunken on the fine, old air of freedom."[26] The strong appeal of personal and sexual freedom that France represented to young Americans at this time might be due to the particular social and cultural conditions of the immediate postwar years in the United States. Historian Beth Bailey notes that in various ways traditional gender relations were reinforced as a response to an increase in women working and entering higher education and to insecurity generated by the Cold War. That is, young American men and women in the 1950s generally conformed to an ideal of masculine authority and responsibility and its obverse of feminine passivity and submission.[27] Yet they also experienced a mass consumer culture that encouraged pleasure and the satisfaction of personal desires, including sexual desires as evidenced in the glamorized and erotic representations of women, especially in mass media.[28] One way to escape these confinements and contradictions was to study abroad and follow the appeal of the "legend" of Paris.

This is precisely what journalist Stanley Karnow did in 1947, when he took advantage of the GI Bill to study in France. He wrote recently of what Paris represented for him at that time: It "promised something for everyone—beauty, sophistication, culture, cuisine, sex, escape and that indefinable called ambience." Additionally, he wrote: "I was further gulled by the real or exaggerated recollections of GIs and their doughboy fathers of compliant French women—the eternal Mademoiselle from Armentières."[29] His fantasies were confirmed at the sight of prostitutes openly plying their trade in the streets with no shame or furtiveness: "This was the permissive Paris of my imagination and, stereotyped though it may have been, I treasured it."[30] Although Karnow acknowledged that "the permissive Paris of [his] imagination" was indeed a stereotype, his later job as a correspondent for *Time* magazine led him to inquire further into French attitudes and practices regarding sexuality. He noted that the French bourgeoisie upheld the appearance of social propriety, but the French were also generally more open about sexuality than were Americans. He cited a young French woman who had studied in the United States as saying: "In the United States . . . girls are obsessed with sex. My sorority sisters talked about nothing else. Here in France we don't talk—we do." As Karnow explained in his controversial report on French youth in 1955, "By prudish American norms, French youths were immoral. By French norms, they were realistic."[31]

It is difficult to determine exactly how widespread such sexual liberation was among French students, the vast majority of whom were middle class, in the 1950s and 1960s. Numerous articles in the popular French press reassured readers that young people were by no means as rebellious, criminal, and sexually promiscuous as represented in the 1958 film *Les Tricheurs* [The Cheaters] by Marcel Carné.[32] A 1960 article on middle-class dating practices asserts that social groupings were bounded by class and neighborhood; that is, residents of the upscale Parisian neighborhood of Passy associated with one another, and similar patterns occurred in other parts of Paris and of France. Although young women had greater freedom of movement and independence than those of earlier eras, they were not as lax as the reputedly sexually liberated Swedes. According to the article, many social encounters between young men and women started in student-related places and activities, such as university restaurants or dances. Dates might then be arranged to go to a movie, a night club, or for a walk, either with a group or as a couple. A good-night kiss at the end of an evening was labeled an "American" practice, fraught with ambiguity as to whether it signified an important milestone in the relationship or a perfunctory gesture. The article concluded: "Girls today offer their hands or their lips with such abandon that boys would be wrong to see in it a move promising a thousand joys [*un geste prometteur de mille bonheurs*]."[33]

Other articles in the late 1950s indicated that among French youth, students in particular were very serious; they were concerned about passing exams and were far more conformist than previous generations. Women especially expressed traditional ideas about marriage, expecting fidelity on the part of their husbands.[34] This emphasis on studying as the only means to combat an insecure future led to new attitudes toward sex, love, and marriage, according to Bertrand Poirot-Delpech. Like other commentators, he noted the disappearance of the nineteenth-century practice of male students finding sexual gratification from prostitutes or *grisettes* (poor, working-class girls). He found that students of both sexes idealized and desired marriage, but women especially feared that marriage and children would hinder their careers. Under these circumstances, then, students engaged in sex to find comfort and support. Poirot-Delpech wrote that, "In 1960 youth do not choose to have fun in the classic sense; they are constrained by the fatality of modern life. It is marriage that appears as the temptation to be avoided." He quoted a student as saying that he cannot visit prostitutes, so he seeks "women who abandon their virginity with all the risks on their side."[35]

Sexuality is highly individual, and it is difficult to generalize about more or less sexual liberation on the part of large groups, like Americans studying in France or French in the United States. Following World War II in both France and the United States, the family and reproduction within marriage were publicly celebrated and, to some extent, these ideals temporarily or superficially overwhelmed discussion of alternative sexual practices.[36] But challenges to this norm were also evident, as Wini Breines and Susan Weiner (among other scholars) demonstrate in their studies of feminine sexuality as portrayed in American sociology and

French popular media, respectively, following World War II.[37] Historian Richard Ivan Jobs asserts that Brigitte Bardot and her films and Françoise Sagan and her novels scandalized the French public in the early 1950s because they represented young women exercising sexual autonomy, suggesting that popular opinion considered such behavior inappropriate.[38] In addition, publication of the Kinsey Reports on male and female sexual behavior in 1948 and 1953 respectively generated public discussion on sexuality in the United States and, to a lesser extent in France, after their immediate translations into French.[39] American students often arrived in France with notions of French sexual immorality that were both affirmed and contradicted by personal experience. Additionally, French students in the United States occasionally confronted such stereotypes among the Americans with whom they lived and studied. On both sides of the transatlantic exchange, students encountered heterosocial practices that were strange to them and that became part of their study abroad experience.

Public acknowledgement of sexual misunderstandings was more widespread and explicit than before the war. A common example was the behavior of American young women. Both Americans and French noted that young American women failed to understand the cultural differences surrounding kissing in France and the United States. Whereas in the United States, kissing was a normal part of dating and not expected to lead necessarily to additional sexual acts, French men regarded it as a come-on, a clear indication that a young woman was available for more. According to a report on study abroad published in 1959, American women students frequently got into misunderstandings or trouble over this: "Some American girls, conditioned by kissing games at adolescent parties, consider osculation a casual and mildly enjoyable game or part of the ritual of thanking a boy for taking them to the movies. When they submit to the embraces of a European who has never played Post Office or Spin-the-Bottle, they are sometimes rudely shocked by what follows."[40]

From the other side of the Atlantic, such American practices implied rampant sexuality among students. During her visit to the United States in 1947, Simone de Beauvoir asked a French professor at a women's college if, as she had heard, Americans were so sexually active that "there are certain parts of the campus where you find piles of condoms?" Her respondent demurred and then told of the confusion American women students experienced when she took them to study in France: "They would return in tears from their outings with young Frenchmen: after generously accepting and even initiating kissing, necking, and petting—which, in America, didn't lead anywhere—they'd been totally astonished when their dates ignored the rules of the game and made open attempts on their virtue. Such loutish behavior made them sob."[41] By contrast, according to Karnow, French women regarded a kiss as a prelude to sex; he quoted an American GI on relations with French women: "No nonsense. If you kiss a girl on the lips, you sleep with her."[42] According to a survey conducted in 1954–55, French students thought that relations between a man and a woman should be either strictly platonic or frankly sexual. This study quoted a French student's bewilderment at American students' attitudes and practices: "A young American woman told me that in America, when a girl has gone out four or five times with the same boy, she considers herself dishonored if he doesn't kiss her. We find that totally shocking."[43]

Sociologist Eric Fassin offers some insights into the apparent contradictions of American dating practices and why they could be misinterpreted. He notes first the difference between a Protestant belief in the pleasure of sex that must be deferred until marriage and the Catholic tradition of considering sex a necessary evil within marriage—and certainly something to be avoided outside of marriage. In addition, although American Puritanism entailed a practice of sexual self-control, especially among women, he indicates that American modernity celebrated pleasure, including erotic and sexual pleasure.[44] Thus, dating throughout much of the twentieth century in the United States was a means for young people to enjoy sexual behavior while (usually) refraining from intercourse. By contrast, as the French articles of the 1950s and early 1960s suggest, heterosociability among French youth either avoided sex entirely or involved intercourse as a primary objective.

Although French people had a reputation in the United States for sexual libertinism, practices such as kissing and dating in general genuinely shocked some French students who came to the United States. When Micaela Blay-Thorup first arrived at the University of Arizona in 1953 as a Fulbright student, she noted with surprise the scene outside of the house where she was to live with other women students at the time of the 10:00 P.M. curfew: "all the girls were kissing the boys outside. I had never seen that, never done that."[45] According to Blay-Thorup, American-style dating "was hardly acceptable in France," because in France "you went out with a group of friends." She said of her experience at the University of Arizona: "I remember that the girls had told me on a Saturday night that, if you don't have a date, you'd better hide in a closet, because 'shame on you.'"[46] Similarly, in 1961–62 another Fulbright student, Marie-José Taube, found strange the feeling among American students that they must have a date every week. In France, she explained, sometimes young women had "boyfriends" [in English], and the couple went out together or with other friends, but "it was not systematic, and one was not obliged to have a boyfriend; that is, among groups that got together on a Saturday night some girls were alone and some boys were alone."[47] She continued in a recent interview: "What was very funny and also symbolic of the importance of going out on Saturday night was to see all the girls and young women in the streets with curlers in their hair on Saturday morning—outside! In the street with curlers! This was shocking to us."[48] Identifying the consumerist and competitive aspects of college dating in the United States, Gérard François, who studied at Ball State University from 1973–75, explained that Americans had greater material means for dating than did most French students because they worked part-time and had cars. By contrast, "in France you don't have time to date in high school because, number one, until I left high school, all the high schools were segregated, boys and girls. So you never see a girl in school, and you are so submerged with homework and tight discipline, you really don't have time to do that. And then you go to college, and then you have a lot more time, but don't have any money, and you don't have any car."[49]

Students variously did or did not adapt to the different heterosocial practices of each country. French Fulbright students tended to be older than American undergraduates and generally concentrated on their studies, finding American dating practices interesting but not necessarily feeling a need to conform to them. A Fulbright engineering student who studied in the United States encouraged future grantees to spend as much time as possible with Americans but "never to look for a flirtation with an American girl (it's extremely fruitless [*c'est d'une stérilité à en pleurer*])."[50] Gérard François said that he associated more with Latin American students than with Americans at Ball State University because they practiced a group sociability similar to what he was familiar with in France, though he eventually met and married an American student.[51] Author Philippe Labro, a younger Fulbright student, described in his autobiographical novel the challenge of negotiating the complex rituals of dating at an elite, Southern men's college in 1954. He quickly learned that men must pay all dating expenses, and women, while acceding to kisses and caresses in the back seat of a car, were also expected to resist sexual intercourse. In Labro's book, *L'Etudiant étranger* (*The Foreign Student*) American student Preston Cate explains premarital intercourse between white college men and women this way: "Rule number 1, he said. Good girls don't 'do it.' And yet, rule number 2: only with a good girl is it important and interesting to 'do it.' A real college boy does not 'do it' with dogs or with sows."[52] The narrator managed to gain the respect and friendship of his fellow American men students by adhering to these rules, although he radically violated them by having a secret love affair with a young black woman off campus.

Although many American women students suffered from misunderstanding surrounding the role of kissing in heterosociality, others adjusted more easily to the less formal social practices of French students. Elizabeth Simmons regaled her mother with accounts of her active social life in Paris in 1949–50, including dates with American men and, increasingly, as the academic year progressed, with Frenchmen. By June 1950 she had "met the most darling French boy," and she wrote: "We've been biking, dancing, walking all over Paris seeing things I would never have gotten to see without him, which makes the perfect ending to a perfect year."[53] Miriam Halbert also socialized extensively with French persons during her stay in Paris in 1947–48 and had a romance with a young French man whom she came close to marrying.[54] During her junior year in France in 1956–57, Anne Rittershofer became seriously attached to a young Frenchman. She wrote to her parents about an early date with him, noting what she considered a more grown-up attitude in their relationship than she experienced in the United States: "He treats me like a queen & yet respects me for the intellectual & spiritual. I am *not* a silly 'girlfriend'! Je suis une *femme* [I am a *woman*]."[55] Nonetheless, awkward situations did occur. Writing home to her mother during her junior year in Pau and Bordeaux in 1966–67, Barbara Boonstopple poignantly explained her anxiety over communication and etiquette while having coffee in a café with another American woman and two French men. When the check arrived, she argued with herself: "shall I pay, yes (I'm reaching for my purse); no, better not, he'll think I'm one of those Americans flaunting my money; but yes, I'd better, French girls always pay their own way." She captured the agony of negotiating cultural differences with burgeoning language skills, writing, "And so the mental battle goes on as you sit there with one hand in your purse and the other foot in your mouth."[56]

In her final report to the Fulbright Commission in 1962, Karen Stedtfeld tried to prepare future American Fulbrighters for different heterosocial and heterosexual practices in France:

> Dating habits are not as developed as in the U.S., and the social patterns observed here are the following: you're either with a group mixed, paying your own way, or damn near engaged. In many respects, the level of mixed-sex relationships here is on the par with ours in junior high school. And if you *are* a gal, and are invited somewhere by one guy alone, watch out, because the "je t'aime's" can flow pretty fast and don't mean much. If you are a guy, investigate the philosophy of dating practices with the local French boys before you invite that cute jeune fille to go to the cinema. You just might pull a terrible boo-boo and not even realize it.[57]

The experiences of students of one country socializing with members of the opposite sex in the other country often hinged upon the persistent stereotypes of promiscuous American women and seductive French men. No doubt the accepted norm of kissing as part of dating in the United States contributed to a French image of young American women as promiscuous. Additionally, middle-class American women were used to greater freedom of movement, alone and in public places, than were many of their French counterparts. Young American women who studied in France after World War II no longer adhered to the strict regulations that governed their prewar antecedents. A Smith College graduate from the first Junior Year in France group of 1925–26 bemoaned this as detrimental to the mastery of the language, to understanding the French, and to establishing good relations between French and Americans: "the idea of being a *jeune fille bien élévée*, of being a member of the family with whom one lived and participating in French life with one's family and the families of friends seems to have been lost."[58] Although the students of the 1940s and 1950s did not regret restrictions they had never known, they sometimes complained about the difficulty of meeting French persons and of greater vulnerability to unwanted advances from men in public places. Smith College student Martha Churchill's first letter to her parents from Paris in 1948 mentioned an encounter with two strangers seated near her and her friend in a café. The men readily identified the two women as Americans and invited them to a dance; the women refused.[59]

Freedom of movement and the obvious appearance of Americanness invited encounters that American women did not entirely welcome. But these conditions also allowed for more desirable relations between American women and French men. Mary Coan, a Smith College junior in France in 1949–50, indicated the following: "In France Smith students could date three or four boys in one day, which was a great liberation from Smith."[60] Coan's classmate Mary Ann Hoberman echoed these sentiments, noting, "I had many French boyfriends; that was part of the fun."[61] Also in 1949–50 Elizabeth Simmons was unabashed in writing to her mother about traveling with two Smith classmates and a French professor: "Originally Martha and Olivier were going alone but now Jackie Bouvier and I are going along with them—as chaperons."[62]

For many American women, study abroad in France—away from family, friends, and American colleges and universities—represented independence and liberation. In 1956 Smith College student Anne Rittershofer wrote to her family from Paris: "Never before have I realized such complete independence, such freedom. It is a *normal* life here—no dormitories, no Bermuda shorts, no grey-suited professors, no rising bells, no house meetings & *no* college weekends. Hurrah!"[63] Nonetheless, Anne Atheling, a Smith College junior in France in 1949–50, thought that her classmates still observed American bourgeois proprieties of that time. She said in a recent interview, "out of my group, I can hardly imagine anybody that had a love affair, but maybe they did. But I just can't imagine it. Because it was a different era."[64] With hindsight Lucy Carr explained how the freedom of movement in public that American women expected and exercised could be interpreted differently in France. In 1960–61 Carr reveled in the independence she felt as a student in Paris, in contrast to Mount Holyoke, where "you are still signing in and out for your dates and when you went for the weekends ... it was a very controlled atmosphere and you had to be in at a certain time." But that same independence also exposed her to unusual social encounters. Discussing how she was approached on the streets by African men in Paris, Carr explained how she thought it was her availability as a white woman, which was not common for French women of her social class, that precipitated these interactions: "they're preying on me because nobody else is available and that lack of availability had something to do with color."[65]

Barbara Boonstopple was dismayed at the representation in a popular French magazine in 1966 of American women as solely interested in sex. Translating the title of the article as "American girls—they call it SEX not love," she explained to her mother that it "proceeds in outlandish fashion to prove that all American girls believe that boys don't even want to marry virgins, that the U.S. is the home of the Pill and LSD is for everybody and *every* college campus has its 'sex club' and so on." Boonstopple was clearly outraged at this stereotype and wrote that she hoped the French didn't believe the article because she feared it would hinder her efforts to befriend young French women; it implied that young American women came to France only to seduce young French men. "And as for the boys," she wrote, "I sure hope they haven't read it as they like to chase Americans enough as it is, thinking we have lower standards. That one article may have set back International Relations ten years."[66]

Boonstopple and others noticed that young French women were more closely supervised than their counterparts in the United States throughout the 1950s and into the 1960s. Laura Sherman remembered that during her junior year in France in 1949–50, in her host family "the young women didn't date without a chaperon."[67] Although much about the new university in Pau reminded Boonstopple of the University of California at Davis ("a college campus under construction in a quiet town"), she wrote in 1966 that the dorm "rules are a bit more strict, like 3 hours earlier on lock-out every night."[68] Similarly, Carolyn Washer and Marilyn Ganetsky, Fulbright students in Bordeaux in 1960–61, claimed that traditional notions of appropriate heterosocial behavior hindered their social interactions with French men: "it is not considered good form, in Bordeaux at least, to approach a man on the street or in a café and announce, 'I am here to further Franco-American relations.'" Referring to Simone de Beauvoir as no doubt approving of such a break with conventional restraints on women, the two nonetheless decided that, "given present-day French society, we found that the best approach is to wait passively; i.e., let the man come to you!"[69]

The opposite of this French stereotype of promiscuous American women was a persistent American view of French men as seducers. In the 1962 film *Take Her, She's Mine,* James Stewart plays the father of Sandra Dee, and he suffers through the vagaries of her college career as she dabbles in folk music and popular protest and then decides to study in France. The father has a nightmare of his daughter seduced by a bereted Frenchman in a café, and the plot of this family comedy involves his traveling to Paris to meet (or rescue his daughter from) her French boyfriend, who has honorable intentions of marrying her. The American stereotype of adulterous French men is evident in a 1963 account by Molly Debon, written after she returned to the United States from a junior year abroad with a French boyfriend. Shortly thereafter the two were engaged, and during wedding preparations at Debon's parents' home, the following exchange took place between her mother's friends and her mother: The "solicitous matrons" deemed the future son-in-law "charming" but asked, "'My dear, does your daughter understand what will happen eventually? The French are delightful, they really are, but does she realize what is bound to happen?' My mother, innocent and concerned, would reply in the negative. 'Why, my dear, it's common knowledge! In ten years' time he'll have a mistress, and then where will your dear girl be?'"[70] This exchange reiterated almost exactly the sentiments of John Lee Clarke about "Latin men" in 1928 (see above).

French men who came to the United States to study confronted the stereotype of the seductive French man and occasionally benefited from it. Paul Benhamou, a French Fulbright student in the United States in 1961–62, was amused by the American stereotype of French men as avid lovers. At the University of Iowa, he said, "I was invited more in sororities [than fraternities] because I was a male French person; they were interested in seeing one in real life—touch me—see if all the misconceptions are true or not." This "misconception" that he found "was rampant in the classrooms" was as follows: "A French man spends his time making love to a woman, and changes many times. The French lover stereotype that's been spread around by Hollywood and in literature, not by the French."[71] In 1954 Philippe Labro immediately realized that his American peers assumed that he had "considerable experience of women and of sex," and he noted that when American students did something sexually suggestive, they said, "'let's get French.'" Labro took advantage of this situation by going out on several blind dates on the strength of being French, but he wrote, "My act of warrior and seducer *frenchie* did not last long," and he was revealed to be like others of his age: "inexperienced, bumbling, hesitant, sometimes forward, often reserved, and especially, like everyone else, respecting the rules of proper behavior in a policed, puritan, and watched-over society."[72]

Gérard François suggested that, contrary to American stereotypes of the hypersexual French, he and his peers were either too busy studying or too poor to engage in sex the way that young Americans did in the mid-1970s. In a recent interview he said, "I think we were less sexually open in France at the time. I'm sure this has changed today, but back then . . . I found Americans to be a lot more active than we were. So much for the romantic French."[73] American imaginings of the sexually experienced and interesting French were not limited to men. In French author

Christine de Rivoyre's novel of 1961, *The Wreathed Head,* the main character, Charlotte, is a young French woman studying at the University of Syracuse. She comments on being the object of fascination on an American campus: "a French girl . . . is very much sought after—she is asked out a great deal. (It is part of the Oo-la-la complex, which will last until the end of the world, or at least until the end of the Atlantic.)"[74] In short, the evidence suggests that the other (French or American) is always more sexually dangerous than the self. Or, as Karen Stedtfeld succinctly put it in 1961: "The French have the same opinion of Americans that we have of the French—that they are very free."[75]

Sexual imaginings associated with national identity and gender profoundly affected study abroad experiences for women and men throughout the twentieth century. They were often part of the process of discovering the limitations of stereotypes and sometimes led to a clearer understanding and appreciation of cultural differences. Different heterosocial practices were also exotic and could contribute to potential romance, as was the case with Lucy Carr in 1961. She recently described her encounter with a French man of similar social background in one of her courses on French theater. He found her behavior unorthodox by French standards but attractive for that reason. Carr recalled, "he took me to the Champs-Elysées, to a bar there, and I didn't think twice about going into a bar on the Champs-Elysées in jeans, and he thought it was totally out of this world, that it was fabulous that I would ever do such a thing." In addition, it was precisely her experiences of freedom, of "breaking the rules," and of successfully extricating herself from uncomfortable situations that inspired Carr to continue traveling, to volunteer at a work camp in Kenya, and, eventually, to earn a degree in African studies and live in Ethiopia for five years. "Absolutely, I think it was Paris," she said about the cause of her subsequent actions; "how could I have dreamed of doing such a thing back in Mount Holyoke?"[76]

Few students followed Carr's trajectory from study abroad in Paris to African Studies, but for some Americans the experience of studying in France and witnessing or engaging in mixed-race relations precipitated consideration of larger social and political issues. As before World War II, American students noticed mixed-race couples in France immediately following the war; however, the civil rights movement in the United States and the Algerian War involving France led some to reflect upon issues of race at home and abroad. In 1948 Miriam Halbert noted about French attitudes toward blacks: "I am happy about the friendly feeling that exists toward the Negro, much more tolerant than ours in the States."⁷⁷ Richard Robbins discovered the limits of French racial tolerance as a Fulbright Fellow to France in 1949: "Two cheers for that happy French indifference, far better than either prejudice or patronization, displayed towards strolling interracial couples. But in more mundane matters of jobs and housing, the writer James Baldwin, a close friend, and other blacks in France both American and from the colonies, spoke of serious problems."⁷⁸

Letters home from Karen Stedtfeld, a Fulbright student at the University of Nancy in 1961–62, reveal a developing awareness of the complexity of race relations in both France and the United States. After barely two weeks in Paris, she remarked upon the acceptability of mixed-race couples in France, just as other Americans had before: "the thing that you see *so* much around here are black boys with *good looking* white girls; not just any old slob of a white girl, but real cool chicks."⁷⁹ One month later, after settling into student life in Nancy, Stedtfeld began to realize the effects of the Algerian War on social relations in France and compared them with race relations in the United States: "We have an Algerian quarter here in Nancy which is strictly taboo—just like in the USA, good white girls don't go out with black boys, here in France a good French girl doesn't go out with Algerians—if she does, the social consequences are exactly the same. You see the Algerian problem is in essence a civil war."⁸⁰

Although French students of the 1960s were acutely aware of segregation in the United States, I have less evidence of their interaction with blacks while studying in the United States. In Rivoyre's fictional account of a French exchange student at Syracuse University in the early 1960s, one of the characters, a white student, locates Charlotte, the French student, in the "Negro quarter" because, according to another American, "The French love Negroes." Charlotte defends her association with blacks on campus because when she first arrived her only American friend was a black student named Kay: "I would have perished in Syracuse, America, but for her," Charlotte asserts to some white students.⁸¹ In his novel reflecting at least something of his actual experience as a Fulbright student in the United States in 1954, Philippe Labro clearly understands how transgressive was his sexual relationship with a young black woman in the American South of that time.

Although inter-race relations were rare in accounts of study abroad, homosexual relations were even more so. Miriam Halbert, who in 1947 studied in Paris on a scholarship from the Institute of International Education after she graduated from Miami University of Ohio, found a broader understanding of sexuality there, though she had difficulty communicating that to her mother back home in Indiana. Responding to her mother's concern about the fact that Halbert socialized frequently with men and with several different men, Halbert reassured her somewhat enigmatically:

> I laughed when I learned that you think I spend an awful lot of time with boys. It's just that the more interesting things I do are with boys. They must be more adventurous. I assure you I haven't abandoned my own sex! It is after all natural, normal and human, and I'm glad I find it so because God knows there exist a lot of abnormalities here. One finds them in artistic centers, among those with sensitive, talented minds, even at the Fondation des Etats-Unis, but it's life, and to understand life one has to observe it and know it. It is a part of my education. You may be glad that I am learning from observation rather than experience.[82]

Much became clearer about "abnormalities" when I interviewed Miriam Halbert Bales a few years ago. At that time she indicated that she learned only later that two friends with whom she spent the Christmas holiday, Yves Bompeix and Gray Phillips, were lovers, and that she had been propositioned by a Portuguese woman in the Cité Universitaire.[83] According to historian Antony Copley, although French laws criminalized pederasty from Vichy through the Fifth Republic and homosexuality was often publicly condemned, its practice was generally more tolerated than in the United States, particularly in literary and artistic circles.[84] And although opportunities existed in the United States for both discursive and actual expressions of homosexuality, Cold War fears of subversion and decadence also pathologized, punished, and condemned it.[85] Still, Halbert framed her introduction to homosexuality as part of her learning experience during study abroad.

As Michael Seidman, Arthur Marwick, Beth L. Bailey, and Didier Fischer have shown, various concerns regarding sexuality troubled students in both France and in the United States long before the demonstrations of 1968, and they were also an important subtext, if not the cause, of that political and social turbulence.[86] Study abroad reveals varied manifestations of student sexuality before the many breakthroughs of the late 1960s. Scholars including Levenstein and Casta-Rosaz see less difference in sexual behaviors between France and the United States after the 1960s as youth culture increasingly globalized, transportation and communication became easier and faster, and the Pill was available in both countries. Nonetheless, the sexual allure of France affected Alice Kaplan, a scholar in French Studies. In her 1993 memoir she wrote about studying in France in the early 1970s: "everyone knew that liberty really meant liberty to have sex, and life in France without sex was inconceivable to me."[87]

In American imaginings, France was associated with sexual license throughout the twentieth century and, most notably, after World War I. An important part of the study abroad experience for American students in the 1920s and 1930s was discovering the limits of this stereotype, as well as the cultural underpinnings of alternative social norms and behaviors. After World War II, this image was amplified, so that France (and especially Paris) was also imagined as a site of personal freedom, a liberating alternative to the particular social and political conditions of middle America in the late 1940s and early 1950s. Certainly being far from home had a liberating effect on many young persons, but the American (and French) imaginings of the other also influenced experiences of students abroad by providing a fantasy or expectation against which to measure observations on the ground. Specifically, American students confronted different meanings associated with practices that they assumed were universal, such as kissing during or at the end of a date or young women's freedom of movement in public places. Although many students found these experiences uncomfortable or incomprehensible, most realized at the very least that cultural differences existed in even similar Western, modern societies such as France and the United States. French students, too, found American dating practices strange, and in all cases students from both countries had to decide to what extent they would adapt to the other country's practices. Students also often dealt with gendered expectations that American women were promiscuous and French men were seductive, which they did in a variety of ways, including taking advantage of or manipulating these stereotypes or trying to change them through personal example or teachings.

The fantasies and misunderstandings involved in study abroad between France and the United States stemmed from perhaps inherently superficial or incomplete information that circulated in popular culture on both sides of the Atlantic. Even as transatlantic travel and communication accelerated and improved over the course of the twentieth century, information from hearsay or from the media still could not replace or reproduce the kind of understanding often achieved through study abroad. The nuances and even contradictions of complex societies are evident in the accounts of students over the course of the twentieth century. For example, there is an apparent contradiction in the claims of late-nineteenth-century American graduate students that they learned to enjoy life while studying in Europe, in contrast to undergraduates in the 1920s and 1930s who complained about how hard they worked in their courses in France. Similarly, French students in the 1950s and 1960s commented on the frivolity of undergraduate life in the United States but also appreciated a more interactive pedagogy in American universities. All of these observations are true; they reflect differences in the ages of the students and in the two higher educational systems. Students who articulated these cultural differences were penetrating quite deeply into the host society, more so than most tourists and even travel writers, who provided much of the information available to the general public in each country about the other country. Extensive commentary on the United States in the French press, and courses on French language and literature in American schools and colleges, often ignited the interest of young people in the opposite country. But it was the profound personal transformation of adapting to another culture, confronting preconceptions and stereotypes, and reconstructing individual and national identities that enabled young people to achieve a new level of understanding of their own and the other society.

Difference is precisely the appeal—and the challenge—of study abroad. Study abroad between France and the United States has persisted throughout the twentieth century because young people are still captivated by imaginings of the other country and because they value the understanding gained from this particular experience, with its attendant surprises, confusions, and challenges. As this book reveals, objectives of study abroad have changed over time to include (variously and simultaneously) professional enhancement, exchange of knowledge, national interest, cultural broadening, and improved international relations. By and large, study abroad achieved these goals. But student experiences influenced the evolution of institutional objectives and produced alternative meanings for study abroad. They also provide a new interpretation of Franco-American relations in the twentieth century that the more familiar narratives of Americanization and anti-Americanism fail to capture.

This book has also developed an interpretation of internationalism that includes ordinary persons, appreciation for difference, and the capacity to reassess national identities. It suggests that analyzing study abroad between other countries might also offer alternative or enhanced understandings of foreign relations, particularly between the United States and some other countries, that have become increasingly fraught, if not downright antagonistic, since the terrorist attacks of September 11, 2001. I am not proposing that study abroad is a panacea for the many legitimate tensions and perilous conditions in the world today. But this case study offers the possibility that governments need not be the sole arbiters of transnational relations.

Abbreviations Used in Notes

AFAC	Archives of the Franco-American Commission, Paris, France
AJ/16	Académie de Paris
AN	Archives Nationales, Paris, France
JYA	Junior Year Abroad
MAE	Archives of the Ministère des Affaires Étrangères, Paris and Nantes, France
NARA	National Archives and Records Administration, College Park, Maryland
SC	Smith College Archives, Northampton, Massachusetts
UD	University of Delaware Archives, Newark, Delaware

Notes

Introduction

1. Open Doors Online, "Report on International Education Exchange," http://opendoors.iienetwork.org/, accessed April 2, 2009. This site has links to additional contemporary data on Americans studying abroad and international students in the United States.
2. W. Reginald Wheeler, Henry H. King, and Alexander B. Davidson, eds., *The Foreign Student in America* (New York: Association Press, 1925), xv–xvi.
3. Open Doors Online, "Report," http://opendoors.iienetwork.org/, accessed April 2, 2009.
4. Sharon S. Witherell, director, Public Affairs, Institute of International Education, e-mail to the author, August 1, 2005. Witherell refers to the National Association for Foreign Student Affairs (NAFSA) changing its name to Association of International Educators in 1990.
5. Akira Iriye, *Cultural Internationalism and World Order* (Baltimore: Johns Hopkins University Press, 2001); see also Akira Iriye, *Global Community: The Role of International Organizations in the Making of the Contemporary World* (Berkeley: University of California Press, 2002).
6. Leila J. Rupp, *Worlds of Women: The Making of an International Women's Movement* (Princeton, NJ: Princeton University Press, 1997), 108.
7. Brent Hayes Edwards, *The Practice of Diaspora: Literature, Translation, and the Rise of Black Internationalism* (Cambridge, MA: Harvard University Press, 2003).
8. Christopher Endy, "Travel and World Power: Americans in Europe, 1890–1917," *Diplomatic History* 22 (Fall 1998): 565–94; Frank Costigliola, *Awkward Dominion: American Political, Economic, and Cultural Relations with Europe, 1919–1933* (Ithaca, NY: Cornell University Press, 1984); Emily S. Rosenberg, *Spreading the American Dream: American Economic and Cultural Expansion,*

1890–1945 (New York: Hill and Wang, 1982); Frank A. Ninkovich, *The Diplomacy of Ideas: United States Foreign Policy and Cultural Relations, 1938–1950* (New York: Cambridge University Press, 1981).

9. Suzanne Balous, *L'Action culturelle de la France dans le monde* (Paris: Presses universitaires de France, 1970); Alain Dubosclard, *L'Action culturelle de la France aux Etats-Unis, de la première guerre mondiale à la fin des années 1960*, thèse d'histoire, Université Paris 1, November 2002; François Chaubert, *La Politique culturelle française et la diplomatie de la langue: L'Alliance Française (1883–1940)* (Paris: L'Harmattan, 2006). See also Ruth Emily McMurry and Muna Lee, *The Cultural Approach: Another Way in International Relations* (Chapel Hill: University of North Carolina Press, 1947).

10. Jessica C. E. Gienow-Hecht, "Shame on U.S.? Academics, Cultural Transfer, and the Cold War: A Critical Review," *Diplomatic History* 24 (Summer 2000): 491. Many other recent works locate the history of the United States within an international framework, including the following: Victoria de Grazia, *Irresistible Empire: America's Advance Through Twentieth-Century Europe* (Cambridge, MA: Belknap Press of Harvard University Press, 2006); Jeremi Suri, *Power and Protest: Global Revolution and the Rise of Détente* (Cambridge, MA: Harvard University Press, 2003); Elizabeth Cobbs Hoffman, *All You Need Is Love: The Peace Corps and the Spirit of the 1960s* (Cambridge, MA: Harvard University Press, 1998); Kristin Hoganson, "Cosmopolitan Domesticity: Importing the American Dream, 1865–1920," *American Historical Review* 107 (February 2002): 55–83.

11. Benedict Anderson, *Imagined Communities: Reflections on the Origin and Spread of Nationalism*, rev. ed. (London: Verso, 1991).

12. Kwame Anthony Appiah, *The Ethics of Identity* (Princeton, NJ: Princeton University Press, 2005).

13. To mention only a few examples from this extensive body of literature: Richard Kuisel, *Seducing the French: The Dilemma of Americanization* (Berkeley: University of California Press, 1993); Richard Pells, *Not Like Us: How Europeans Have Loved, Hated, and Transformed American Culture Since World War II* (New York: Basic Books, 1997); Gienow-Hecht, "Shame on U.S.?". On the political and economic influence of the United States in France following World War II, see Irwin M. Wall, *The United States and the Making of Postwar France, 1945–1954* (New York: Cambridge University Press, 1991); Frank Costigliola, *France and the United States: The Cold Alliance Since World War II* (New York: Twayne Publishers, 1992); Gérard Bossuat, *La France, l'aide américaine et la construction européenne, 1944–1954*, vol. 1 (Paris: Comité pour l'histoire économique et financière de la France, 1992); Jean-Pierre Rioux, *The Fourth Republic, 1944–1958*, trans. Godfrey Rogers (Cambridge: Cambridge University Press; Paris: Editions de la Maison des Sciences de l'Homme, 1987), ch. 9.

14. Harvey Levenstein, *Seductive Journey: American Tourists in France from Jefferson to the Jazz Age* (Chicago: University of Chicago Press, 1998); Harvey Levenstein, *We'll Always Have Paris: American Tourists in France Since 1930* (Chicago: University of Chicago Press, 2004); Christopher Endy, *Cold War Holidays: American Tourism in France* (Chapel Hill: University of North Carolina Press, 2004).

15. Jacques Portes, *Une Fascination réticente: Les Etats-Unis dans l'opinion française* (Nancy: Presses universitaires de Nancy, 1990); Levenstein, *Seductive Journey*; Bernadette Galloux-Fournier, "Un Regard sur l'Amérique: Voyageurs français aux Etats-Unis (1919–1939)," *Revue d'histoire moderne et contemporaine* 37 (April–June 1990): 308–23. Bertram M. Gordon, "The Decline of a Cultural Icon: France in American Perspective," *French Historical Studies* 22 (Fall 1999): 625–51. See also Raymonde Carroll, *Cultural Misunderstandings: The French-American Experience*, trans. Carol Volk (Chicago: University of Chicago Press, 1987).

16. For a recent study of Franco-American relations and internationalism in the 1950s and early 1960s through film, see Vanessa R. Schwartz, *It's So French: Hollywood, Paris, and the Making of Cosmopolitan Film Culture* (Chicago: University of Chicago Press, 2007).

17. Paul Fussell, "Travel, Tourism, and 'International Understanding,'" in *Thank God for the Atom Bomb and Other Essays* (New York: Summit Books, 1988), 151–76; Eric J. Leed, *The Mind of the Traveler: From Gilgamesh to Global Tourism* (New York: Basic Books, 1991); Shelley Baranowski and Ellen Furlough, eds., *Being Elsewhere: Tourism, Consumer Culture, and Identity in Modern Europe and North America* (Ann Arbor: University of Michigan Press, 2001); Rudy Koshar, "Seeing, Traveling, and Consuming: An Introduction," in *Histories of Leisure*, ed. Rudy Koshar (New York: Berg Publishers, 2002), 1–24.

18. Jürgen Herbst, *The German Historical School in American Scholarship: A Study in the Transfer of Culture* (Ithaca, NY: Cornell University Press, 1965). See also Julie A. Reuben, *The Making of the Modern University: Intellectual Transformation and the Marginalization of Morality* (Chicago: University of Chicago Press, 1996).

19. Carl Diehl, "Innocents Abroad: American Students in German Universities, 1810–1870," *History of Education Quarterly* 16 (1976): 321–41; Thomas Neville Bonner, *To the Ends of the Earth: Women's Search for Education in Medicine* (Cambridge, MA: Harvard University Press, 1992); Gabriel Weisberg, Jane Becker, Catherine Fehrer, and Tamar Garb, *Overcoming All Obstacles: The Women of the Académie Julian* (New York: Dahesh Museum, 1999).

20. Carl Diehl, *Americans and German Scholarship, 1770–1870* (New Haven, CT: Yale University Press, 1978); Peter Novick, *That Noble Dream: The "Objectivity Question" and the American Historical Profession* (New York: Cambridge University Press, 1988); Bonnie G. Smith, *The Gender of History: Men, Women, and Historical Practice* (Cambridge, MA: Harvard University Press, 1998);

Daniel T. Rodgers, *Atlantic Crossings: Social Politics in a Progressive Age* (Cambridge, MA: The Belknap Press of Harvard University Press, 1998).

21. Christophe Charle, *La République des universitaires, 1870–1914* (Paris: Seuil, 1994); George Weisz, *The Emergence of Modern Universities in France, 1863–1914* (Princeton, NJ: Princeton University Press, 1983); Charles E. McClelland, *State, Society, and University in Germany, 1700–1914* (Cambridge: Cambridge University Press, 1980); James C. Albisetti, *Schooling German Girls and Women: Secondary and Higher Education in the Nineteenth Century* (Princeton, NJ: Princeton University Press, 1988), esp. ch. 7; Martha Hanna, "French Women and American Men, 'Foreign' Students at the University of Paris, 1915–1925," *French Historical Studies* 22 (Winter 1999): 87–112. On the academic culture of France, see Fritz K. Ringer, *Fields of Knowledge: French Academic Culture in Comparative Perspective, 1890–1920* (Cambridge: Cambridge University Press and Paris: Editions de la Maison des Sciences de l'Homme, 1992).

22. There are too many of these works to list here, but following are a few examples: David A. Robertson, "The Junior Year Abroad: A Successful Experiment," *Educational Record* 9 (January 1928): 32–45; Roxana Holden, "Ten Years of Undergraduate Study Abroad," *Modern Language Journal* 19 (November 1934): 117–22; John A. Garraty and Walter Adams, *From Main Street to the Left Bank: Students and Scholars Abroad* (East Lansing: Michigan State University Press, 1959); Dennison Nash, "The Personal Consequences of a Year of Study Abroad," *Journal of Higher Education* 2 (March–April 1976): 191–203. See also Arthur Power Dudden and Russell R. Dynes, eds., *The Fulbright Experience, 1946–1986: Encounters and Transformations* (New Brunswick, NJ: Transaction Books, 1987).

23. Joan W. Scott, "The Evidence of Experience," *Critical Inquiry* 17 (Summer 1991): 773–97.

24. Scholars in a variety of disciplines have recently examined women and gender in international relations. See, for example, Cynthia Enloe, *Bananas, Beaches and Bases: Making Feminist Sense of International Politics* (Berkeley: University of California Press, 1989); Mrinalini Sinha, Donna Guy, and Angela Woollacott, eds., *Feminisms and Internationalism* (Oxford: Blackwell, 1999); Rupp, *Worlds of Women*. An extensive literature addresses the association among "modernity," women, and America in Europe, especially in the 1920s and 1930s. Mary Louise Roberts, *Civilization Without Sexes: Reconstructing Gender in Postwar France, 1917–1927* (Chicago: University of Chicago Press, 1994); Lynne Frame, "Gretchen, Girl, Garçonne? Weimar Science and Popular Culture in Search of the Ideal New Woman," in *Women in the Metropolis: Gender and Modernity in Weimar Culture*, ed. Katharina von Ankum (Berkeley: University of California Press, 1997), 12–40; Emily S. Rosenberg, "Consuming Women: Images of Americanization in the 'American Century,'" *Diplomatic History* 23 (Summer 1999): 479–97.

Chapter 1

1. John W. Burgess, *Reminiscences of an American Scholar: The Beginnings of Columbia University* (New York: Columbia University Press, 1934), 84–86.

2. Edward Alsworth Ross, *Seventy Years of It: An Autobiography* (New York: D. Appleton-Century Company, 1936), 25.

3. Horace M. Kennedy, "Studying in Germany," *Popular Science Monthly* 26 (January 1885): 347, 352.

4. Morris B. Crawford, "American Students in Germany," *Century Magazine* 34 (May–October 1887): 475–76.

5. Jürgen Herbst, *The German Historical School in American Scholarship: A Study in the Transfer of Culture* (Ithaca, NY: Cornell University Press, 1965). Carl Diehl asserts that only a later generation of Americans studying in Germany after the 1840s was psychologically prepared to accept German philological scholarship, much less incorporate it to some extent into American universities. Carl Diehl, *Americans and German Scholarship, 1770–1870* (New Haven, CT: Yale University Press, 1978). See also Bonnie G. Smith, *The Gender of History: Men, Women, and Historical Practice* (Cambridge, MA: Harvard University Press, 1998); Peter Novick, *That Noble Dream: The "Objectivity Question" and the American Historical Profession* (Cambridge: Cambridge University Press, 1988).

6. Julie A. Reuben, *The Making of the Modern University: Intellectual Transformation and the Marginalization of Morality* (Chicago: University of Chicago Press, 1996). See also Laurence R. Veysey, *The Emergence of the American University* (Chicago: University of Chicago Press, 1965); W. Bruce Leslie, *Gentlemen and Scholars: College and Community in the "Age of the University," 1865–1917* (University Park: Pennsylvania State University Press, 1992).

7. Konrad H. Jarausch, "Higher Education and Social Change: Some Comparative Perspectives," in *The Transformation of Higher Learning, 1860–1930*, ed. Konrad H. Jarausch (Chicago: University of Chicago Press, 1983), 9–36.

8. Thomas Neville Bonner, *To the Ends of the Earth: Women's Search for Education in Medicine* (Cambridge, MA: Harvard University Press, 1992).

9. Natalia Tikhonov, "Les Universités suisses, pionnières de l'introduction de la mixité dans l'enseignement supérieur (1870–1930)," in *Ecoles et mixités*, ed. Annik Houel and Michelle Zancarini-Fournel (Lyon: Presses universitaires de Lyon, 2001), 27–35; Patricia M. Mazón, *Gender and the Modern Research University: The Admission of Women to German Higher Education, 1865–1914* (Stanford: Stanford University Press, 2003); Pierre Moulinier, *La Naissance de l'étudiant moderne (XIXe siècle)* (Paris: Belin, 2002), chs. 2–3; Carole Lécuyer, "Une nouvelle figure de la jeune fille sous la IIIe République: l'étudiante," *Clio: Histoire, femmes et sociétés* 4 (1996): 166–76. Significant numbers of American women also went to France for art education. Gabriel P. Weisberg and Jane R. Becker, eds.,

Overcoming All Obstacles: The Women of the Académie Julian (New York: The Dahesh Museum, and New Brunswick, NJ: Rutgers University Press, 1999).

10. Daniel T. Rodgers, *Atlantic Crossings: Social Politics in a Progressive Age* (Cambridge, MA: Belknap Press of Harvard University Press, 1998), esp. ch. 3.

11. Adam R. Nelson, "Nationalism, Transnationalism, and the American Scholar in the Nineteenth Century: Thoughts on the Career of William Dwight Whitney," *New England Quarterly* 78 (September 2005): 341–76.

12. Harvey Levenstein, *Seductive Journey: American Tourists in France from Jefferson to the Jazz Age* (Chicago: University of Chicago Press, 1998), ch. 10; Mark Rennella and Whitney Walton, "Planned Serendipity: American Travelers and the Transatlantic Voyage in the Nineteenth and Twentieth Centuries," *Journal of Social History* 38 (Winter 2004): 365–83. See also Basil Woon, *The Frantic Atlantic: An Intimate Guide to the Well-known Deep* (New York: Alfred A. Knopf, 1928).

13. William W. Stowe analyzes writings by Americans to discern how travel to Europe helped shape a variety of identities, including personal, national, bourgeois, and female. William W. Stowe, *Going Abroad: European Travel in Nineteenth-century American Culture* (Princeton, NJ: Princeton University Press, 1994). Several scholars distinguish between travel and tourism, viewing the former as an individual voyage of discovery of others and of the self and the latter as less challenging because capitalist enterprises structure its expected itinerary of iconic sites and shield tourists from anything uncomfortable or unfamiliar. James Buzard, *The Beaten Track: European Tourism, Literature, and the Ways to Culture, 1800–1918* (Oxford: Clarendon Press, 1993); Paul Fussell, *Abroad: British Literary Traveling Between the Wars* (New York: Oxford University Press, 1980); Wolfgang Schivelbusch, *The Railway Journey: The Industrialization of Time and Space in the 19th Century* (Berkeley: University of California Press, 1986). Rudy Koshar, among others, challenges this dichotomy, arguing that tourism does not necessarily preclude the making of individual meaning out of travel experience. Rudy Koshar, *German Travel Cultures* (New York: Berg, 2000). My own thinking is similar to that of Koshar in accepting varieties of travel as constructive of new meanings.

14. Bertram M. Gordon, "The Decline of a Cultural Icon: France in American Perspective," *French Historical Studies* 22 (Autumn 1999): 625–51.

15. Levenstein, *Seductive Journey*, chs. 10–12.

16. James A. Harrison, "The American Student in France," *Chautauquan* 30 (March 1900): 580.

17. Russell M. Jones, "American Doctors in Paris, 1820–1861: A Statistical Profile," *Journal of the History of Medicine and Allied Sciences* 25 (April 1970): 143–57; Nancy L. Green, "The Comparative Gaze: Travelers in France Before the Era of Mass Tourism," *French Historical Studies* 25 (Summer 2002): 423–40.

18. "Getting a Doctor's Degree in Germany," *The Nation* 20 (May 20, 1875): 344.
19. Kennedy, "Studying in Germany," 351.
20. Diehl, *Americans and German Scholarship*; Crawford, "American Students in Germany."
21. "Going Abroad for an Education," *Century, a popular quarterly* 24, no. 5 (September 1882): 795.
22. Kennedy, "Studying in Germany," 352.
23. Burgess, *Reminiscences of an American Scholar*, 146, 192–223.
24. Ross, *Seventy Years of It*, 27.
25. Nicholas Murray Butler, *Across the Busy Years: Recollections and Reflections*, vol. 1 (New York: Charles Scribner's Sons, 1939), 105.
26. Ibid., 113, 133.
27. Richard T. Ely, *Ground Under Our Feet: An Autobiography* (New York: The Macmillan Company, 1938), 40. It is not clear in the autobiography whether Ely earned his doctorate in Heidelberg in 1878 or 1879 (46).
28. M. Carey Thomas, *The Making of a Feminist: Early Journals and Letters of M. Carey Thomas*, ed. Marjorie Housepian Dobkin with a foreword by Millicent Carey McIntosh (Kent, OH: Kent State University Press, 1979), 189.
29. Ibid., 208–11.
30. Ibid., 162. Thomas's feminism is clear in the next sentence: "Mary, before I die one book shall be written to try to protest against the misery and oppression of a girl's life."
31. Ibid., 208–19, 242–45, 252–53, 260–65. Helen Lefkowitz Horowitz, *The Power and Passion of M. Carey Thomas* (Urbana: University of Illinois Press, 1994; Illini books edition, 1999), chs. 6 and 8. The importance of politics in the history of women's admission into the decentralized German universities is evident in Mazón, *Gender and the Modern Research University*.
32. J. B. S., "Women at the German Universities," *Nation* 58 (February 15, 1894): 117.
33. Ibid., 116.
34. Lydia Lois Tilley, "Woman's Work at a German University," *Outlook* 69 (1901): 368–70; J. B. S., "Women at the German Universities," 116–17; J. B. S., "Women at the University of Paris," *Nation* 58 (March 1, 1894): 151–52; J. B. S., "Women Students and Women Teachers in Germany," *Nation* 59 (September 27, 1894): 232–33; Martha Krug Genthe, "Women at German Universities," *Forum* 33 (March–June 1902): 243–54.
35. Adele Luxenberg, "Women at Leipzig," *Nation* 59 (October 4, 1894): 247–48.
36. Mazón, *Gender and the Modern Research University*.
37. Natalia Tikhonov, "The Benefits of Foreign Study: American Women in Swiss Universities Prior to the First World War," paper presented at the American

Historical Association annual meeting, Chicago, January 4, 2003; Moulinier, *La Naissance de l'étudiant moderne*, chs. 2–3.

38. J. B. S., "Women at the University of Paris," 51; Tikhonov, "The Benefits of Foreign Study"; Moulinier, *La Naissance de l'étudiant moderne*; Bonner, *To the Ends of the Earth*.

39. Moulinier, *La Naissance de l'étudiant moderne*, 77–86 ; Carole Christen-Lécuyer, "Les Premières étudiantes de l'Université de Paris," *Travail, Genre et Sociétés* 4 (October 2000): 35–50.

40. Weisberg and Becker, *Overcoming All Obstacles*. See also dossiers in the Bibliothèque Marguerite Durand, Paris, France, on American women studying art in Paris in the late nineteenth century. DOS Enseignement supérieur 370 ENS.

41. Aimée Fabrègue, "Les Etudiantes étrangères à Paris," *Fronde*, June 24, 1898, and June 25, 1898, clippings found in DOS Enseignement supérieur 370 ENS in the Bibliothèque Marguerite Durand.

42. Augustus Saint-Gaudens, *The Reminiscences of Augustus Saint-Gaudens*, vol. 1 (New York: The Century Co., 1913), 93–94.

43. Jocelyne Rotily, *Artistes américains à Paris, 1914–1939* (Paris: L'Harmattan, 1998).

44. G. Stanley Hall, *Life and Confessions of a Psychologist* (New York: D. Appleton and Company, 1923), 219.

45. Ibid., 221, 222–23.

46. Ely, *Ground Under Our Feet*, 54.

47. Ibid., 43.

48. Ross, *Seventy Years of It*, 29–30.

49. Lincoln Steffens, *The Autobiography of Lincoln Steffens* (New York: The Literary Guild, 1931), 127.

50. Ibid., 151.

51. Ibid., 162.

52. Ely, *Ground Under Our Feet*, 117–18.

53. "Post-graduate Work in Germany: A Symposium," *Technology Review* 1 (1899): 300–13.

54. William Wallace Whitelock, "Taking a Degree in a German University," *Chautauquan* 35 (April–September 1902): 553.

55. Peter Drewek, "Limits of Educational Internationalism: Foreign Students at German Universities Between 1890 and 1930," *German Historical Institute Bulletin* 27 (Fall 2000): 39–63.

56. George Weisz, *The Emergence of Modern Universities in France, 1863–1914* (Princeton, NJ: Princeton University Press, 1983).

57. Alain Dubosclard, *L'Action culturelle de la France aux Etats-Unis de la Première Guerre mondiale à la fin des années 1960*, thèse d'Histoire, Université Paris I—Panthéon Sorbonne, November 2002; François Chaubet, *La Politique*

culturelle française et la diplomatie de la langue: L'Alliance Française (1883–1940) (Paris: L'Harmattan, 2006).

58. Archives Nationales [hereafter AN] AJ/16/6973, Propagande française à l'étranger, 1895–1916, Harry J. Furber, Jr., "Concerning the Attendance of Americans at the Universities of France," 1895.

59. AN AJ/16/6973, Propagande française à l'étranger, 1895–1916, "Notes sur les étudiants américains en France," November 30, 1896. James A. Harrison credits Furber with precipitating the French university reforms that drew more American students. Harrison, "The American Student in France," 580–82.

60. Weisz, *The Emergence of Modern Universities in France*; Christophe Charle, *La République des universitaires, 1870–1940* (Paris: Seuil, 1994).

61. Weisz, *The Emergence of Modern Universities in France,* ch. 7; Moulinier, *La Naissance de l'étudiant moderne*, chs. 2–3.

62. Weisz, *The Emergence of Modern Universities in France*, 258; Moulinier, *La Naissance de l'étudiant moderne*, 56.

63. Moulinier, *La Naissance de l'étudiant moderne*, 53.

64. Weisz, *The Emergence of Modern Universities in France*, 252–68; Moulinier, *La Naissance de l'étudiant moderne*, ch. 2; Charle, *La République des universitaires*, 343–59; Chaubet, *L'Alliance Française*, 74–9; AN AJ/16/6968–6975, Instituts français à l'étranger, Relations internationales de l'Université de Paris (1843–1965); Etats-Unis (1895–1960).

65. Henry Johnson, *The Other Side of Main Street: A History Teacher from Sauk Centre* (New York: Columbia University Press, 1943), 166.

66. Ibid., 167, 168.

67. Ibid., 186.

68. AN AJ/16/6968, Etats-Unis, Letter from Paul Boyer to the rector of the University of Paris, October 31, 1904.

69. AN AJ/16/6973, Les étudiants américains à Paris pendant la guerre de 1916–1918; 1918; 1936, Letter from G. Chinard to the rector of the University of Paris, February 17, 1916. An American law professor also suggested that French universities provide services similar to those of American universities to help students find lodgings, navigate the university, and promote sociability. Robert Ferrari, "De l'avenir des relations universitaires entre la France et l'Amérique," *Revue politique et parlementaire* 71 (1917): 444–52.

70. Gustave Lanson, *Trois mois d'enseignement aux Etats-Unis. Notes et impressions d'un professeur français* (Paris: Hachette, 1912), 193–210. For a similar view on American receptivity to French pedagogy, see Emile Legouis, *Impressions de Harvard* (Paris: Librarie Edouard Champion, Editeur, 1914), 10, printed pamphlet, located in AN AJ/16/6970, Université d'Harvard, 1907–60.

71. Maurice Caullery, "Les Clubs universitaires; la vie intellectuelle aux Etats-Unis," *Revue de Paris* 24, pt. 4 (1917): 333–48; Louis Vigouroux, "Les Universités américaines et la réforme de l'éducation en France," *Revue scientifique* 56 (1918):

164–67; Ch. Guignebert, "Les Universités américaines et les notres," *Revue politique et littéraire* 56 (March 16, 1918): 171–73.

72. Lanson, *Trois mois d'enseignement aux Etats-Unis*, 193–210.

73. Ch. Petit-Dutaillis,"Les Conditions de notre expansion intellectuelle," *Revue politique et parlementaire* 91 (April–May 1917): 22.

74. L. Houllevigue, "Les Etudiants étrangers dans nos universités," *La Revue de Paris* 24, pt. 3 (May 15, 1917): 362–77.

75. AN AJ/16/6973, Les étudiants américains à Paris pendant la guerre de 1916–1918; 1918; 1936, Letter from G. Chinard to the rector of the University of Paris, February 17, 1916.

76. Maurice Caullery, "French Universities and American Students," *Harvard Graduates' Magazine* 26 (December 1917): 208–20.

77. Mark Meigs, *Optimism at Armageddon: Voices of American Participants in the First World War* (Washington Square: New York University Press, 1997), 69.

78. Stephen H. Bush, "Un Détachement de l'armée américaine dans les écoles de Paris," *Revue internationale de l'enseignement* 74 (1920): 345; C. Bouglé, "L'Université Franco-Américaine," *La Revue de Paris* 26, pt. 3 (1919): 751–52.

79. Weisz, *The Emergence of Modern Universities in France*, 259.

80. Martha Hanna, "French Women and American Men: 'Foreign' Students at the University of Paris, 1915–1925," *French Historical Studies* 22 (Winter 1999): 87–112.

81. AN AJ/16/6973, Les étudiants américains à Paris pendant la guerre de 1916–1918; 1918; 1936, "Rapport à M. le Doyen de la Faculté des lettres sur la réception des étudiants américains pendant la période de démobilization," accompanying a letter by the dean of the Faculty of Letters to the rector of the University of Paris, November 23, 1918.

82. Ibid.

83. Bouglé, "L'Université Franco-Américaine," 750–53.

84. Bush, "Un Détachement de l'armée américaine," 346–47.

85. Bouglé, "L'Université Franco-Américaine," 750–65.

86. Robert J. Menner, "American Soldiers in French Universities," *The Sewanee Review* 28 (January–March 1920): 21–26.

87. Ibid., 20.

88. Ibid., 26–29.

89. AN AJ/16/6973, Les étudiants américains à Paris pendant la guerre de 1916–1918; 1918; 1936, letter from Samuel Lloyd to L. Poincaré, July 22, 1919.

90. Hanna, "French Women and American Men."

91. Bouglé, "L'Université Franco-Américaine," 757.

92. "Les Etudiants américains à l'Université de Toulouse," *Revue internationale de l'enseignement* 73 (1919): 230–34.

93. Bush, "Un Détachement de l'armée américaine," 348–58.

94. AN AJ/16/6974, Bourses pour les jeunes filles aux Etats-Unis, 1918–1924, Letter from Director of ONUEF to rectors of all universities, July 22, 1918; Letter/notice from minister of Public Instruction to rector of the University of Paris, June 7, 1918.

95. C. Cestre, "Une Mission aux Etats-Unis," *Revue internationale de l'enseignement* 73 (1919): 62–64.

Chapter 2

1. AN AJ/16/7020 and AJ 16/7021.
2. *Albert Kahn, 1860–1940: Réalités d'une utopie* (Boulogne: Musée Albert Kahn, 1995), 10, 141–42.
3. Akira Iriye, "A Century of NGOs," *Diplomatic History* 23 (Summer 1999): 421–35; Frank Costigliola, *Awkward Dominion: American Political, Economic, and Cultural Relations with Europe, 1919–1933* (Ithaca, NY: Cornell University Press, 1984); Emily S. Rosenberg, *Spreading the American Dream: American Economic and Cultural Expansion, 1890–1945* (New York: Hill and Wang, 1982); Frank A. Ninkovich, *The Diplomacy of Ideas: U.S. Foreign Policy and Cultural Relations, 1938–1950* (Cambridge: Cambridge University Press, 1981); Merle Curti, *American Philanthropy Abroad: A History* (New Brunswick, NJ: Rutgers University Press, 1963). See also Daniel T. Rodgers, *Atlantic Crossings: Social Politics in a Progressive Age* (Cambridge, MA: Belknap Press of Harvard University Press, 1998).
4. Historian Volker R. Berghahn, for one, charts the path of major American foundations in the twentieth century: from complementing U.S. foreign policy with independent support for transnational legal and scientific research, educational exchanges and development, and international medical assistance to partnering with the government after World War II to combat communism and spread democratic values, capitalist practices, and American culture. In another recent study, avoiding the dichotomy between American cultural imperialism and naive idealism as explanations for internationalist efforts, Oliver Schmidt contends that American philanthropic support for educational exchanges between Europe and the United States after 1945 combined stabilization favorable to American interests with satisfying European academics' desire for access to American science and knowledge. Contributors to Giuliana Gemelli's edited collection on the Ford Foundation from the 1950s to the 1970s generally conclude that the Foundation reshaped U.S. government policy away from cultural transplant toward a more interactive process of exchange or selective transfer so that transatlantic research and education became internationalized rather than Americanized. Recent work by Ludovic Tournès is notable for addressing the period before World War II. He explains how the Rockefeller Foundation laid the groundwork for Big Science in France through its financial

support of selected French biochemistry laboratories and especially through its fellowships for young French researchers to study in the United States during the 1920s and 1930s. Volker Berghahn, "Philanthropy and Diplomacy in the 'American Century,'" *Diplomatic History* 23 (Summer 1999): 393–419; Oliver Schmidt, "Small Atlantic World: U.S. Philanthropy and the Expanding International Exchange of Scholars after 1945," in *Culture and International History*, ed. Jessica C. E. Gienow-Hecht and Frank Schumacher (New York: Berghahn Books, 2003), 115–34; Giuliana Gemelli, ed., *The Ford Foundation and Europe (1950s–1970s): Cross-fertilization of Learning in Social Science and Management* (Brussels: European Interuniversity Press, 1998); Ludovic Tournès, "Le réseau des boursiers Rockefeller et la recomposition des saviors biomédicaux en France (1920–1970)," *French Historical Studies* 29 (Winter 2006): 77–108.

5. Jay Winter, *Dreams of Peace and Freedom: Utopian Moments in the Twentieth Century* (New Haven, CT: Yale University Press, 2006).

6. Costigliola, *Awkward Dominion*; Rosenberg, *Spreading the American Dream*; Richard F. Kuisel, *Seducing the French: The Dilemma of Americanization* (Berkeley: University of California Press, 1993); Denis Lacorne, Jacques Rupnik, and Marie-France Toinet, eds., *The Rise and Fall of Anti-Americanism: A Century of French Perception*, trans. Gerry Turner (New York: St. Martin's Press, 1990); Philippe Roger, *The American Enemy: A Story of French Anti-Americanism*, trans. Sharon Bowman (Chicago: University of Chicago Press, 2005); Seth D. Armus, *French Anti-Americanism, 1930–1948: Critical Moments in a Complex History* (Lanham, MD: Rowman & Littlefield Publishers, 2007).

7. *Albert Kahn, 1860–1940*; Sophie Cœuré and Frédéric Worms, eds., *Henri Bergson et Albert Kahn, correspondances* (Strasbourg: Desmaret and Boulogne: Musée Départemental Albert-Kahn, 2003); Winter, *Dreams of Peace and Freedom*, ch. 1.

8. Akira Iriye, *Global Community: The Role of International Organizations in the Making of the Contemporary World* (Berkeley: University of California Press, 2002), 9–19; Stephen Kern, *The Culture of Time and Space, 1880–1919* (Cambridge, MA: Harvard University Press, 1983); Leila J. Rupp, *Worlds of Women: The Making of an International Women's Movement* (Princeton, NJ: Princeton University Press, 1997).

9. Thomas J. Schaeper and Kathleen Schaeper, *Rhodes Scholars, Oxford and the Creation of an American Elite* (New York: Berghahn Books, 2004), 1, 13–16; Robert I. Rotberg, *The Founder: Cecil Rhodes and the Pursuit of Power* (New York: Oxford University Press, 1988), 665–69; Eugen Weber, "Pierre de Coubertin and the Introduction of Organised Sport in France," *Journal of Contemporary History* 5 (1970): 3–26; Allen Guttmann, *The Olympics: A History of the Modern Games*, 2nd ed. (Urbana: University of Illinois Press, 2002), 8–19; Iriye, *Global Community*, 9–19. See also Lee Shai Weissbach, "The Nature of Philanthropy in Nineteenth-century France and the *Mentalité* of the Jewish Elite,"

Jewish History 8 (1994): 191–204. The research of F. S. L. Lyons indicates that nongovernmental international organizations in Europe multiplied around the turn of the century, and though they did not prevent World War I, they nonetheless accustomed a small minority of Europeans to international practices. F. S. L. Lyons, *Internationalism in Europe 1815–1914* (Leyden: A. W. Sythoff, 1963), 14–15, 203–45, 366–69. According to Merle Curti American philanthropy was primarily humanitarian at the turn of the century in the sense of providing disaster relief in troubled areas. A more cosmopolitan and internationalist orientation started with the founding of the Carnegie Endowment for International Peace in 1910. Curti, *American Philanthropy Abroad*, 178–97.

10. Fondation Albert Kahn, *Autour du Monde*, par les boursiers de voyage de l'Université de Paris (Paris: Felix Alcan, 1904), i.

11. Ibid., ii–iii.

12. Ibid.

13. Ibid., ii.

14. Nathalie Clet-Bonnet, attachée de conservation, Musée départemental Albert-Kahn, assembled data on the *boursiers*. See also Nathalie Clet-Bonnet, "Les Bourses Autour du Monde, la fondation française, 1898–1930," in *Albert Kahn*, 137–51.

15. *Albert Kahn*, 143–50; Fondation Albert Kahn, *Autour du Monde*, i–iii.

16. Albert Kahn to Louis Liard, June 2, 1905, quoted in Clet-Bonnet, "Les Bourses Autour du Monde," 142.

17. Clet-Bonnet, "Les Bourses autour du Monde," 142.

18. Theodore Roosevelt, *The Strenuous Life: Essays and Addresses* (New York: The Century Co., 1918 [orig. 1899]), 1.

19. Fabian Hilfrich, "Manliness and 'Realism': The Use of Gendered Tropes in the Debates on the Philippine-American and Vietnam Wars," in Gienow-Hecht and Schumacher, eds., *Culture and International History*, 60–78; Gary Gerstle, *American Crucible: Race and Nation in the Twentieth Century* (Princeton, NJ: Princeton University Press, 2001); John F. Kasson, *Houdini, Tarzan, and the Perfect Man: The White Male Body and the Challenge of Modernity in America* (New York: Hill and Wang, 2001), 4–10; Christopher Endy, "Travel and World Power: Americans in Europe, 1890–1917," *Diplomatic History* 22 (Fall 1998): 565–94. See also John Milton Cooper, *The Warrior and the Priest: Woodrow Wilson and Theodore Roosevelt* (Cambridge, MA: Belknap Press of Harvard University Press, 1983), 7–13, 31–39. Jacques Portes claims that Theodore Roosevelt was unknown in France until 1900 when he ran for vice president on the Republican ticket and then became the most popular American politician in France until Woodrow Wilson. Jacques Portes, *Une Fascination réticente: Les Etats-Unis dans l'opinion française* (Nancy: Presses universitaires de Nancy, 1990), 192–93.

20. Roosevelt, *The Strenuous Life*, 4, 6.

21. AN AJ/16/7021, Allard-Bourgogne, Jeanne Antoine. Similarly Henri Labroue titled a newspaper article that recounted his travels, "New York, la vie intense," *L'Avenir de la Dordogne*, March 9, 1908, in AN AJ/16/7023, Labroue-Meyer, Henri Labroue 1907. Pierrette Sapy wrote from Boston in 1906, "One can have initiative, be energetic and lead the 'strenuous' life more cheaply in the United States than in France." AN AJ/16/7023, Ronze-Weurlesse, Pierrette Sapy. See also the published travel account by Abbé Félix Klein, *Au Pays de "la vie intense"* (Paris: Plon, 1904). Klein described his meeting with President Theodore Roosevelt in the White House; he wrote that his proposal to name his book after Roosevelt's phrase pleased the president, and that he allowed Klein to dedicate the book to Roosevelt (238).

22. Jean-Baptiste Duroselle, *France and the United States from the Beginning to the Present*, trans. Derek Coltman (Chicago: University of Chicago Press, 1978), 76–77.

23. Georges Duhamel, *America the Menace: Scenes from the Life of the Future*, trans. Charles Miner Thompson (Boston: Houghton Mifflin Company, 1931 [orig.1930]). As many scholars have shown, Duhamel's critique of American materialism and cultural conformity was not new or unique in 1930. Pascal Ory, "From Baudelaire to Duhamel: An Unlikely Antipathy," in *The Rise and Fall of Anti-Americanism*, 42–54; Portes, *Une Fascination réticente* ; Bernadette Galloux-Fournier, "Un Regard sur l'Amérique: Voyageurs français aux Etats-Unis (1919–1939)," *Revue d'histoire moderne et contemporaine* 37 (April–June 1990): 308–23; Ralph Schor, *L'Opinion française et les étrangers en France, 1919–1939* (Paris: Publication de la Sorbonne, 1985).

24. Mlle. Clément, "Quelques réflexions sur la vie intense aux Etats-Unis," *Bulletin de la Société Autour du Monde* (July 1914): 169–70.

25. Ibid., 174–76, 182.

26. AN AJ/16/7021, Bourquin-Comuel, Georges Burchard [sic] 1899.

27. Emile Hovelaque, "La Situation économique de la France à l'extérieur," in Fondation Albert Kahn, *Autour du Monde*, 207–30.

28. G. Weulersse, "L'Education publique aux Etats-Unis, impressions et réflexions," in Fondation Albert Kahn, *Autour du Monde*, 385–418.

29. Albert Kahn Museum archives, dossiers français M-W, Madeleine Mignon.

30. Jo Burr Margadant, *Madame le professeur: Women Educators in the Third Republic* (Princeton, NJ: Princeton University Press, 1990), 204–18, 222–26.

31. Portes, *Une Fascination réticente*, chs. 8–9; Galloux-Fournier, "Un regard sur l'Amérique."

32. James Albisetti argues that because French universities were admitting women beginning in the 1860s, French travelers to the United States did not usually consider women's colleges to be a desirable or necessary alternative. James C. Albisetti, "American Women's Colleges through European Eyes, 1865–1914," *History of Education Quarterly* 32 (Winter 1992): 439–58. Barbara Miller Solomon

asserts that coeducational universities were the dominant trend in the United States around the turn of the century. Barbara Miller Solomon, *In the Company of Educated Women: A History of Women and Higher Education in America* (New Haven, CT: Yale University Press, 1985), 47, 58. Lynn D. Gordon maintains that women students in the United States cultivated a separate women's culture in coed universities (that was also institutionally constructed) that enhanced women's self-confidence and led them to demand equal resources for women and men and eventually to challenge gender separation itself. Lynn D. Gordon, *Gender and Higher Education in the Progressive Era* (New Haven, CT: Yale University Press, 1990), 190. Natalia Tikhonov examined 211 American women who studied in Switzerland between the 1870s and World War I, and she maintains that most went abroad to get medical degrees in coeducational universities, which was not possible at that time in the United States. On returning to the United States, these graduates were influential in increasing women's access to higher education in coeducational universities. Natalia Tikhonov, "The Benefits of Foreign Study: American Women in Swiss Universities Prior to the First World War," paper presented at the American Historical Association annual meeting in Chicago, January 4, 2003.

33. AN AJ/16/7021, Bourquin-Comuel, Marguerite Clément.

34. AN AJ/16/7021, Bourquin-Comuel, Annette-Marie Cartan. Nathalie Clet-Bonnet notes that Cartan's legal first name was Anna, Albert Kahn Museum Archives.

35. AN AJ/16/7022, Couchoud-Eggli, Jeanne Darlu 1908.

36. AN AJ/16/7023, Mignon-Nogard, Madeleine Mignon.

37. Ibid.

38. AN AJ/16/7023, Mignon-Nogard, Lucy Nicole, 1912.

39. AN AJ/16/7023, Piriou-Renaud [sic], Jeanne Renauld.

40. AN AJ/16/7023, Labrou-Meyer, Alice Lapotaire, 1913.

41. AN AJ/16/7022, Couchoud-Eggli, Jeanne Darlu, 1908.

42. AN AJ/16/7023, Mignon-Nogard, Madeleine Mignon.

43. AN AJ/16/7022,Couchoud-Eggli, Jeanne Darlu, 1908.

44. AN AJ/16/7021, Bourquin-Comuel, Marguerite Clément.

45. Mary Lynn Stewart and Kathleen Alaimo have found that despite expert opinion on the benefits of exercise for young women in late nineteenth- and early twentieth-century France, the general public feared it might harm women's childbearing capabilities. Mary Lynn Stewart, *For Health and Beauty: Physical Culture for Frenchwomen, 1880's–1930's* (Baltimore: Johns Hopkins University Press, 2001), 153–56; Kathleen Alaimo, "The Authority of Experts: The Crisis of Female Adolescence in France and England, 1880–1920," in *Secret Gardens, Satanic Mills: Placing Girls in European History, 1750–1969*, ed. Mary Jo Maynes, Birgitte Soland, and Christina Benninghaus (Bloomington: Indiana University Press, 2004), ch. 9.

46. AN AJ/16/7021, Bourquin-Comuel, Annette-Marie Cartan.

47. AN AJ/16/7023, Mignon-Nogard, Madeleine Mignon.

48. AN AJ/16/7023, Labrou-Meyer, Alice Lapotaire, 1913.

49. AN AJ/16/7021, Bourquin-Comuel, Annette-Marie Cartan.

50. Albert Kahn Museum Archives, Boursiers français M-W, Madeleine Mignon.

51. AN AJ/16/7021, Allard-Bourgogne, Rachel Victoire Allard.

52. AN AJ/16/7023, Ronze-Weurlesse, Pierrette Sapy.

53. Amieux wrote: "To be sure, French feminism has accomplished a lot, but all is not yet done! Between the American [women] and the Swedish [women] no doubt closer to the latter than the former, a place is reserved for us that we have not yet conquered. Is the time not yet ripe for us, or have we not oriented and coordinated our efforts as we should? Perhaps both! But I hope and I believe that the time will come when we will know how to work for their advancement." AN AJ/16/7021, Allard-Bourgogne, Anna Amieux.

54. Rebecca Rogers, *From the Salon to the Schoolroom: Educating Bourgeois Girls in Nineteenth-century France* (University Park: Pennsylvania State University Press, 2005), 215–18.

55. Helen Lefkowitz Horowitz, *Alma Mater: Design and Experience in the Women's Colleges from Their Nineteenth-century Beginnings to the 1930s*, 2nd ed. (Amherst: University of Massachusetts Press, 1993), 147, 159–63, 169, xxiv; Gordon, *Gender and Higher Education*, 190; Solomon, *In the Company of Educated Women*, ch. 8.

56. Carole Lécuyer, "Une Nouvelle figure de la jeune fille sous la IIIe République: l'étudiante," *Clio: Histoire, femmes et sociétés* 4 (1996): 166–76. See also the two dossiers, DOS Enseignement supérieur, 370, AGR Agrégées and DOS Enseignement supérieur, 370, ENS held in the Bibliothèque Marguerite Durand, Paris, France, and Françoise Lelièvre and Claude Lelièvre, *Histoire de la scolarisation des filles* (Paris: Nathan, 1991).

57. AN AJ/16/7021, Bourquin-Comuel, Annette-Marie Cartan.

58. *Kahn Foundation for the Foreign Travel of American Teachers, Reports* vol. 1, no. 1 (New York: Printed by the Trustees, 1912), 1; *Albert Kahn, 1860–1940*, 151.

59. While the trustees of the Kahn Foundation in the United States were affiliated with universities and institutions on the East Coast, they selected fellows largely from central locations within the country, like Indiana, Texas, Georgia, Colorado, and Missouri. See Clet-Bonnet's data on *boursiers*, and *Kahn Foundation for the Foreign Travel of American Teachers. Reports*, vol. 1, no. 1 (New York: Printed by the Trustees, 1912), 1.

60. Walter Williams, "The World's Journalism," *Kahn Foundation for the Foreign Travel of American Teachers, Reports*, vol. 3, no. 1 (New York: Printed by the Trustees, 1919), 16.

61. Ivan M. Linforth, "Report to the Trustees," *Kahn Foundation for the Travel of American Teachers, Reports*, vol. 2, no. 1 (New York: Printed by the Trustees, 1913), 25–26. This report was translated into French: Ch.-M. Garnier, "Le Rapport de M. Ivan M. Linforth," *Bulletin de la Société Autour du Monde* (July 1914): 238–40.

62. Sandi E. Cooper, *Patriotic Pacifism: Waging War on War in Europe, 1815–1914* (New York: Oxford University Press, 1991); James A. Field, Jr., "Transnationalism and the New Tribe," in *Transnational Relations and World Politics*, ed. Robert O. Keohane and Joseph S. Nye, Jr. (Cambridge, MA: Harvard University Press, 1972), 10; Lyons, *Internationalism in Europe*.

63. Emile Hovelaque, "L'Opinion américaine et la guerre," *Bulletin de la Société Autour du Monde* (January–April 1916): 48–68.

64. Anne Main, "De la neutralité à la guerre: Notes d'un séjour à New York, 1916–1917," *Bulletin de la Société Autour du Monde*, [pencilled November 1918]: 37–56. Located in Albert Kahn Museum Archives, Boursiers français M-W, Main, Anne. Lauréate 1914.

65. Ibid.

66. Iriye, *Global Community*, 20–36.

67. Charles Garnier, "Société des Nations: Section de l'éducation et des relations intellectuelles," *Bulletin de la Société Autour du Monde*, (April–December 1920): 37–45.

68. R. P. Brooks, a copy of his statement published in *Bulletin de la Société Autour du Monde*, (June 14, 1931): xiv–xv. Located in Albert Kahn Museum Archives, file on Brooks, R.P.

69. "Allocation de M. Félicien Challaye, au nom de la fondation française," *Bulletin de la Société Autour du Monde*, (June 14, 1931): xvi.

70. Ivan M. Linforth, "Nouvelle Expérience d'entente internationale," *Bulletin de la Société Autour du Monde* (June 14, 1931): 37–42.

71. Clet-Bonnet, "Les Bourses Autour du Monde," 137–51.

72. Quoted in *Albert Kahn*, 238.

73. Quoted in *Albert Kahn*, 163.

74. Quoted in *Albert Kahn*, 163.

75. Quoted in *Albert Kahn*, 151.

76. Edmée Hitzel, "Extrême-Orient," *Bulletin de la Société Autour du Monde*, (1929–30): 1.

77. AN AJ/16/7022, Couchoud-Eggli, Jeanne Darlu, 1908.

78. AN AJ/16/7023, Ronze-Weurlesse, Simone Téry, 7.

79. William Henri Goy, "Le Monde de demain en formation," *Bulletin de la Société Autour du Monde* (July–October 1917): 68–69. This appears to be Goy's presentation of Williams's report.

80. André Siegfried, *Les Etats-Unis d'aujourd'hui* (Paris: Armand Colin, 1927); Georges Duhamel, *Scènes de la vie future* (1930). According to Pascal Ory,

Duhamel's book was first published in April 1930. Pascal Ory, "From Baudelaire to Duhamel: An Unlikely Antipathy," in *The Rise and Fall of Anti-Americanism*, 42–54.

81. Edmée Hitzel, "Deuxième partie: Etats-Unis," *Bulletin de la Société Autour du Monde* (129–30): 48.

82. Clet-Bonnet, "Les Bourses Autour du Monde," 137–52; Sophie Coeuré, "La société Autour du Monde, 1906–1949," *Albert Kahn*, 237–41.

83. Costigliola, *Awkward Dominion*; Rosenberg, *Spreading the American Dream*; Ory, "From Baudelaire to Duhamel"; Richard Pells, *Not Like Us: How Europeans Have Loved, Hated, and Transformed American Culture Since World War II* (New York: Basic Books, 1997); Kuisel, *Seducing the French*; Armus, *French Anti-Americanism*; Roger, *The American Enemy*. See also Victoria de Grazia, *Irresistible Empire: America's Advance Through Twentieth-century Europe* (Cambridge, MA: Belknap Press of Harvard University Press, 2005).

84. Rupp, *Worlds of Women*; Mrinalini Sinha, Donna Guy, and Angela Wollacott, eds., *Feminisms and Internationalism* (Oxford: Blackwell, 1999); Emily S. Rosenberg, "Consuming Women: Images of Americanization in the 'American Century,'" *Diplomatic History* 23 (Summer 1999): 479–97; Gienow-Hecht and Schumacher, eds., *Culture and International History*.

Chapter 3

Material from this chapter was published earlier as "Internationalism and the Junior Year Abroad: American Students in France in the 1920s and 1930s," *Diplomatic History* 29 (April 2005): 255–78. Many thanks for the kind permission to reproduce it here.

1. University of Delaware Archives [hereafter UD], Foreign Study Plan Records, 1922–48. Numbers of students on the University of Delaware Foreign Study Plan are as follows: 8 in 1923–24; 5 in 1924–25; 14 in 1925–26; 45 in 1926–27; 44 in 1927–28; 67 in 1928–29; 67 in 1929–30; 60 in 1930–31; 91 in 1931–32; 65 in 1932–33; 42 in 1933–34; 34 in 1934–35; 41 in 1935–36; 35 in 1936–37; 57 in 1937–38; 51 in 1938–39; and 42 in 1939 for a total of 768 from 125 different colleges and universities. Brief Report on the Delaware Foreign Study Plan, May 13, 1948, in UD AR 448, vol. 20, 1947–48. Approximately 450 Smith College students went to France from 1925–39; 32 in 1925–26; 32 in 1926–27; 42 in 1927–28; 38 in 1928–29; 38 in 1929–30; 47 in 1930–31; 33 in 1931–32; 46 in 1932–33; 31 in 1933–34; 18 in 1934–35; figures missing for 1935–36; 23 in 1936–37; 26 in 1937–38; and figures missing for 1938–39. Smith College Archives [hereafter SC], Junior Year Abroad France, 1927–present, Box 1132.

2. Alain Dubosclard, *L'Action culturelle de la France aux Etats-Unis, de la Première Guerre mondiale à la fin des années 1960*, thèse d'Histoire, Université Paris 1—Panthéon Sorbonne, November 2002; Alain Dubosclard, "Diplomatie

culturelle et propagande française aux Etats-Unis pendant le premier vingtième siècle," *Revue d'Histoire Moderne et Contemporaine* 48 (January–March 2001): 102–19; François Chaubet, *La Politique culturelle française et la diplomatie de la langue: L'Alliance Française (1883–1940)* (Paris: L'Harmattan, 2006); Suzanne Balous, *L'Action culturelle de la France dans le monde* (Paris: Presses Universitaires de France, 1970); George Weisz, *The Emergence of Modern Universities in France, 1863–1914* (Princeton, NJ: Princeton University Press, 1983), 252–68; Ruth Emily McMurry and Muna Lee, *The Cultural Approach: Another Way in International Relations* (Chapel Hill, NC: University of North Carolina Press, 1947); Emily S. Rosenberg, *Spreading the American Dream: American Economic and Cultural Expansion, 1890–1945* (New York: Hill and Wang, 1982); Frank Costigliola, *Awkward Dominion: American Political, Economic, and Cultural Relations with Europe, 1919–1933* (Ithaca, NY: Cornell University Press, 1984).

3. Martha Hanna, "French Women and American Men: 'Foreign' Students at the University of Paris, 1915–1925," *French Historical Studies* 22 (Winter 1999): 87–112; C. Bouglé, "L'Université franco-américaine," *Revue de Paris* 26, pt. 3 (1919): 750–65; Stephen H. Bush, "Un Détachement de l'armée américaine dans les écoles de Paris," *Revue internationale de l'enseignement* 74 (1920): 345–58; Henri Goy, "Les Cours de civilisation," *Foreign Study Notes* 1 (December 1929–March 1930): 7–10.

4. AN AJ/16/6973, Les étudiants américains à Paris pendant la guerre de 1916–1918; 1919; 1936 "Rapport à M. le Doyen de la Faculté des lettres sur la réception des étudiants américains pendant la période de démobilization," accompanying a letter by the dean of the Faculty of Letters to the rector of the University of Paris, November 23, 1918.; AN AJ/16/4752, Registre des actes et déclarations de la Faculté des lettres de Paris, 1914–18.

5. Robert J. Menner, "American Soldiers in French Universities," *Sewanee Review* 28 (January–March 1920): 29.

6. Raymond W. Kirkbride to Walter Hullihen, November 17, 1922, UD AR 330 President's Office, Walter Hullihen, Series 2: Foreign Study Plan Correspondence 1922–37; 1927–28, Volume 1922–37.

7. Walter Hullihen quoted in "Service Citizens plan numerous educational aids," *Morning News* [Wilmington], May 13, 1922. This clipping is in Scrapbook 1, UD AR 42 Scrapbooks.

8. Walter Hullihen, "Undergraduate Foreign Study for Credit Toward the American Baccalaureate Degree," *Educational Record* 5 (January 1924): 45. See also AN AJ/16/6970, University of Delaware, 1930–36.

9. Costigliola, *Awkward Dominion;* Rosenberg, *Spreading the American Dream*; Frank A. Ninkovich, *The Diplomacy of Ideas: U.S. Foreign Policy and Cultural Relations, 1938–1950* (Cambridge: Cambridge University Press, 1981).

10. Stephen P. Duggan, "The Institute of International Education," *School and Society* 12 (July–December 1920): 642.

11. David A. Robertson, "International Educational Relations of the United States," *Educational Record* 6 (1925): 91–153; Institute of International Education, 23rd series, Bulletin No. 1, "Directory of Former Fellows of the American Field Service Fellowships for French Universities, Inc., 1919–1942" (May 1, 1942), 51–55.

12. Institute of International Education, Bulletin No. 3, "Observations on Higher Education in Europe" (1920): 385–86. IIE bulletins and pamphlets published in the 1920s provide information about educational exchanges, especially between France and the United States, and lists of fellowship opportunities, including those for French and American students.

13. Georges Duflot, *Guide illustré de l'étudiant étranger à Paris et en France* (Paris: Labrousse, 1907); Robertson, "International Educational Relations," 136; McMurry and Lee, *The Cultural Approach,* ch. 2; AN AJ/16/6968, Etats-Unis, Echanges universitaires 1902–1957; AN AJ/16/7027–44, Cité Universitaire; within this group, cartons 7039–40, deal with the Fondation des Etats-Unis, 1921–57.

14. Marcus M. Marks, "International Travel and Study—An Official College Extension," *Educational Record* 5 (1924): 40–43.

15. Numbers of Americans studying in France vary widely according to different sources. Part of the reason is that there were so many different forms of study abroad; in addition to students enrolled at French universities, many took courses in art, music, or at technical institutes or in summer schools, and this latter group was not always counted. A conservative estimate of the number of Americans studying in France in April 1922 was between 600 and 700; the director of the American University Union in Paris counted 3,002 Americans studying in France in 1923–24; and unofficial figures for 1927–28 noted 4,000 American students enrolled in French universities. W. Reginald Wheeler, Henry H. King, and Alexander B. Davidson, eds., *The Foreign Student in America* (New York: Association Press, 1925), 23; Horatio S. Krans, "L'Américan University Union à Paris et son nouveau domicile," *Revue internationale de l'enseignement* 78 (1924): 242; AN AJ/16/6973, John L. Gerig, "De l'utilité d'une maison française à l'Université Columbia," n.d., mimeographed report. A British publication put the figure of Americans studying in France in 1922 at 1,392, in contrast with 407 Americans at British universities. "The Universities and International Relations," *Nature* 115 (April 11, 1925): 523.

16. Horatio S. Krans, "The American University Union in Paris," Institute of International Education Bulletin, 17th series, no. 4 (October 1, 1936): 11.

17. Hullihen, "Undergraduate Foreign Study," 48–51.

18. Typed list of years, number of students, and directors, in Junior Year in France. 50 JYA France, SC Junior Year Abroad [JYA] France, 1927–present, box 1132.

19. Typed report dated May 22, 1929, in Junior Year in France. 50 JYA France, SC JYA France, 1927–present, box 1132.

20. "When the President Went to France," *Smith Alumnae Quarterly* 17 (May 1926): 288.
21. Raymond W. Kirkbride to Walter Hullihen, March 5, 1923, in Foreign Study Plan Records, UD AR 330, Hullihen Papers, 1922–37.
22. "When the President Went to France," 291.
23. Report to the President, December 18, 1927, SC JYA France, Neilson Papers, box 49.
24. David O. Levine, *The American College and the Culture of Aspiration, 1915–1940* (Ithaca, NY: Cornell University Press, 1986).
25. Katherine S. Bolman, "Juniors in France," *Journal of the American Association of University Women* 23 (October 1929): 24.
26. Ibid.
27. Christopher Endy, "Travel and World Power: Americans in Europe, 1890–1917," *Diplomatic History* 22 (Fall 1998): 572.
28. Katharine A. Morrison, excerpts from letters, 1930, UD AR 68, folder 540.
29. Beatrice F. Davis, oral interview by Myron L. Lazarus, July 15, 1970, UD AR 97, folder 1646.
30. Marian Sage to her family, August 29, 1927, SC JYA, Marian Sage Seewoster, Letters 1927–28, box 2019.1.
31. Delia Brown to Hélène Cattenès, July 14, 1926, SC JYA France, Neilson Papers, box 49..
32. Helen P. Roads, excerpt from a letter to George E. Brinton, May 5, 1930, responding to his request that parents share portions of the letters from their children on the Delaware Foreign Study Plan, UD AR 68, folder 540, p. 6.
33. Florence Elizabeth Bragdon to her family, November 14, 1929, SC, box 2029.
34. Harvey Levenstein, *Seductive Journey: American Tourists in France from Jefferson to the Jazz Age* (Chicago: University of Chicago Press, 1998). While Levenstein dates the stereotype of France as a place of decadent pleasures to the late nineteenth century, William Keylor attributes this to returning American veterans from World War I. William R. Keylor, "'How They Advertised France': The French Propaganda Campaign in the United States During the Breakup of the Franco-American Entente, 1918–1923," *Diplomatic History* 17 (Summer 1993): 351–73.
35. Raymond W. Kirkbride to Walter Hullihen, March 4, 1923, from UD AR 330, Hullihen Papers, Foreign Study, 1922–37.
36. Hélène Cattanès, "Twenty-Five Years Ago: Thirty-Two Innocents Abroad," *Smith Alumnae Quarterly* 42 (February 1951): 74.
37. Beatrice F. Davis, oral interview.
38. Sarah Alice Johnston to her family, November 9, 1938, in "Sally Goes to France: Letters from a Junior Year, 1938–1939," ed. Ellen J. Maycock, 2003, typed manuscript.

39. Eleanor Daniels to her parents, January 9, 1938, SC, box 2116.

40. Common French stereotypes of Americans were the following: Americans were rich; American men especially were interested only in business, and they were missionaries of modernization; they were uncouth, arrogant. Ralph Schor, *L'Opinion française et les étrangers en France, 1919–1939* (Paris: Publications de la Sorbonne, 1985), 161–64. Although American movies reached Parisian audiences in the 1930s, French imaginings about Americans usually came from published accounts by French persons who had traveled in the United States. Bernadette Gailloux-Fournier, "Un Regard sur l'Amérique: Voyageurs français aux Etats-Unis (1919–1939)," *Revue d'histoire moderne et contemporaine* 37 (April–June 1990): 308–23; Jacques Portes, *Fascination and Misgivings: The United States in French Opinion, 1870–1914*, trans. Elborg Forster (New York: Cambridge University Press, 2000).

41. Dorothy Tebbets to her parents, January 31, 1926, SC, box 1994.

42. Sarah Alice Johnston to her sister, October 20, 1938, in "Sally goes to France."

43. Elizabeth Bragdon to her parents, September 11, 1929, SC, box 2029.

44. Mary Louise Cahill to her parents, November 4, 1936, SC, box 2110.

45. Caroline Miller Stabler to her mother, November 29, 1925, SC, box 1990. French popular opinion against paying off the war debt to the United States resulted in attacks on American tourists in Paris in 1926. Costigliola, *Awkward Dominion*, 133–35.

46. Caroline Miller Stabler to her family, February 14, 1926, SC, box 1990.

47. "Foreign Study Members Broadcast in Paris," *University of Delaware Review*, May 25, 1928. Johnston's speech was titled, "What an American Student Gains in France," and was published in its entirety. UD AR 42, Printed and Duplicated material. Scrapbook, vol. 1.

48. Dorothy Tebbets to her parents, October 17 and 20, 1925, SC, box 1994.

49. Phebe Adams to her parents, February [n.d.] 1931, SC, box 2041.

50. Henry Kirkpatrick, excerpt of a letter to his parents, September 15, 1929; enclosed with a letter from his father, William F. Kirkpatrick in Storrs, CT, to George E. Brinton of June 26, 1930, UD AR 68, Miscellaneous historical Material, folder 540: Letters to parents from students 1929–30 (Group VII).

51. Dorothy Tebbets to her parents, November 22, 1925, SC, box 1994.

52. Hilda Donahue to W. A. Neilson, February 4, 1927, SC JYA, Neilson Papers, box 49.

53. Ibid.

54. Weisz, *The Emergence of Modern Universities in France;* Fritz Ringer, *Fields of Knowledge: French Academic Culture in Comparative Perspective* (Cambridge: Cambridge University Press, and Paris: Editions de la Maison des Sciences de l'homme, 1992).

55. Julie A. Reuben, *The Making of the Modern University: Intellectual Transformation and the Marginalization of Morality* (Chicago: University of Chicago Press, 1996); Laurence R. Veysey, *The Emergence of the American University* (Chicago: University of Chicago Press, 1965).

56. Levine, *The American College and the Culture of Aspiration*.

57. Christophe Charle, *La République des universitaires, 1870–1940* (Paris: Seuil, 1994).

58. Helen Lefkowitz Horowitz, *Campus Life: Undergraduate Cultures from the End of the Eighteenth Century to the Present* (New York: Alfred A. Knopf, 1987); Paula Fass, *The Damned and the Beautiful: American Youth in the 1920s* (New York: Oxford University Press, 1977). Pierre Moulinier presents the public, social, and political life of Parisian students before World War I, but he also notes the competitive, individualistic nature of higher education in France. Pierre Moulinier, *La Naissance de l'étudiant moderne (XIXe siècle)* (Paris: Belin, 2002), 152–153 and chs. 9–11.

59. X., "Examens de conscience," *Foreign Study Notes* 1 (August–November 1929): 38.

60. Z., "Examens de conscience," *Foreign Study Notes* 1 (August–November 1929): 43.

61. Alice A. Woodard, "The Second Group of Juniors in France," *Smith Alumnae Quarterly* 18 (May 1927): 288.

62. Mary Louise Cahill to her parents, January 11 and February 22, 1937, SC, box 2110. The last letter also indicates that this phonetics course was dropped from the program.

63. Fass, *The Damned and the Beautiful*, 18–20 and ch. 8; Frederick Lewis Allen, *Only Yesterday: An Informal History of the 1920s* (New York: Harper & Row Publishers, 1931); Horowitz, *Campus Life*, esp. 161, 164, and ch. 7; Levine, *American College and the Culture of Aspiration*, chs. 6, 9, pp. 205–6; Helen Lefkowitz Horowitz, *Alma Mater: Design and Experience in the Women's Colleges from Their Nineteenth-century Beginnings to the 1930s* (Boston: Beacon Press, 1984), 281–82.

64. Edith Pardee, "Our Foreign Correspondents," *Smith Alumnae Quarterly* 25 (May 1934): 292.

65. Sarah Alice Johnston to the family, November 24–25, 1938, in "Sally Goes to France."

66. Florence Elizabeth Bragdon to her family, March 5, 1930, SC, box 2029.

67. Unknown student to parents, 1929 or 1930, UD AR 68, folder 539.

68. Miriam Allen, excerpt of a letter to her parents, August 24, 1929, sent by W. Ray Allen in Chicago to George Brinton, UD AR 68, folder 540: Letters to parents from students 1929–30 (Group VII).

69. Frances Hurrey to her family, August 24, 1929, Frances Hurrey Philips Papers, Mount Holyoke College Archives and Special Collections, South Hadley,

MA. Many thanks to Emily Brush for this research. Hurrey's preference for the American cemetery over the rest of the Verdun battlefield site supports Mark Meigs's contention that the American Graves Registration Service intended the graveyard to be separate from and grander than those of other nationalities, reflecting the nature of the United States' engagement in World War I. Mark Meigs, *Optimism at Armageddon: Voices of American Participants in the First World War* (New York: New York University Press, 1997), 185–86.

70. Eleanor Daniels to her family, November 14, 1937, SC, box 2116.

71. Stephen L. Harp, *Marketing Michelin: Advertising and Cultural Identity in Twentieth-Century France* (Baltimore: Johns Hopkins University Press, 2001), ch. 3; David W. Lloyd, *Battlefield Tourism: Pilgrimage and the Commemoration of the Great War in Britain, Australia and Canada, 1919–1939* (New York: Berg, 1998); George L. Mosse, *Fallen Soldiers: Reshaping the Memory of the World Wars* (New York: Oxford University Press, 1990). See also Rudy Koshar, *German Travel Cultures* (New York: Berg, 2000); Adrian Gregory, *The Silence of Memory: Armistice Day, 1919–1946* (Providence, RI: Berg, 1994); G. Kurt Piehler, "The War Dead and the Gold Star: American Commemoration of the First World War," in *Commemorations: The Politics of National Identity,* ed. John R. Gillis (Princeton, NJ: Princeton University Press, 1994), 168–85; Daniel J. Sherman, *The Construction of Memory in Interwar France* (Chicago: University of Chicago Press, 1999).

72. Gregory, *The Silence of Memory;* Piehler, "The War Dead and the Gold Star"; Sherman, *The Construction of Memory in Interwar France.*

73. Laurence Wylie, excerpts of letters to his mother, Maud Stout Wylie, who wrote to George E. Brinton, May 16, 1930, UD AR 68, folder 540.

74. Phebe Elizabeth Adams, diary entry, November 7, 1930, SC, box 2041.

75. Unknown author, UD AR 68, folder 540.

76. Frances Hurrey to her family, August 2, 1929, Frances Hurrey Philips Papers, Mount Holyoke College Archives and Special Collections, South Hadley, MA.

77. Dorothy Tebbets to her parents, November 11, 1925, SC, box 1994.

78. Katherine M. Pratt, excerpts from letters, UD AR 68, folder 539. The letter was probably written in 1929 since all the excerpts in this folder came from the 1929–30 group, and the "first excursion" probably occurred in the first part of the year.

79. Dorothy Tebbets to her parents, June 14, 1926, SC, box 1994.

80. AN AJ/16/6968, Association d'Accueil aux Etudiants des Etats-Unis, 14e Assemblée Générale, 17 Juin 1936. Rapport de la Secrétaire Générale, p. 7.

81. Office national des universités et écoles françaises, dispatch to the director of the Services des oeuvres françaises à l'étranger, May 17, 1932, in folder 0-160-3, 1932 Etats-Unis bourses, Ministère des Affaires Étrangères [MAE], carton 426, Section des services des oeuvres françaises à l'étranger, Ecoles, Etats-Unis, 1920–40.

82. AN AJ/16/6970, University of Delaware, 1930–36, Sebastien Charléty, draft of a letter. When George Brinton, the director of the Delaware Foreign Study Plan, sent a copy of the publication to Charléty, he wrote in the accompanying letter of April 9, 1930: "I hope that this little publication will impress you favorably, and that it will serve effectively to make known in America the education offered to foreigners at the Sorbonne." AN AJ/16/6970, University of Delaware, 1930–36. The published version of Charléty's letter appears in *Foreign Study Notes* 1 (December 1929–March 1930): 3.

83. AN AJ/16/6970, University of Delaware, 1930–36; UD AR 96 and 97, Delfor Alumni Association; SC JYA France, Association of Former Juniors in France, boxes 1133 and 1134.

84. W. A. Neilson, president of Smith College, "Educator Sees Wide Benefits in Study Abroad," New York *Herald Tribune,* August 16, 1931, located in UD AR 42, printed and duplicated material, vol. 2 scrapbook, 1929–54.

85. Walter Hullihen, "Present Status of the 'Junior Year Abroad,'" typed manuscript [printed in *French Review,* January 1928], UD AR 67, folder 522, p. 7.

86. Pierre Bourdieu, *Distinction: A Social Critique of the Judgement of Taste*, trans. Richard Nice (Cambridge, MA: Harvard University Press, 1984). On American students' (especially women's) sense of freedom and selfhood, see Peter G. Filene, *Him/Her/Self: Gender Identities in Modern America*, 3rd ed. (Baltimore: Johns Hopkins University Press, 1998), 143; Fass, *The Damned and the Beautiful*, 23 and ch. 5.

87. Joan W. Scott, "The Evidence of Experience," *Critical Inquiry* 17 (Summer 1991): 773–97.

88. "Reactions on Year in France," UD AT 67, folder 536, History of Anciens Elèves des Groupes Delaware en France 1923–36. It is worth noting that Beatrice F. Davis stated that her motivation for participating in the Delaware Foreign Study Plan in 1931 was a long-standing desire for a career in the Foreign Service. However, she claims that after she graduated from the University of Delaware, the Depression and a prohibition against hiring married women prevented her from fulfilling this goal. Beatrice F. Davis, oral interview.

89. UD AR 97, Delfor Alumni Association, folder 1637, Delfor Alumni Questionnaire, January 26, 1933, A-D. See also David A. Robertson, "The Junior Year Abroad: A Successful Experiment," *The Educational Record* 9 (January 1928): 32–45.

90. Ginny Stearns to Hélène Cattenès, July 16, 1926, SC JYA France, Neilson Papers, box 49.

91. Louise Whitney to Hélène Cattenès, July 19, 1926, Neilson Papers, SC JYA France, box 49.

92. Louis V. Blum, "Blum Gives Impressions of France; Foreign Study Student Writes to Review," *University of Delaware [Review]*, March 22, 1929, UD AR 42, Scrapbook, vol. 1.

93. "Excerpts taken from questionnaire to Groups I, II, III," UD AR 45, Operations File, Selected Papers, 1922–48.

94. Althea B. Avery, "The Junior Year in France," *Bryn Mawr Alumnae Bulletin* 15 (1935): 6.

95. Herbert H. Lank, oral interview by Myron L. Lazarus, August 20, 1970, UD AR 97, folder 1646.

96. Eleanor Daniels to her family, September 16, 1937, SC, box 2116.

97. Elizabeth Murphy, "Ten Years Ago the Juniors Went to France," *Smith Alumnae Quarterly* (May 1935): 241 (reproduced and located in Junior Year Abroad France 1927–present, SC, box 1132).

98. Benedict Anderson, *Imagined Communities: Reflections on the Origin and Spread of Nationalism*, rev. ed. (London: Verso, 1991).

99. Margaret White, "The Junior Year in France," *Modern Language Forum* 18 (April 1933): 131.

100. David Allan Robertson, "The Junior Year Abroad," *Educational Record* 7 (April 1926): 98–113; David A. Robertson, "The Junior Year Abroad: A Successful Experiment," *The Educational Record* 9 (January 1928): 32–45; Edwin C. Byam and Marine Leland, "American Undergraduates in France," *French Review* 3 (February 1930): 261–69; Ruth E. Young, "The Juniors Spend a Year Abroad," *American Association of University Women Journal* 31 (June 1938): 216–19; White, "The Junior Year in France"; Horatio Smith, "The Junior Year Abroad," *World Affairs* 96 (March 1933): 30–32; Roxana Holden, "Ten Years of Undergraduate Study Abroad," *Modern Language Journal* 19 (November 1934): 117–22; Paul Hazard, "Undergraduate Study in France," *Légion d'honneur* 4 (1935): 262–67. A more skeptical assessment of independent study abroad but not of the junior year abroad is Olaf Axelgaard, "Study Abroad: The American Scholastic Tourist Trade," *Harper's Magazine* 165 (June–November 1932): 696–709.

101. C. Robert Pace, *The Junior Year in France: An Evaluation of the University of Delaware–Sweet Briar College Program* (Syracuse, NY: Syracuse University Press, 1959), 16.

Chapter 4

Material from this chapter was published earlier as "American Girls and French *jeunes filles*: Negotiating National Identities in Interwar France," *Gender & History* 17 (August 2005): 325–53. Many thanks for the kind permission to reproduce it here.

1. Dorothy Tebbets to her parents, November 11, 1925, Smith College Archives [hereafter SC], box 1994.

2. Leila J. Rupp, *Worlds of Women: The Making of an International Women's Movement* (Princeton, NJ: Princeton University Press, 1997). See also Anne

Summers, "Critique. Gaps in the Record: Hidden Internationalisms," *History Workshop Journal* 52 (Autumn 2001): 217–27.

3. Emily S. Rosenberg, "Consuming Women: Images of Americanization in the 'American Century,'" *Diplomatic History* 23 (Summer 1999): 479–97; Lynne Frame, "Gretchen, Girl, Garçonne? Weimar Science and Popular Culture in Search of the Ideal New Woman," in *Women in the Metropolis: Gender and Modernity in Weimar Culture*, ed. Katharina von Ankum (Berkeley: University of California Press, 1997), 12–40; Mary Louise Roberts, *Civilization Without Sexes: Reconstructing Gender in Postwar France, 1917–1927* (Chicago: University of Chicago Press, 1994); Miriam Silverberg, "The Modern Girl as Militant," in *Recreating Japanese Women, 1600–1945*, ed. Gail Lee Bernstein (Berkeley: University of California Press, 1991), 239–66; "The Modern Girl Around the World," University of Washington Institute for Transnational Studies (2004), www.depts.washington.edu/its/moderngirl.htm.

4. In her consideration of how historians can most effectively use experience as evidence, Joan Scott proposes that they seek to understand how experience itself is constructed. She recommends that "historians take as their project *not* the reproduction and transmission of knowledge said to be arrived at through experience, but the analysis of the production of that knowledge." Joan W. Scott, "The Evidence of Experience," *Critical Inquiry* 17 (Summer 1991): 797.

5. In 1928–29 there were 270 American students enrolled in the Faculty of Letters of the University of Paris. Of those, 102 were men and 168 were women. "Faculté des Lettres. Rapport annuel du doyen, année scolaire 1928–1929," *Annales de l'Université de Paris* 3 (May–June 1930): 206.

6. For numbers of students, see Chapter 3, footnote 1. A list of alumni of the Delaware Foreign Study Plan indicates that 185 men and 532 women participated in the program from 1923 to 1939; however, this list does not include "special" students—for example, graduate students. Both Smith College and the University of Delaware started study abroad programs in Germany in the 1930s, but low enrollments caused them to merge into a consortium for study in Germany, and political tensions eventually caused a shift from Germany to Switzerland. Smith College also began programs in Spain and Italy after the success of the French venture, though they were smaller, and the war in Spain precipitated a move to Mexico. Trinity College in Washington, DC, started a small program in France in 1928 for women from Catholic colleges in the United States. "The Trinity College Group at the Sorbonne," *Foreign Study Notes* 1 (April–July 1930): 11.

7. "Statistique générale des étudiants de l'Université de Paris au 31 juillet 1932. . . ." *Annales de l'Université de Paris* 6 (November–December 1932): 575.

8. C. Robert Pace, *The Junior Year in France: An Evaluation of the University of Delaware—Sweet Briar College Program* (Syracuse, NY: Syracuse University Press, 1959), 16. See also Francis M. Rogers, *American Juniors on the Left Bank* (Sweet Briar, VA: Sweet Briar College, 1958), 16.

9. Martha Hanna, "French Women and American Men: 'Foreign' Students at the University of Paris, 1915–1925," *French Historical Studies* 22 (Winter 1999): 87–112.

10. Dorothy M. Brown, *Setting a Course: American Women in the 1920s* (Boston: Twayne Publishers, 1987), 133, 151; Susan Ware, *Holding Their Own: American Women in the 1930s* (Boston: Twayne Publishers, 1982), 56–60, 72. See article titled, "Many Americans Study French in College Towns. Prospective Pedagogues Now Flocking to France," *Chicago Tribune, European Edition,* Paris, June 16, 1922, p. 3, in AN AJ/16/6975. Relations avec les universités des Etats-Unis (suite) (1895–1960). See also Emma Gertrude Kunze, "Summer Study Abroad," *Modern Language Journal* 13 (February 1929): 353–59, with advice to teachers of Spanish, French, and German. Barbara Miller Solomon, *In the Company of Educated Women: A History of Women and Higher Education in America* (New Haven, CT: Yale University Press, 1985), 60, 81, ch. 9.

11. Paula S. Fass, *The Damned and the Beautiful: American Youth in the 1920s* (New York: Oxford University Press, 1977), ch. 5.

12. Diplomats and others serving in the French Ministry of Foreign Affairs noted that American women's colleges were more interested in student exchanges with France than were men's colleges or coed universities. "The majority of scholarships [for French students to study in the United States] are funded by women's colleges," wrote S. Léger of the Service des oeuvres françaises à l'étranger, section des écoles. Dispatch of June 13, 1932, to the Director of the Office National des Universités, Archives du Ministère des Affaires Etrangères, Services des oeuvres françaises à l'étranger 1912–1940 (Nantes), carton 426, folder 0-160-3.1932, Etats-Unis, Bourses [hereafter MAE with box and folder nos.].

13. Pierre Bourdieu, *La Distinction: Critique sociale du jugement* (Paris: Editions de minuit, 1979), 121.

14. Harvey Levenstein, *Seductive Journey: American Tourists in France from Jefferson to the Jazz Age* (Chicago: University of Chicago Press, 1998); William R. Keylor, "'How They Advertised France': The French Propaganda Campaign in the United States During the Breakup of the Franco-American Entente, 1918–1923," *Diplomatic History* 17 (Summer 1993): 351–73. By contrast, no evidence for gender differences in American views of France appears in Bertram M. Gordon, "The Decline of a Cultural Icon: France in American Perspective," *French Historical Studies* 22 (Fall 1999): 625–51.

15. Beatrice F. Davis, oral interview by Myron L. Lazarus, July 15, 1970, University of Delaware Archives [hereafter UD] AR 97, folder 1646.

16. Yvonne Knibiehler, et al., *De la pucelle à la minette: Les jeunes filles de l'âge classique à nos jours* (Paris: Temps Actuels, 1983); Susan Weiner, *Enfants Terribles: Youth and Femininity in the Mass Media in France, 1945–1968* (Baltimore: Johns Hopkins University Press, 2001), 2–8.

17. Siân Reynolds, *France Between the Wars: Gender and Politics* (London: Routledge, 1996), 92–118, 136–49; Roberts, *Civilization Without Sexes;* Edmée Charrier, *L'Evolution intellectuelle féminine*, thèse pour le doctorat en droit, Université de Paris, faculté de droit (Paris: Mechelinck, 1931).

18. James F. McMillan, *Housewife or Harlot: The Place of Women in French Society, 1870–1940* (New York: St. Martin's Press, 1981), 163–74; Eugen Weber, *The Hollow Years: France in the 1930s* (New York: W. W. Norton, 1994), 80–84.

19. Jacques Portes, *Une Fascination réticente: Les Etats-Unis dans l'opinion française* (Nancy: Presses universitaires de Nancy, 1990), ch. 9; Bernadette Galloux-Fournier, "Un Regard sur l'Amérique: Voyageurs français aux Etats-Unis (1919–1939)," *Revue d'histoire moderne et contemporaine* 37 (April–June 1990), 319; Roberts, *Civilization Without Sexes,* 9; Frame, "Gretchen, Girl, Garçonne?"

20. Fass, *The Damned and the Beautiful;* Brown, *Setting a Course,* 31–43.

21. Walter Hullihen, "Undergraduate Foreign Study for Credit Toward the American Baccalaureate Degree," *Educational Record* 5 (January 1924), 45; Raymond W. Kirkbride in Paris to Walter Hullihen in Newark, November 30, 1922, and March 2, 1923, UD AR 330 President's Office, Walter Hullihen. Series 2: Foreign Study Plan Correspondence, 1922–37.

22. Walter Hullihen to Raymond W. Kirkbride, January 11, 1923, and March 28, 1923, UD AR 330, Correspondence, 1922–37.

23. Rapport à M. le Doyen de la Faculté des lettres sur la réception des étudiants américains pendant la periode de démobilisation, submitted to the rector of the University of Paris on November 23, 1918, AN AJ/16/6973, Les étudiants américains à Paris pendant la guerre de 1916–18; 1918; 1936; Hanna, "French Women and American Men."

24. "Select Miss to Study in France: Wilmington Girl Wins First Foreign Study Group Honor at U of D," *Delmarva Star,* April 6, 1924, Clipping in UD AR 42 Scrapbooks.

25. Pace, *The Junior Year in France,* 16; UD, Foreign Study Plan Records, 1922–48.

26. Typed report dated May 22, 1929, located in folder, "Junior Year in France. 50 JYA France," SC JYA France, box 1132.

27. Madeleine Guilloton to W. A. Neilson, third report, December 18, 1927, SC JYA France, Neilson Papers, box 49.

28. "Règlement pour les jeunes filles," in UD AR 68, Mimeographed notices, 1926–48, folder 522. The closest thing to such restrictions on male behavior was a note from Director Raymond Kirkbride to President Walter Hullihen, March 5, 1923, on the three requirements for University of Delaware students: "the student will be expected to conduct himself as a gentleman at all times"; "he must work, and work hard"; "he must absolutely avoid speaking English." UD AR 330, President's Office—Walter Hullihen. Series 2: Foreign Study Plan Correspondence, 1922–37.

29. Mrs. Robert H. Richards, Jr., oral interview by Myron L. Lazarus, August 21, 1970, UD AR 97, folder 1646.

30. W. Emerson Wilson, oral interview by Myron L. Lazarus, August 9, 1970 (Wilson was a student in 1929–30), UD AR 97, folder 1646.

31. Notice No. 2a (To Women), n.d.; Notice No. 2b (To Men), n.d.; Notice no. 3a (To Women), June 1, 1931, UD AR 68, folders 550 and 545. It is worth noting that the Delaware Foreign Study Plan advised women to bring plenty of silk stockings with them, since French varieties were very expensive. No evidence exists as to whether Smith College students received the same advice. However, letters from several Smith College students begged their parents to mail them stockings, even to send them prewashed and enclosed, one by one, in an envelope in order to avoid paying customs duty.

32. William Allan Neilson, "When the President Went to France," *Smith Alumnae Quarterly* 17 (May 1926): 291.

33. Mary Louise Cahill to her family, September 6, 1936, SC, box 2110.

34. "A Chronicle of American Student Life in France," *Foreign Study Notes*, 1 (April–July 1930): 31.

35. Marie Claudia Holslag to her family, June 14, 1931, SC, box 2041.

36. Florence Elizabeth Bragdon to her family, November 3, 1929, SC, box 2029.

37. Florence Elizabeth Bragdon to her family, March 16, 1930, SC, box 2029.

38. Miriam Putnam Emerson to her parents, September 30, 1930, SC, box 2041.

39. [Report] no. 9, Second Semestre à Paris, Paris, le 15 Juin 1926, SC JYA France, box 1132.

40. [Report] no. 6, Novembre et Décembre à Paris, Paris, le 30 décembre 1925, SC JYA France, box 1132.

41. Diary from a woman student, November 12, 1927, UD AR 67, folder 524.

42. Minutes of the Foreign Study Committee meeting of January 30, 1929, UD AR 49 Operations File, folder 46.

43. Ibid.

44. Third report, December 18, 1927, SC JYA France, Neilson Papers, box 49.

45. Brown, *Setting a Course*, 138; Fass, *The Damned and the Beautiful*, 196.

46. Hélène Cattanès, "Vers d'autres horizons," *Mémento de l'année en France* by the Association of Former Juniors in France of Smith College, New York–Paris 1965, 11, SC JYA France, box 1133.

47. Alexis de Tocqueville, *Democracy in America*, trans. George Lawrence, ed. J. P. Mayer (Garden City, NY: Doubleday & Company, 1969), 590–92; Portes, *Une Fascination réticente*, ch. 9; Galloux-Fournier, "Un Regard sur l'Amérique," 319. See also Ralph Schor, *L'Opinion française et les étrangers en France, 1919–1939* (Paris: Publications de la Sorbonne, 1985), 163.

48. Florence Elizabeth Bragdon to her family, September 11, 1929, SC, box 2029.

49. Sarah Alice Johnston to her aunt and uncle, February 27, 1939, in "Sally Goes to France: Letters from a Junior Year, 1938–1939," ed. Ellen J. Maycock, 2003, typed manuscript.
50. Hélène Cattanès to Dean F. F. Benard, March 1, 1926, SC JYA France, box 1132, folder B49F5. According to student Dorothy Tebbets, the other students managed to persuade Cattanès to give the offenders two demerits but not send them home. Dorothy Tebbets to her parents, March 7, 1926, SC, box 1994.
51. Mary Louise Cahill to her parents, December 1, 1936, SC, box 2110.
52. Neilson, "When the President Went to France," 291.
53. Eleanor Daniels to her family, September 26, 1937, SC, box 2116.
54. Peter G. Filene, *Him/Her/Self: Gender Identities in Modern America*, 3rd ed. (Baltimore: Johns Hopkins University Press, 1998), 131–34; Solomon, *In the Company of Educated Women*, ch. 11; Brown, *Setting a Course*, 39–42; Ware, *Holding Their Own*, 60–80, 180–87; Helen Lefkowitz Horowitz, *Alma Mater: Design and Experience in the Women's Colleges from Their Nineteenth-Century Beginnings to the 1930s* (Boston: Beacon Press, 1984), 280–92; Roberts, *Civilization Without Sexes;* Reynolds, *France Between the Wars;* McMillan, *Housewife or Harlot*, 116–25; Lucien Romier, *Promotion de la femme* (Paris: Hachette, 1930); Charrier, *L'Evolution intellectuelle féminine*, 160–217.
55. Marian Sage Seewoster to her family, September 5, 1927, SC, box 2019.1.
56. Eleanor Daniels to her family, November 28, 1937, SC, box 2116.
57. Margaret Goddard to her family, November 7, 1935, SC, box 2106.
58. Raymonde Carroll, *Cultural Misunderstandings: the French-American Experience*, trans. Carol Volk (Chicago: University of Chicago Press, 1987).
59. Dorothy Tebbets to her parents, September 11, 1925, SC, box 1994.
60. Dorothy Tebbets to her parents, October 3, 1925, SC, box 1994.
61. W. Emerson Wilson, oral interview, UD AR 97, folder 1646.
62. Marian Sage Seewoster to her family, September 5, 1927, SC, box 2019.1.
63. Elizabeth Brown to her mother, excerpt of a letter in a letter from Harriet M. Brown, East Orange, NJ, to George Brinton, May 16, 1930, UD AR 68, folder 540.
64. Beth L. Bailey, *From Front Porch to Back Seat: Courtship in Twentieth-century America* (Baltimore: Johns Hopkins University Press, 1988), ch. 4; Peter N. Stearns, *Battleground of Desire: The Struggle for Self-Control in Modern America* (New York: New York University Press, 1999), esp. ch. 7. For an extensive analysis of American dating practices from a French perspective, see Eric Fassin, "Un Échange inégal: Sexualité et rites amoureux aux Etats-Unis," *Critique* 596–97 (January–February 1997): 48–65.
65. Beatrice F. Davis, oral interview.
66. Brown, *Setting a Course*, 143; Fass, *The Damned and the Beautiful*, ch. 6; Solomon, *In the Company of Educated Women*, 161. See also Ware, *Holding Their Own*, 62–63; Filene, *Him/Her/Self*, 140–41; Stearns, *Battleground of Desire*,

199–204, 227–28; Steven Seidman, *Romantic Longings: Love in America, 1830–1980* (New York: Routledge, 1991), 71, 94.

67. Eleanor Daniels to her family, October 19, 1937, SC, box 2116.

68. Fassin, "Un échange inégal," 50.

69. Mary Lynn Stewart, *For Health and Beauty: Physical Culture for Frenchwomen, 1880s–1930s* (Baltimore: Johns Hopkins University Press, 2001), 77.

70. Jean Elisabeth Pedersen, "Something Mysterious: Sex Education, Victorian Morality, and Durkheim's Comparative Sociology," *Journal of the History of the Behavioral Sciences* 34 (Spring 1998): 135–51; Anne-Marie Sohn, *Du premier baiser à l'alcove: La Sexualité des Français au quotidien (1850–1950)* (Paris: Aubier, 1996); Fabienne Casta-Rosaz, *Histoire du flirt: Les Jeux de l'innocence et de la perversité, 1870–1968* (Paris: Bernard Grasset, 2000), 31, pt. 2; Fassin, "Un Échange inégale," 50.

71. Casta-Rosaz, *Histoire du flirt*, 135–38; Dominique Desanti, *La Femme au temps des Années Folles* (Paris: Stock, 1984), 138–41.

72. Eleanor Daniels to her parents, October 19, 1937, SC, box 2116.

73. McMillan, *Housewife or Harlot*, 127–28; Romier, *Promotion de la femme*, 237–40.

74. Frances Hurrey to her family, November 4, 1929, from Frances Hurrey Philips Papers, Mount Holyoke College Archives and Special Collections, South Hadley, MA. Many thanks to Emily Brush for providing this source.

75. Sarah Alice Johnston to her family, December 3, 1938, in "Sally Goes to France."

76. Simone de Beauvoir, *Memoirs of a Dutiful Daughter*, trans. James Kirkup (New York: Harper & Row Publishers, 1958), 287. Annie Kriegel, who came from a petty bourgeois Jewish family and also grew up in Paris, wrote on the close supervision her family exercised over her brief courtship with an aspiring Ecole Polytechnique student during World War II. As a boarding student at the Ecole Normale Supérieure de Sèvres from 1945–47, Kriegel adhered to the school's strict rules governing the women students. Annie Kriegel, *Ce que j'ai cru comprendre* (Paris: Robert Laffont, 1991), 150, 286–88.

77. Eleanor Daniels to her family, January 2, 1938, SC, box 2116. See also Casta-Rosaz, *Histoire du flirt*, 138.

78. Sarah Alice Johnston to her family, April 24, 1939, in "Sally Goes to France."

79. Hilda Donahue to David A. Robertson, February 4, 1927, SC JYA France, Neilson Papers, box 49.

80. Delia Brown to Mademoiselle Cattenès, July 14, 1926, SC JYA France, Neilson Papers, box 49.

81. Mary Louise Cahill to her family, November 4, November 10, and November 17, 1936, SC, box 2110.

82. Eleanor Daniels to her family, October 10, 1937, SC, box 2116.

83. Louise Cruppi, "La Jeunesse universitaire féminine," *Annales politiques et littèraires* 84 (1925): 31–32.

84. Odette Pascaud, "Etudiantes de Paris," *Revue des deux mondes* 27 (May 15, 1935): 358.

85. Françoise Lelièvre and Claude Lelièvre, *Histoire de la scolarisation des filles* (Paris: Nathan, 1991), 131, 153.

86. Pascaud, "Etudiantes de Paris," 363; many newspaper clippings in the Dossier 370, Enseignement supérieur, of the Bibliothèque Marguerite Durand in Paris.

87. Carole Lécuyer, "Une nouvelle figure de la jeune fille," *Clio: Histoire, femmes et sociétés* 4 (1996): 166–76.

88. Marguerite d'Escola, "Un thé chez les étudiantes parisiennes," *Clio: Histoire, femmes et sociétés* 4 (1996): 202–14; reprinted from *La Revue belge*, 15 mai 1926 and annotated by Carole Lécuyer.

89. Pascaud, "Etudiantes de Paris," 375.

90. Beauvoir, *Memoirs of a Dutiful Daughter*, 287. Kriegel echoes the narrow focus on studies in her memoir of student life at the Ecole Normale Supérieure de Sèvres in 1945–47: "In the postwar years, 'chiader'—to work hard . . . was the primordial obligation." Kriegel, *Ce que j'a cru*, 290.

91. Beauvoir, *Memoirs of a Dutiful Daughter*, 272.

92. Lécuyer, "Une nouvelle figure de la jeune fille"; Jo Burr Margadant, *Madame le Professeur: Women Educators in the Third Republic* (Princeton, NJ: Princeton University Press, 1990).

93. Horowitz, *Alma Mater*, 147, 159–63, 169, xxiv; Solomon, *In the Company of Educated Women*, ch. 8; Lynn D. Gordon, *Gender and Higher Education in the Progressive Era* (New Haven, CT: Yale University Press, 1990), 190 and ch. 2.

94. Dorothy Tebbets to her parents, November 22, 1925, SC, box 1994.

95. Caroline Stabler to her family, November 29, 1925, SC, box 1990.

96. Eleanor Daniels to her family, November 14, 1937, SC, box 2116.

97. Z, "Examens de conscience," *Foreign Study Notes* 1 (August–November 1929): 43.

98. Hélène Cattanès, "Twenty-Five Years Ago: Thirty-Two Innocents Abroad," *Smith Alumnae Quarterly* 42 (1950): 74.

99. Schor, *L'Opinion française*, 163; Galloux-Fournier, "Un Regard sur l'Amérique," 319; Casta-Rosaz, *Histoire du flirt*, 183–85.

100. Laboulaye of the French embassy in the United States to Monsieur Tardieu, president of the council, Ministry of Foreign Affairs, dispatch of April 12, 1932, no. 22. MAE, Services des ouevres française à l'étranger 1912–40, Section des Ecoles, Etats-Unis, box 431, folder 0-161-3, 1932 Etats-Unis, Relations universitaires franco-américaines. Du Verneuil, Service des oeuvres françaises à l'étranger to director of Office national des universités, June 13, 1932; Charles Petit-Dutaillis, reply, May 17, 1932, MAE, Services des ouevres française à

l'étranger 1912–40, Section des Ecoles, Etats-Unis, box 426, folder 0-160-3, 1932, Etats-Unis, Bourses.

101. Ibid. Sebastian Charléty, rector of the University of Paris, wrote at least two addresses on the benefits of American junior year abroad programs. "Etudiants américains à Paris," draft of a speech or article, AN AJ/16/6975; "Aux Etudiants de la section d'études à l'étranger de l'Université de Delaware," *Foreign Study Notes* 1 (December 1929–March 1930): 3. See also letters of appreciation from former students to the Association d'Accueil aux Etudiants des Etats-Unis, AN AJ/16/6968.

102. SC JYA France, Association of Former Juniors in France A-Meet and Mem-Z, boxes 1133–34; UD, Delfor Alumni Association, AR 96–97.

103. Elizabeth Murphy, "Ten Years Ago the Juniors Went to France," *Smith Alumnae Quarterly* (May 1935): 239–44 (reproduced and located in JYA France 1927–present, SC, box 1132).

104. Roxana Holden, "Ten Years of Undergraduate Study Abroad," *Modern Language Journal* 19 (November 1934): 117–18.

105. See also replies to a questionnaire sent to Delaware Foreign Study Plan alumni in 1933, UD AR 97, folders 1637–40; Betty Klinefelter, "Where O, Where Are the 1930 Juniors-in-France?" *Smith Alumnae Quarterly* 21 (July 1930): 416–17.

106. Aureta E. Lewis, "Letters from a Junior in France, 1937–1938," printed pamphlet, UD AR 44, folder C15.

107. She said: "Well, I never made it. Actually, when I got out of college in '33, it was the depths of the Depression, there were no openings whatsoever in the foreign service in Washington." She took the foreign service exams and got on a waiting list, and then she married. "And then they were not making appointments for married women." Beatrice F. Davis, interview.

108. Murphy, "Ten Years Ago," 241. See also Delfor Alumni Questionnaire, January 26, 1933, UD AR 97, folders 1638–40.

109. Ginny Stearns, in response to Hélène Cattanès's request for an answer to the question: What did you gain from a year in France? July 16, 1926, SC, Neilson Papers, box 49.

110. Summers, "Critique: Gaps in the Record"; Rosenberg, *Spreading the American Dream*.

111. Althea B. Avery, "The Junior Year in France," *Bryn Mawr Alumnae Bulletin* 15 (1935): 6.

112. Rogers, *American Juniors on the Left Bank*; Pace, *The Junior Year in France*; John A. Garraty and Walter Adams, *From Main Street to the Left Bank: Students and Scholars Abroad* (East Lansing: Michigan State University Press, 1959); responses to a questionnaire sent to Delaware Foreign Study Plan alumni in 1933, UD AR 97, folders 1637–40.

113. Eric J. Leed, *The Mind of the Traveler: From Gilgamesh to Global Tourism* (New York: Basic Books, 1991), ch. 8; Sidonie Smith, *Moving Lives: Twentieth-century Women's Travel Writing* (Minneapolis: University of Minnesota Press, 2001), ch. 1; Frances Bartkowski, *Travelers, Immigrants, Inmates: Essays in Estrangement* (Minneapolis: University of Minnesota Press, 1995).

114. Marie Holslag to her sister [orig. in French], March 3, 1931, SC, box 2041.

115. Marie Holslag to her family, July 12, 1931, SC, box 2041.

116. Caroline Stabler to her parents, October 3, 1925, SC, box 1990.

117. Dorothy Tebbets to her parents, November 17, 1925, SC, box 1994.

118. Eleanor Daniels to her family, December 19, 1937, SC, box 2116. In a letter of August 1937, Daniels wrote: "It really is awfully good for me to be over here alone—I have had too little experience and am so dumb about doing things. . . . I do think I am slowly learning how to take care of myself."

119. René de Messières, cultural consul in New York, to the minister of Foreign Affairs, General Direction of Cultural Relations, March 18, 1948, MAE, Direction générale des relations culturelles, scientifiques et techniques, Enseignement, 1948–59, Etats-Unis, 512, Bourses, étudiants, échanges, stages, 1948–49. Although this particular passage referred to the Sweet Briar program, his letter of January 12, 1948, made similar requests for support for the Smith College Junior Year in France.

Chapter 5

1. Liping Bu, *Making the World Like Us: Education, Cultural Expansion, and the American Century* (Westport, CT: Praeger, 2003), 24–25, 145–48; Frank A. Ninkovich, *The Diplomacy of Ideas: United States Foreign Policy and Cultural Relations, 1938–1950* (New York: Cambridge University Press, 1981).

2. Irwin M. Wall, *The United States and the Making of Postwar France, 1945–1954* (New York: Cambridge University Press, 1991); Jean-Pierre Rioux, *The Fourth Republic, 1944–1958*, trans. Godfrey Rogers (Cambridge: Cambridge University Press; Paris: Editions de la Maison des Sciences de l'Homme, 1987); Gérard Bossuat, *La France, l'aide américaine et la construction européenne, 1944–1954* (Paris: Comité pour l'histoire économique et financière de la France, 1992), vol. 1. See also Detlef Junker, "Introduction: Politics, Security, Economics, Culture, and Society—Dimensions of Transatlantic Relations," in *The United States and Germany in the Era of the Cold War, 1945–1990*, vol. 1, ed. Detlef Junker (Washington, DC: German Historical Institute; New York: Cambridge University Press, 2004), 1–28.

3. Frank Costigliola, *France and the United States: The Cold Alliance Since World War II* (New York: Twayne Publishers, 1992); Brian Angus McKenzie,

Remaking France: Americanization, Public Diplomacy, and the Marshall Plan (New York: Berghahn Books, 2005).

4. Giles Scott-Smith, *Networks of Empire: The U.S. State Department's Foreign Leader Program in the Netherlands, France, and Britain 1950–70* (Brussells: P.I.E. Peter Lang, 2008); Bu, *Making the World Like Us*.

5. Similarly, Christopher Endy notes that after World War II, governments and civilians involved in tourist industries in France and the United States found American tourism in France beneficial to both countries; it signaled the United States' wealth and power through the democratization of overseas tourism and affirmed French cultural preeminence because France was as a favored tourist destination. Christopher Endy, *Cold War Holidays: American Tourism in France* (Chapel Hill: University of North Carolina Press, 2004).

6. Alain Dubosclard, *L'Action culturelle de la France aux Etats-Unis, de la Première Guerre mondiale à la fin des années 1960*, thèse d'Histoire, Université Paris 1—Panthéon Sorbonne, November 2002.

7. Account of a spring banquet of the Association of Former Juniors, May 17, 1943, in *Le Trait d'Union*, printed pamphlet, September 1943, SC, Junior Year Abroad, France, Association of Former Juniors in France, A—Meet, box 1133.

8. Beatrice Howell to Mrs. D. C. Stapleton, June 8, 1944, SC, Junior Year Abroad, France, Association of Former Juniors in France, A-Meet, box 1133.

9. *Le Trait d'Union*, February 1946; short document dated February 5, 1944, titled, "Association of Former Juniors in France of Smith College," SC, Junior Year Abroad, France, Association of Former Juniors in France, Mem-Z, box 1134.

10. Carbon copy of a report on the junior year in France program, 1947, UD AR 330 President's Office, Walter Hullihen. Series 2: Foreign Study Plan correspondence 1922–37, vol. 1; UD AR 448, President's Office William S. Carlson, 1946–48, vol. 19, 1946–47.

11. "Brief Report on the Delaware Foreign Study Plan, prepared for the Committee on Foreign Studies, May 13, 1948," UD AR 448, vol. 20, 1947–48; "Report on the Foreign Study Plan Presented to President William S. Carlson by the Chairman of the Committee on Foreign Study, July 1, 1946," UD AR 334, Hullihen Papers, 1939–48; "Committee on Foreign Study Suggested Outline of Discussion at the Meeting of October 18, 1944," and additional meeting minutes in UD AR 49, folder 46; several letters between William S. Carlson and Martha B. Lucas, 1947, UD AR 334, President's Office, Walter Hullihen, 1938; 1939–48, vol. 1939–48.

12. American Paris Study Center, Special Course for American Soldier-Students under the patronage of the Sorbonne, June 15, 1945–March 31, 1946; Report of M. Charles Cestre, director of the Course, Sorbonne Archives, folder: Seconde guerre mondiale, Fonctionnement, Cours de français pour armées alliées, 1945–46. This folder was intended for transfer to the National Archives at Fontainebleau in fall 2004. See also General Joseph T. McNarney to

Monsieur Roussy, rector of the University of Paris, February 25, 1946, in the same folder.

13. Harvey Levenstein, *We'll Always Have Paris: American Tourists in France Since 1930* (Chicago: University of Chicago Press, 2004), 84–93; Costigliola, *France and the United States*, 39–42; Rioux, *The Fourth Republic*, 8; Wall, *The United States and the Making of Postwar France*, 37; Alice Kaplan, *The Interpreter* (New York: Free Press, 2005).

14. Francis Lacoste, chargé d'affaires de France aux Etats-Unis to Georges Bidault, ministre des Affaires Etrangères, dispatch of July 30, 1945, Sorbonne Archives, folder: Seconde guerre mondiale, Fonctionnement, Cours de français pour armées alliées, 1945–46. See also Richard Pells, *Not Like Us: How Europeans Have Loved, Hated, and Transformed American Culture Since World War II* (New York: Basic Books, 1997), 22–31.

15. Joseph T. McNarney to Roussy, February 25, 1946, Sorbonne Archives, Seconde guerre mondiale. Fonctionnement. Cours de français pour armées alliés, 1945–46.

16. "Veterans' Education in France" by Major Ian F. Fraser, in AN AJ/16/6973, Etudiants américains à Paris pendant la guerre de 1916–18; Reid Hall correspondence, etc.; in the same location, see "Le Centre universitaire américain: Facteur essentiel du rapprochement culturel franco-américain"; Keith W. Olson, *The G.I. Bill, the Veterans, and the Colleges* (Lexington: University Press of Kentucky, 1974), 17.

17. René de Messières to the minister of Foreign Affairs, General Direction of Cultural Relations, January 12, 1948, Archives of the Ministry of Foreign Affairs [hereafter MAE], Direction générale des relations culturelles, scientifiques et techniques, Enseignement, 1948–59, Etats-Unis, 512, Bourses, étudiants, échanges, stages 1948–49, file: 1948.

18. Albert Chambon to Henri Bonnet, December 30, 1950, forwarded from Bonnet to Robert Schuman, minister of Foreign Affairs, General Direction of Cultural Relations, January 12, 1951, file: Etats-Unis 163-3, 1951, MAE, Paris, Direction Générale des Relations Culturelles, 1948–59, Ensiegnement, Etats-Unis, 513, 163.3, Bourses.

19. René de Messières to the minister of Foreign Affairs, General Direction of Cultural Relations, March 18, 1948, MAE, Direction générale des relations culturelles, scientifiques et techniques, Enseignement, 1948–59, Etats-Unis, 512, Bourses, étudiants, échanges, stages 1948–49, file: 1948.

20. R. John Matthew, *Twenty-five Years on the Left Bank*, n.p., n.d. [probably 1973], 14–17.

21. Joseph E. Barker, director, Junior Year Abroad, Sweet Briar College, to Jean Sarrailh, rector, University of Paris, including catalogue from Sweet Briar College, February 25, 1948, AN AJ/16/6971, Relations avec les universités étrangères, Etats-Unis (1895–1960), file on Sweet Briar College, 1948–55.

22. House Committee on Foreign Affairs, *International Office of Education: Hearings Before the Committee on Foreign Affairs*, 79th Cong., 1st sess., 1945; House Committee on Foreign Affairs, *Interchange of Knowledge and Skills Between People of the United States and Peoples of Other Countries: Hearings Before the Committee on Foreign Affairs*, 79th Cong., 1st and 2d sess., 1945 and 1946.

23. House Committee on Expenditures in the Executive Departments, *Disposal of Surplus Property Abroad*, report prepared by Mr. Manasco, 79th Cong., 2d sess., 1946; Arthur Power Dudden and Russell R. Dynes, eds., *The Fulbright Experience, 1946–1986: Encounters and Transformations* (New Brunswick, NJ: Transaction Books, 1987), 1.

24. Walter Johnson and Francis J. Colligan, *The Fulbright Program: A History* (Chicago: University of Chicago Press, 1965), 12–14.

25. J. William Fulbright, interview by Leonard Sussman, 1991, in Leonard R. Sussman, *The Culture of Freedom: The Small World of Fulbright Scholars* (Lanham, MD: Rowman & Littlefield Publishers, 1992), 55–56.

26. From the *Journal Officiel*, January 23, 1949, in *Dix années d'échanges Fulbright, 1949–1959*, printed pamphlet by Lucien Jambrun, loaned by him to the author, p. 6.

27. Typed explanation of the Fulbright Law and the agreement between France and the United States, in a file folder titled, "Loi Fulbright. Affiches 1948"; Direction Générale des relations culturelles, No. 1620C/1.AA, to French ambassador in Washington, April 23, 1948, file: "Etats Unis 1948," MAE (Paris), Direction générale des relations culturelles, scientifiques et techniques, Cabinet du Directeur général, 1948–68, Enseignement, 1948–61, Etats-Unis, 509, Affaires générales, 3.163.1; Johnson and Colligan, *The Fulbright Program*, 115. The Ministry of Foreign Affairs appointed the six French members of the Commission.

28. Untitled, undated [probably early 1970s], typed manuscript by Lucien Jambrun, loaned by him to the author, pp. 2–3; Johnson and Colligan, *The Fulbright Program*, 31–33.

29. *Dix années d'échanges Fulbright, 1949–1959*, printed pamphlet by Lucien Jambrun, 42. Figures vary slightly in different documents located in the archives of the Franco-American Commission in Paris.

30. Clipping titled, "Quand M. Yvon Delbos se fait controler par l'ambassadeur d'Amérique," *L'Humanité*, May 1949 [no date]. The article claims that, "American 'professors' and 'students' are, for the most part, as every informed man knows, current or future agents of the American information services." File: "Bourses Fulbright, 1949–1958," AN AJ/16/6974, Comité de l'Université de Paris pour les échanges avec les grandes universités américaines, 1948–53.

31. Jean Baillou to E. Audra, recteur d'Académie, Office National des Universités, June 17, 1948, no. 1625 RC3b, MEA, Direction générale des relations culturelles, scientifiques et techniques, Enseignement, 1948–59, Etats-Unis, 512, Bourses, étudiants, échanges, stages, 1948–49.

32. Chairman, United States Advisory Commission on Educational Exchanges, Department of State, "Sixth Semiannual Report on Education Exchange Activities," January 8, 1952, House document No. 321, MEA, Amérique 1952–63—Etats-Unis, 539, questions culturelles, 9-11-1. A report proposing an American University Center in Paris enumerates the benefits of exposing the French to American academics and academic practices: "If one accepts the rather obvious premise that a country is best understood and liked by those who have visited or know about it through a qualified friendly medium, it can be claimed that France has many more friends in the U.S. than the U.S. has in France since France has sent and we have brought many professors to this country to inform us about herself on the one hand, and on the other she has educated and received as guests thousands of our students and hundreds of thousands of travelers, while the reverse of this is not true." "Report on the Proposal to Establish an American University Center in Paris," National Archives and Records Administration [hereafter NARA], R659, Stack 250 Decimal file 811.42751, 1945–49, pp. 5–6.

33. Dispatch of December 29, 1951, Supplement to USIE Semi-Annual Evaluation Report for Period June 1, 1951–December 1, 1951, NARA, 511.51/8-51, box 2384, p. 6. The report also stated, "There can be little doubt that, whatever the merits—and there are many—of sending Americans to France, it is infinitely more important to send French citizens to the United States. And this, of course, is where, by its very nature, the Fulbright program is weakest." The author recommended additional, private funding as the means to maintain the hard-won near parity of exchange persons.

34. Paris to the secretary of state, telegram, September 8, 1952, NARA, 511.51/1-252; 511.51/12-3052, box 2385.

35. U.S. Embassy in Paris to the Department of State, January 13, 1953, from the "USIS Semi-Annual Evaluation Report for Period June 1–November 30, 1952," NARA, 511.51/1-1353, box 2386, p. 31.

36. Paris to Department of State, July 6, 1951, NARA, 511.51/7-651, box 2384. This report also indicates that for academic year 1950–51, 227 French students, scholars, teachers, and researchers went to the United States on Fulbright grants, while 312 Americans went to France.

37. Johnson and Colligan, *The Fulbright Program*, 69. This appears to be a quote from the Board, though no source is offered.

38. Ibid., 71–83.

39. American Embassy in Paris to the Department of State, August 18, 1955, "Educational Exchange: Semi-Annual Report on the International Exchange Program, January 1, 1955–June 30,1955." NARA, 511.513/8-1855 France General #4, p. 4. The report later mentioned an increase in unnamed problems with American students in France, attributing them to students' immaturity and recommending that screening must address this issue better.

40. Henri Bonnet, French ambassador to the United States, to Robert Schuman, minister of Foreign Affairs, December 31, 1952, no. 5767/RC, General Direction of Cultural Relations, MEA, Paris, Amérique 1952–63, Etats-Unis, 540, Relations culturelles 9-11-2.

41. Minister of Foreign Affairs to Henri Bonnet, French ambassador to the United States, April 4, 1952, no. 1255, MAE, Paris, Amérique 1952–63, Etats-Unis, 540, Relations culturelles 9-11-2.

42. Yves-Henri Nouailhat, "Aspects de la politique culturelle des Etats-Unis à l'égard de la France de 1945 à 1950," *Relations internationales* 25 (Spring 1981): 87–111.

43. Boxes labeled, "Reid Hall Press Books and unclassified material" and "Reid Hall—Correspondence, Minutes, Rapports, 1917–1950," in Reid Hall, 4, rue de Chevreuse, Paris. I am grateful to Danielle Haase-Dubosc, director of Reid Hall, for graciously allowing me access to this material.

44. Miriam Halbert to her mother, October and November 1947, copies in author's possession. Many thanks to Miriam Halbert Bales for sharing her letters and her memories.

45. Martha Churchill to her parents and brother, November 14, 1948, SC, box 2172.

46. Laura Sherman [pseudonym], telephone interview by author, September 15, 2004.

47. Arndt, "Tilting at Myths," in Dudden and Dynes, *The Fulbright Experience*, 42.

48. Folder: Westerburg, Sister Anne Louise [pseudonym], in file: U.S. Students [19]63–64, Archives of the Franco-American Commission, Paris.

49. "What the Year Has Meant to Me," *American Association of University Women Journal* 39 (Summer 1946): 215. She also stated: "Those fellowships are the best publicity that can be made for your country and at the same time for France." Ibid., 216.

50. Dorothy W. Woodruff, "French Students Here from Wartime France," *Smith Alumnae Quarterly* 37 (February 1946): 67.

51. Richard Kuisel, *Seducing the French: The Dilemma of Americanization* (Berkeley: University of California Press, 1993), 16–17. Philippe Roger asserts that by the end of World War I, anti-Americanism in France was in fact a cumulative discourse since the late eighteenth century that was so pervasive that it actually shaped particular events in Franco-American relations, rather than being caused by them. Nonetheless, he acknowledges that even in the present (2002), "anti-Americanism remains less secure in the country's popular strata than with intellectuals." Philippe Roger, *The American Enemy: A Story of French Anti-Americanism*, trans. Sharon Bowman (Chicago: University of Chicago Press, 2005), 450. Roger's book addresses French anti-Americanism as a discourse; by contrast, I seek to understand it in individual transnational relations.

52. Laura Sherman, telephone interview by author, September 15, 2004.

53. Mary Bishop Coan, telephone interview by author, notes, January 6, 2003.

54. Barbara Nosanow, telephone interview by author, September 18, 2004.

55. Mary Ann Hoberman, telephone interview by author, September 10, 2004.

56. Anne Rittershofer to her family, October 29, 1956, SC, box 2214. Many thanks to FlorenceMae Waldron for providing the citation for this source.

57. David O. Levine, *The American College and the Culture of Aspiration, 1915–1940* (Ithaca, NY: Cornell University Press, 1986), 215–18; Christopher J. Lucas, *American Higher Education: A History* (New York: St. Martin's Griffin, 1994), ch. 7.

58. Helen Lefkowitz Horowitz, *Campus Life: Undergraduate Cultures from the End of the Eighteenth Century to the Present* (New York: Alfred A. Knopf, 1987).

59. Burton J. Bledstein, *The Culture of Professionalism: The Middle Class and the Development of Higher Education in America* (New York: W. W. Norton & Company, 1976).

60. Didier Fischer, *L'Histoire des étudiants en France de 1945 à nos jours* (Paris: Flammarion, 2000).

61. Jean-Marie Domenach, "Les Etudiants," 20th year special issue, *Esprit* (April 1952): 529.

62. Jean-Marie Domenach, "Conclusion," 20th year special issue, *Esprit* (April 1952): 677–78.

63. "La Jeunesse de France parle," special issue, *Arts, Spectacles* 608 (February 27–March 5, 1957): 1, 7.

64. "Une génération éprise d'efficacité et de sérieux renie l'intellectualisme," *Arts, Spectacles* 611 (March 20–26, 1957): 9.

65. "Sommes-nous américanisés?" special issue, *Arts, Spectacles* 613 (April 3–9, 1957): 6.

66. James Donnedieu, "Quand américains et français échangent maîtres et professeurs," *Rapports France-Etats-Unis* 42 (September 1950): 39.

67. "Enquête sur les problèmes d'enseignement en France et aux Etats-Unis," *Bulletin de l'Association amicale universitaire France-Amérique* [typed, mimeographed booklet], Octobre 1956, pp. 1–23, NARA, R659, Records of Plan and Development 1955–60, Lot 62D 321, box 13, file: Unclassified Effectiveness, 1957.

68. Micheline Jammes, "Etudiante aux USA," *Bulletin de l'Association amicale universitaire France-Amérique* (May 1956): 14–16.

69. Bernard Poll, "De l'autre côté de la barrière," *Rives. Bulletin de l'Association amicale universitaire France-Amérique* 9 (April 1959): 22.

70. Stanley Karnow, *Paris in the Fifties* (New York: Times Books, Random House, 1997), 12. He noted later that he spent much of his time "with my American chums, most of whom were riding the GI Bill and studying—or pretending to study—such subjects as art, literature, ballet, even haute cuisine" (19).

71. Henriette Nizan, "Quand la jeunesse américaine vient respirer l'air de Paris," *Rapports France-Etats-Unis* 42 (September 1950): 47.

72. Olson, *The G.I. Bill*, 49–54. Olson indicates that between 1945 and 1955, 2,232,000 veterans were educated on the GI Bill, and of that number 64,728 were women. He does not indicate how many studied abroad (43).

73. Ernest O. Hauser, "G.I. Jim's in Love with Paris," *Saturday Evening Post* 222 (August 6, 1949): 48.

74. Martha Churchill to her family, January 18, 1949, SC, box 2172.

75. Nizan, "Quand la jeunesse américaine vient respirer l'air de Paris," 45.

76. Matthew, *Twenty-five Years on the Left Bank*, 16–17.

77. Miriam Halbert to her mother, January 20, 1948, in author's possession.

78. Laura Sherman, interview.

79. Mary Ann Horenstein, telephone interview by author, September 16, 2004.

80. Mary Bishop Coan, telephone interview by author, October 13, 2003.

81. Elizabeth Cannon to her family, December 3, 1949, and May 6, 1950, among others, copies in author's possession. I am grateful to Elizabeth Cannon Simmons for sending me the letters she wrote from France and Europe to her family while she studied abroad and allowing me to copy them.

82. Elizabeth Cannon to her mother and family, February 23 and March 24 and 31, 1950, copies in author's possession.

83. Elizabeth Cannon to her mother and family, June 19, 1950, copy in author's possession.

84. Martha Churchill wrote to her family of her friend Molly's romance with a French student she had met at the Institut des Sciences Politiques, indicating that Molly did not want her own parents to know of the liaison. Martha Churchill to her family, March 10, 1949, SC, box 2172. Several women on the Smith group of 1949–50 mentioned classmates with foreign boyfriends, and an engagement of one in the group to a future French president, Valéry Giscard d'Estaing, though this relationship ended before the marriage took place. Cynthia Bartlett Barnett, interview by author, September 26, 2004; Mary Bishop Coan, interview by author, January 6, 2003; Helen Davidson [pseudonym], interview, October 13, 2004; Margaret Home Chapin [pseudonym], interview by author, October 18, 2004, and others.

85. Miriam Halbert to her mother, August 5, 1948, in author's possession. Similarly, Richard T. Arndt wrote of the many things he learned from living in France as a Fulbright researcher in 1949–50, including this statement about his

professors at the University of Dijon: "They lived a provincial French version of the life of the mind, they lived it with genuine style and in it found a peculiar kind of richness." Arndt, "Tilting at Myths," 48.

86. Thomas Page Smith, "I Saw Your Daughter in Paris," *Smith Alumnae Quarterly* 40 (February 1949): 85.

87. Nizan, "Quand la jeunesse américaine vient respirer l'air de Paris," 45–50.

88. Michel Y. Roy, "Impressions d'un interne," *Rives. Bulletin de l'Association amicale universitaire France-Amérique* (February 1956): 12.

89. Department of State translation of selected portions of "Voyage aux Etats-Unis et au Canada" graduating class of the Ecole nationale supérieure d'électrotechnique, d'électronique et d'hydraulique de Toulouse, July 18–August 26, 1958, p. 9.

90. Ibid., 6–7.

91. Ibid., 10, 14–15, 21–22, and in original French version, 9.

92. "Etudiants américains à l'étranger," *Rives. Bulletin de l'Association amicale universitaire France-Amérique* 1 (April 1957): 14–19, in NARA, R659, Records of Plans and Development Staff, 1955–60, Lot 62D, box 321; John T. Gullahorn and Jeanne E. Gullahorn, "American Objectives in Study Abroad," *Journal of Higher Education* 29 (1958): 369–74.

93. Gullahorn and Gullahorn, "American Objectives," 369, 374.

94. John A. Garraty and Walter Adams, *From Main Street to the Left Bank: Students and Scholars Abroad* (East Lansing: Michigan State University Press, 1959), 137–47.

95. John T. Gullahorn and Jeanne E. Gullahorn, "American Students in France: A Perspective on Cultural Interchange," *Rives. Bulletin de l'Association amicale universitaire France-Amérique* 9 (April 1959): 4.

96. Garraty and Adams, *From Main Street to the Left Bank*, 173–81; Francis M. Rogers, *American Juniors on the Left Bank* (Sweet Briar, VA: Sweet Briar College, 1958), 23; C. Robert Pace, *The Junior Year in France: An Evaluation of the University of Delaware-Sweet Briar College Program* (Syracuse, NY: Syracuse University Press, 1959), 18–21.

97. Gullahorn and Gullahorn, "Etudiants américains à l'étranger," 16.

98. Ibid., 18.

99. Ibid., 19.

100. Gullahorn and Gullahorn, "American Students in France," 5.

101. Pace, *The Junior Year in France*, 26–27.

102. Ibid., 45–46.

103. Ibid., 26, 44, 48–49.

104. *Le Trait d'Union*, May 1953, SC, Junior Year Abroad, France, Association of Former Juniors in France, Mem-Z, box 1134, folder: JYA France, AFJF: publications, Trait d'Union (Bound Copies), 1938–65.

105. Pace, *The Junior Year in France*, 68–69.

106. For an elaboration of difference in the context of globalization, see Arjun Appadurai, *Modernity at Large: Cultural Dimensions of Globalization* (Minneapolis: University of Minnesota Press, 1996).

Chapter 6

1. Paul Benhamou, interview by author, April 20, 2005, in West Lafayette, IN. *Pied noir*, literally "black foot," is a pejorative term for French citizens who migrated to France from Algeria after Algerian independence.

2. Elizabeth Cobbs Hoffman, *All You Need Is Love: The Peace Corps and the Spirit of the 1960s* (Cambridge, MA: Harvard University Press, 1998).

3. Jeremi Suri, *Power and Protest: Global Revolution and the Rise of Détente* (Cambridge, MA: Harvard University Press, 2003).

4. Ronald Fraser, et al., *1968: A Student Generation in Revolt* (New York: Pantheon Books, 1988); Arthur Marwick, *The Sixties: Cultural Revolution in Britain, France, Italy, and the United States, c. 1958–c. 1974* (New York: Oxford University Press, 1998).

5. Frank Costigliola, *France and the United States: The Cold Alliance Since World War II* (New York: Twayne Publishers, 1992), ch. 4; Charles Cogan, *Oldest Allies, Guarded Friends: The United States and France Since 1940* (Westport, CT: Praeger, 1994), ch. 6.

6. Frank Costigliola, "Kennedy, de Gaulle, and the Challenge of Consultation," Lloyd Gardner, "Lyndon Johnson and de Gaulle," and Anne Sa'adah, "Idées Simples and Idées Fixes: De Gaulle, the United States, and Vietnam," in *De Gaulle and the United States: A Centennial Reappraisal*, ed. Robert O. Paxton and Nicholas Wahl (Providence, RI: Berg, 1994), chs. 8, 11, and 13.

7. Cogan, *Oldest Allies*; James Chace and Elizabeth Malkin, "The Mischief-Maker: the American Media and de Gaulle, 1964–68," in Paxton and Wahl, *De Gaulle and the United States*, ch. 17.

8. Costigliola, *France and the United States*, 142–43.

9. Marwick, *The Sixties*.

10. UNESCO, *Statistics of Students Abroad, 1962–1968. Where They Go, Where They Come From, What They Study. Statistiques des étudiants à l'étranger* (Paris: UNESCO, 1972), 19–20, 24–25, 27, 43.

11. Although the position of assistant secretary of state for Educational and Cultural Affairs continued until 1978, the first holder of this office, Philip H. Coombs, was unable to fulfill the goal of making cultural relations an important part of U.S. foreign policy. The reasons for this failure included inadequate funding, disagreement within the Department of State and the U.S. Congress over the value of cultural exchange versus propaganda, and the Vietnam War. Frank Ninkovich, "U.S. Information Policy and Cultural

Diplomacy," *Headline Series: Foreign Policy Association* 308 (Fall 1994): 28–30; Randolph Wieck, *Ignorance Abroad: American Educational and Cultural Foreign Policy and the Office of Assistant Secretary of State* (Westport, CT: Praeger, 1992), 28–29, 123–32.

12. Institute of International Education, *Open Doors: Report on International Educational Exchange,* 1960–1970.

13. Harvey Levenstein, who has researched American tourists in France from the 1930s to the present, asserts that self-actualization became a paramount objective of youth travel in the late 1960s and 1970s. He argues that the particular attraction of Paris or France as a site for cultural improvement or sexual adventure declined, because the process of discovering oneself, usually in the company of other traveling youth, was more important than a specific location. Harvey Levenstein, *We'll Always Have Paris: American Tourists in France Since 1930* (Chicago: University of Chicago Press, 2004), chs. 11–12. Christopher Endy notes that in the early 1960s, France was the top European destination for American tourists. Later in the decade, diplomatic tensions in Franco-American relations and a French reputation for rudeness affected American public opinion, but de Gaulle's efforts to modernize the French tourism industry were effective in the long term. Christopher Endy, *Cold War Holidays: American Tourism in France* (Chapel Hill: University of North Carolina Press, 2004), ch. 7.

14. William McCormack, "New Directions in Study Abroad: Opportunities for Students in the Professional Schools," *Journal of Higher Education* 37 (October 1966): 369–76.

15. Edward J. Durnall, "Study-abroad Programs: A Critical Survey," *Journal of Higher Education* 38 (November 1967): 450–53.

16. Roger D. Masters, "Toward Improved Franco-American University Exchanges," *International Educational and Cultural Exchange* 7 (Winter 1972): 7–15; Ruth H. Purkaple, "American Students Abroad," *International Educational and Cultural Exchange* 7 (Winter 1972): 67–81.

17. Dennison Nash, "The Personal Consequences of a Year of Study Abroad," *Journal of Higher Education* 47 (March–April 1976): 191–203.

18. Jeanne E. Gullahorn and John T. Gullahorn, "American Students Abroad: Professional versus Personal Development," *Annals of the American Academy of Political and Social Science* 368 (November 1966): 43–59.

19. Annual Report Franco-American Commission for Educational Exchange (P.L. 584, 79th Congress, The Fulbright Act and Franco-American Treaty of May 7, 1965), Program Year 1966 covering Exchanges for the Academic Year September 1, 1966–August 31, 1967, adopted by the Commission November 7, 1967, pp. 33, 59. Located in Archives of the Franco-American Commission, Paris [hereafter AFAC]. However, after the cut in U.S. funding

in 1968–69, numbers of American students funded by Fulbright plummeted and never were restored to 1968 levels. In 1968–69, there were 178 students (out of a total of 210 American grantees); in 1969–70 and 1970–71, there were 0 students (out of a total of 12 and 32 American grantees, respectively); in 1971–72, there were 11 students (out of 53 total American grantees); and in 1972–73, there were 13 students (out of 47 total American grantees). "Franco-American Commission Programs (1968–1973)," file: Histoire du Programme Fulbright 4 (25e anniv de la CFA) located in the office of the director of the Franco-American Commission, Paris.

20. Michael J. Flack, "Results and Effects of Study Abroad," *Annals of the American Academy of Political and Social Science* 424 (March 1976): 117.

21. Ibid.

22. Jeanne Mars, "Les Etudiants français aux Etats-Unis," *Informations et documents* 204 (October 1, 1964): 24–31, copy in file : Histoire du Programme Fulbright 3, AFAC.

23. In answer to the question, "Did you easily find a position upon returning from the United States?", 44 scientists and engineers replied yes, none replied no, and 10 did not answer the question. *Rives. Bulletin de l'Association amicale universitaire France-Amérique* 19 (Autumn 1962): 6. Among those in the liberal professions and managerial fields, 35 said yes, 4 said no, and 5 did not answer the question. *Rives. Bulletin de l'Association amicale universitaire France-Amérique* 20 (Winter 1962): 8.

24. Marie-José Taube, interview by author, May 13, 2005, in Paris, France; Rosine Lorotte, interview by author, May 10, 2005, in Paris, France.

25. Jean-Michel Roche [pseudonym], interview by author, May 4, 2005, in Paris, France.

26. Exact questions on the Fulbright forms changed slightly in the 1960s, and included the following: "Please evaluate your experience in terms of its: (a) professional value; (b) personal or social value; and (c) contribution to international understanding." AFAC. Comparable data from French Fulbrighters in the United States were not made available by the Fulbright archives in Arkansas.

27. J. W. Fulbright, "Education for a New Kind of International Relations," *International Educational and Cultural Exchange* (Winter 1967): 17, quoting Charles Frankel, *The Neglected Aspect of Foreign Affairs* (Washington, DC: Brookings Institution, 1966), 104.

28. Sarah Price [pseudonym], interview by author, July 8, 2002, Paris, France; written interview notes reviewed and corrected by Sarah Price.

29. Steve Whitfield, telephone interview by author, December 13, 2004.

30. Herbert Larson, telephone interview by author, October 19, 2004.

31. Copy of Karen Stedtfeld's final report to the Fulbright Commission in 1962, in author's possession. Many thanks to Karen Offen for sharing her letters and other materials from her Fulbright year in France.

Notes to Chapter 6

32. Folder: Paul Simon [pseudonym], file: U.S. Students 1963–64, AFAC.

33. Folder: Samuel Rutherford [pseudonym], file: U.S. Students 1962–63, AFAC.

34. Jean-Michel Roche [pseudonym], interview by author, May 4, 2005, in Paris, France.

35. Paul Benhamou, interview by author, April 20, 2005, in West Lafayette, IN.

36. Pierre Bourdieu's study of student culture in France, especially Paris, in the early 1960s presents French arts students as relatively closed socially and culturally, yet lacking a shared, collective identity. To compensate for the sense of isolation, and uncertain job prospects, Parisian arts students, he argues, constructed alternative cultural identities outside of the university, with film, music, art, and books. Pierre Bourdieu and Jean-Claude Passeron, *The Inheritors: French Students and Their Relation to Culture*, trans. Richard Nice (Chicago: University of Chicago Press, 1979).

37. Steve Whitfield, telephone interview by author, December 13, 2004.

38. Folder: Jeffrey Coatsworth [pseudonym], file: U.S. Students 1965–66, AFAC.

39. Karla Taudin, interview by author, May 3, 2005, Paris, France.

40. Paul Benhamou, interview by author, April 20, 2005, in West Lafayette, IN.

41. Rosine Lorotte, interview by author, May 10, 2005, in Paris, France.

42. Gérard François, telephone interview by author, November 29, 2004.

43. Karen Offen, telephone interview by author, January 11, 2006.

44. Leslie Roberts, telephone interview by author, February 22, 2007.

45. Sarah Price [pseudonym], interview by author, July 8, 2002, Paris, France; written interview notes reviewed and corrected by Sarah Price.

46. Folder: Nancy S. Hires [pseudonym], file: U.S. Grantees 1963–64, AFAC.

47. Folder: Joy Sellers [pseudonym], file: U.S. Students 1962–63, AFAC. The other misconceptions were that American women were domineering and domestically incompetent, that all Americans were wealthy, and that higher education in the United States was vastly inferior to that in France.

48. Leslie Roberts, telephone interview by author, February 22, 2007.

49. Folder: Anita Maier [pseudonym], file: U.S. Grantees 1963–64, AFAC. She originally studied at the University of Toulouse in 1962–63, when she wrote the final report, but she requested and was granted a teaching fellow position to stay in France for another year in 1963–64.

50. Lucy Carr [pseudonym], telephone interview by author, January 13, 2006.

51. Leslie Roberts, telephone interview by author, February 22, 2007.

52. Rusty L. Monhollon, *"This Is America?" The Sixties in Lawrence, Kansas* (New York: Palgrave, 2004).

53. Folder: Gregory Dean [pseudonym], file: U.S. Students 1965–66, AFAC.

54. Folder: Alison Bennett [pseudonym], file: U.S. Students 1966–67, AFAC.

55. Herbert Larson, telephone interview by author, October 19, 2004.

56. Costigliola, *France and the United States*, 140–47; Paxton and Wahl, *De Gaulle and the United States*.

57. Barbara Boonstoppel to her mother, September 15, 1966, typed manuscript in author's possession. Many thanks to Barbara Diefendorf for sharing her letters.

58. Three different folders in U.S. Students 1966–67, AFAC.

59. Folder: Vivian Scanlon [pseudonym], file: U.S. Grantees 1967–68; Students, AFAC.

60. Yves Legras, "Dans le journal de bord," *Rives. Bulletin de l'Association amicale universitaire France-Amérique* 25 (Spring 1964): 12.

61. Mark Kurlansky, *1968: The Year That Rocked the World* (New York: Ballantine Books, 2004); Hoffman, *All You Need Is Love*; Suri, *Power and Protest*; Didier Fischer, *L'Histoire des étudiants en France de 1945 à nos jours* (Paris: Flammarion, 2000).

62. Michael Seidman, *The Imaginary Revolution: Parisian Students and Workers in 1968* (New York: Berghahn Books, 2004), chs. 1–2.

63. Folder: David Alcan [pseudonym], file: U.S. Grantees 1967–68, AFAC.

64. Folder: Joseph Bender [pseudonym], file: U.S. Grantees 1967–68, AFAC.

65. Fischer, *Histoire des étudiants en France*, 426–32; Seidman, *The Imaginary Revolution*, 277–80.

66. Jean-Michel Roche [pseudonym], interview by author, May 4, 2005, in Paris, France.

67. Seidman, *The Imaginary Revolution*, 277–80; Fischer, *Histoire des étudiants en France*, 416–17.

68. Guy Mermier to Dean Seighardt Reigel and Dean Henry Hill, January 21, 1969, memo regarding visit to Aix, December 11–13, 1968. Bentley Historical Library, University of Michigan, Office of International Programs, 93819 Bimu 2, box 1, Folder: Aix-Director Reports 68–70.

69. Lucien Jambrun, May 5, 2005, interview by author, Vichy, France. See also Seidman, *The Imaginary Revolution*, 277.

70. William W. Davenport, *An Old House in Paris: The Story of Reid Hall* (France: Reid Hall, 1970), 26, in Columbia University Archives.

71. "Annual Report Franco-American Commission for Educational Exchange (P.L. 584, 79th Congress, The Fulbright Act and Franco-American Treaty of May 7, 1965), Program Year 1967 Covering Exchanges for the Academic Year September 1, 1967–August 31, 1968, Adopted by the Commission November 4, 1968," pp. 4–5, AFAC.

72. "Annual Report Franco-American Commission for Educational Exchange (P.L. 584, 79th Congress, The Fulbright Act and Franco-American Treaty of May 7, 1965), Program Year 1968 Covering Exchanges for the Academic Year September 1, 1968–August 31, 1969, Adopted by the Commission October 21, 1969," p. 39, AFAC.

73. "Annual Report Franco-American Commission for Educational Exchange (P.L. 584, 79th Congress, The Fulbright Act and Franco-American Treaty of May 7, 1965), Program Year 1968 Covering Exchanges for the Academic Year September 1, 1968–August 31, 1969, Adopted by the Commission October 21, 1969," p. 50, AFAC.

74. Steven Sadler [pseudonym], telephone interview by author, December 21, 2004.

75. Jean-Michel Roche [pseudonym], interview by author, May 4, 2005, in Paris, France.

76. Folder: Eleanor Allard [pseudonym], file: U.S. Grantees 1968–69; Students, AFAC.

77. Folder: Monica Billings [pseudonym], file: U.S. Grantees 1968–69; Students, AFAC.

78. Folder: Vivian Scanlon [pseudonym], file: U.S. Grantees 1967–68; Students, AFAC.

79. Folder: Geoffrey Aikins [pseudonym], file: U.S. Grantees 1968–69; Students, AFAC.

80. Typed paper entitled, "Commission Franco-American d'Echanges universitaires et culturels, probably dated from 1984 or 1985, and handwritten report on Fulbright budget in France from 1949 to 1974 in file: Histoire du Programme Fulbright 2, AFAC.

81. "Annual Report Franco-American Commission for Educational Exchange (P.L. 584, 79th Congress, The Fulbright Act and Franco-American Treaty of May 7, 1965) Program Year 1969 covering Exchanges for the Academic Year September 1, 1969–August 31, 1970," p. 2, in folder: 1967–73 Annual Reports (con't.), AFAC.

82. "Minutes of the One Hundred and Ninety-first Meeting of the Franco-American Commission for Educational Exchange, Monday April 1, 1968," file: "USEC/F Meetings—1968," folder: 1967–73 Annual Reports (con't.), AFAC.

83. Lucien Jambrun, interview by author, May 5, 2005, Vichy, France.

84. Dr. James R. Roach to William P. Rogers, secretary of state, March 6, 1969, file: Histoire du Programme Fulbright 2, AFAC.

85. Folder: Cynthia Seymour [pseudonym], file: U.S. Grantees 1968–69; Students, AFAC.

86. Folder: Elizabeth Saltzman [pseudonym], file: U.S. Grantees 1968–69; Students, AFAC.

87. *Newsweek*, May 29, 1971, p. 29, copy in file: Histoire du Programme Fulbright 3, AFAC. Another critical period in the history of the Fulbright Program occurred in the lead-up to President Jimmy Carter's decision to merge cultural programs with information activities into a single agency, the International Communication Agency, in 1979. The very initials—ICA—prompted the foreign press to raise the alarm about the affiliation of cultural exchanges like Fulbright with the CIA. Clipping, "'ICA' Often Spells 'CIA' for Foreigners," *International Herald Tribune* (June 1978): 17–18, along with statement by Charles Blitzer, chairman, Council for International Exchange of Scholars, November 4, 1977, and other relevant documents, file: Histoire du Programme Fulbright 1, AFAC. Leonard R. Sussman, *The Culture of Freedom: The Small World of Fulbright Scholars* (Lanham, MD: Rowman & Littlefield Publishers, 1992), 24–26.

88. Folder: Vivian Scanlon [pseudonym], file: U.S. Grantees 1967–68; Students, AFAC.

89. Folder: Steven Sadler [pseudonym], file: U.S. Grantees 1967–68; Students, AFAC.

90. Folder: Shelly Reardon [pseudonym], file: U.S. Grantees 1967–68; Students, AFAC. The expression "a grandiloquent mouthful" comes from the folder of Martin Novak [pseudonym] in U.S. Grantees 1967–68; Students, AFAC.

91. Jonathan H. Ebbets, "A Little More than Four Months Later," *Rives. Bulletin de l'Association amicale universitaire France-Amérique* 29 (Spring–Summer 1965): 33, 35.

92. "Nous entrerons dans la carrière...," *Rives. Bulletin de l'Association amicale universitaire France-Amérique* 22 (Summer 1963): 1–2.

93. Ibid., 2.

94. Ibid., 6–7.

95. Arick Head, "Enquête: 'Comme d'un animal venu de l'Amérique' (La Fontaine)," *Rives. Bulletin de l'Association amicale universitaire France-Amérique* 18 (Spring 1962): 37.

96. Survey results, *Rives. Bulletin de l'Association amicale universitaire France-Amérique* 21 (Spring 1963): 3.

Chapter 7

Material from this chapter was published earlier as "Sexe, genre, et sociabilité: Étudiantes américaines en France après la Seconde Guerre mondiale," *Clio: Histoire, femmes et sociétés* 28 (2008) "Voyageuses": 145–58. Many thanks for the kind permission to reproduce it here.

1. Robert Mengin, "Pour Helen," *Revue des deux mondes* 9 (May 1, 1962): 54.

2. Robert Mengin, "Pour Helen," *Revue des deux mondes* 11 (June 1, 1962): 422.

3. Several studies address love and sexuality in national identities and in Western civilization. A very popular book since its publication in 1939, Denis de Rougemont's *Love in the Western World*, argues that passion, a modern variant of courtly love, threatens to dissolve marriage, a bedrock of Western society. Denis de Rougemont, *Love in the Western World*, trans. Montgomery Belgion, rev. ed. (New York: Pantheon, 1956). More recently Luisa Passerini analyzes how romantic love was integral to a popular conception of European identity in the 1920s and 1930s against threats from communism, fascism, and American feminism. Luisa Passerini, *Europe in Love, Love in Europe: Imagination and Politics Between the Wars* (New York: New York University Press, 1999). George Mosse maintains that Protestant England and Germany took the lead in constructing national identities that included sexual restraint and respectability as part of bourgeois domination in the nineteenth and twentieth centuries. George L. Mosse, *Nationalism and Sexuality: Middle-class Morality and Sexual Norms in Modern Europe* (Madison: University of Wisconsin Press, 1985). Miriam G. Ruemann analyzes the Kinsey Reports on women's and men's sexuality as integral to the construction of American identity in the 1950s. Miriam G. Reumann, *American Sexual Character: Sex, Gender, and National Identity in the Kinsey Reports* (Berkeley: University of California Press, 2005). Dagmar Herzog asserts that post–World War II debates over sexuality in Germany functioned as a means to manage the memory of Nazism and the Holocaust. Dagmar Herzog, *Sex After Fascism: Memory and Morality in Twentieth-century Germany* (Princeton, NJ: Princeton University Press, 2005).

4. Harvey Levenstein, *Seductive Journey: American Tourists in France from Jefferson to the Jazz Age* (Chicago: University of Chicago Press, 1998), 201–09; William R. Keylor, "'How They Advertised France': The French Propaganda Campaign in the United States During the Breakup of the Franco-American Entente, 1918–1923," *Diplomatic History* 17 (Summer 1993): 368–69.

5. Jacques Portes, *Une Fascination réticente: Les Etats-Unis dans l'opinion française* (Nancy: Presses Universitaires de Nancy, 1990); Bernadette Galloux-Fournier, "Un regard sur l'Amérique: Voyageurs français aux Etats-Unis (1919–1939)," *Revue d'histoire moderne et contemporaine* 37 (April–June 1990): 308–23; Gérard de Catalogne, *Dialogue entre deux mondes* (Paris: Librairie la Revue Française, 1931); Richard F. Kuisel, *Seducing the French: The Dilemma of Americanization* (Berkeley: University of California Press, 1993); Richard Pells, *Not Like Us: How Europeans Have Loved, Hated, and Transformed American Culture Since World War II* (New York: Basic Books, 1997).

6. Steven Seidman, *Romantic Longings: Love in America, 1830–1980* (New York: Routledge, 1991); Beth L. Bailey, *From Front Porch to Back Seat: Courtship in Twentieth-century America* (Baltimore: Johns Hopkins University Press,

1988); Paula Fass, *The Damned and the Beautiful: American Youth in the 1920s* (New York: Oxford University Press, 1977); Peter G. Filene, *Him/Her/Self: Gender Identities in Modern America*, 3rd ed. (Baltimore: Johns Hopkins University Press, 1998); John D'Emilio and Estelle B. Freedman, *Intimate Matters: A History of Sexuality in America* (New York: Harper & Row, 1988); Anne-Marie Sohn, *Du premier baiser à l'alcove: La Sexualité des Français au quotidien (1850–1950)* (Paris: Aubier, 1996); Anne-Marie Sohn, *Age tendre et tête de bois: Histoire des jeunes des années 1960* (Paris: Hachette, 2001).

7. Fabienne Casta-Rosaz, *Histoire du flirt: Les Jeux de l'innocence et de la perversité, 1870–1968* (Paris: Bernard Grasset, 2000).

8. Levenstein, *Seductive Journey*, 197–209, 218–19; Keylor, "'How They Advertised France,'" 351–73

9. Raymond W. Kirkbride to Walter Hullihen, March 4, 1923, UD AR 330, Hullihen Papers, Foreign Study, 1922–37.

10. Beatrice F. Davis, oral interview by Myron L. Lazarus, UD AR 97, folder 1646.

11. W. Emerson Wilson, oral interview by Myron L. Lazarus, UD AR 97, folder 1646.

12. Phebe Elizabeth Adams to her family, n.d., probably August 1930, SC, box 2041.

13. J. Edward Davidson, "Letters from a Junior in France, 1936–1937: Paris, France, April 13,1937," printed pamphlet, 3–4, UD AR 44, folder C-14.

14. Y., "Examens de conscience: L'enseignement, la religion, la politique, et l'avenir de la France," *Foreign Study Notes* 1 (August–November 1929): 39.

15. Bailey, *From Front Porch to Back Seat*; Fass, *The Damned and the Beautiful*.

16. J. Edward Davidson, "Letters from a Junior in France."

17. UD AR 68, folder 540, Letters to parents from students 1929–30 (Group VII).

18. Dorothy Tebbetts to her parents, January 24, 1926, SC, box 1994.

19. John Lee Clarke to W. A. Neilson, March 9, 1928, SC JYA France, Neilson Papers, box 49, folder B49F14.

20. This same student noted other preconceptions that her stay in France dispelled. She wrote: "I will never say to my friends in America that all Frenchmen are immoral, wanton, and indelicate." Y., "Examens de conscience: L'enseignement, la religion, la politique, et l'avenir de la France," *Foreign Study Notes* 1 (August–November 1929): 39.

21. Delia Brown to Mademoiselle Cattenès, July 14, 1926, SC JYA France, Neilson Papers, box 49.

22. Hélène Cattenès, *Mémento de l'année en France*, in SC 50 JYA, box 1133.

23. Charles Petit-Dutaillis of the Office national des universités et écoles françaises to his director, M. Marx, February 12, 1935, Ministère des Affaires

Etrangères [MAE] (Nantes), Service des oeuvres françaises à l'étranger, 1912–1940, box 426, folder 0-160-3, 1932, Etats-Unis, Bourses.

24. Sarah Alice Johnston to her family, November 3, 1938, in "Sally Goes to France: Letters from a Junior Year, 1938–1939," ed. Ellen J. Maycock, 2003, typed manuscript.

25. Henriette Nizan, "Quand la jeunesse américaine vient respirer l'air de Paris," *Rapports France-Etats-Unis* 42 (September 1950): 45–50.

26. James Baldwin, "Paris Letter: A Question of Identity," *Partisan Review* 21 (July 1954): 404. Harvey Levenstein claims that American movies, such as *To Catch a Thief* (1955), *An American in Paris* (1951), and *Paris Blues* (1961), represented Paris as a place for romance, love, and sex—freer of conventions and restrictions than the United States. Levenstein, *We'll Always Have Paris*, 160–63.

27. Bailey, *From Front Porch to Back Seat*, ch. 5.

28. Seidman, *Romantic Longings*, 118–40.

29. Stanley Karnow, *Paris in the Fifties* (New York: Times Books, 1997), 3–4.

30. Ibid., 8.

31. Ibid., 235–36.

32. For an analysis of this film in the context of rebellious youth in postwar France, see Susan Weiner, *Enfants Terribles: Youth and Femininity in the Mass Media in France, 1945–1968* (Baltimore: Johns Hopkins University Press, 2001), 163–67.

33. "Cythère 1960: Comment un garçon de la jeunesse dorée conçoit son itinéraire sentimental," *Réalités fémina-illustration* 167 (December 1959): 79–82.

34. Jean-René Huguenin and Renaud Matignon, "La Jeunesse de France parle," *Arts, spectacles* 608 (February 27–March 5, 1957): 7.

35. Bertrand Poirot-Delpech, "Une génération qui ne se paie pas de mots," *Réalités fémina-illustration* 167 (December 1959): 128.

36. Elaine Tyler May, *Homeward Bound: American Families in the Cold War Era* (New York: Basic Books, 1988); Barbara Miller Solomon, *In the Company of Educated Women: A History of Women and Higher Education in America* (New Haven, CT: Yale University Press, 1985); Filene, *Him/Her/Self*; Jean-François Sirinelli, *Les Baby-Boomers: Une Génération, 1945–1969* (Paris: Fayard, 2003), 45–48; Antony Copley, *Sexual Moralities in France 1780–1980: New Ideas on the Family, Divorce, and Homosexuality* (London: Routledge, 1989), 198–99, 204.

37. Wini Breines, *Young, White, and Miserable: Growing Up Female in the Fifties* (Chicago: University of Chicago Press, 1992); Weiner, *Enfants Terribles*; Seidman, *Romantic Longings*, 122–25; Bailey, *From Front Porch to Back Seat*, ch. 5. Beth Bailey also finds that structural changes in the society and within universities contributed to new attitudes toward and practices of sexuality during

the 1950s. Beth Bailey, *Sex in the Heartland* (Cambridge, MA: Harvard University Press, 1999). Similarly, Michael Seidman locates the origins of the 1960s sexual revolution in the late 1950s with the beginnings of claims for personal freedoms and a general atmosphere of tolerance and permissiveness in two Paris university settings. Michael Seidman, "The Pre-May 1968 Sexual Revolution," *Contemporary French Civilization* 25 (Winter/Spring 2001): 20–41. Fabienne Casta-Rosaz presents an extensive analysis of a diary kept by a young French woman in 1946–47 on her flirtatious practices that stopped short of sexual intercourse. She suggests that they were less "institutionalized" than heterosexual flirting in the United States, based on her reading of William Styron's novel *Sophie's Choice* and on Philippe Labro's fictionalized account of a young French man studying at a university in Virginia in 1954. She also notes similar developments of more openness in attitudes and practices surrounding heterosexuality in both the United States and France in the 1950s but also similar contradictions between media presentations of sexualized femininity and a traditionalist orientation of mass consumption. Casta-Rosaz, *Histoire du Flirt*.

38. Richard Ivan Jobs, *Riding the New Wave: Youth and the Rejuvenation of France After the Second World War* (Stanford, CA: Stanford University Press, 2007), ch. 5.

39. D'Emilio and Freedman, *Intimate Matters*, 285–86; Reumann, *American Sexual Character*; Sylvie Chaperon, "Kinsey en France: Les Sexualités féminine et masculine en débat," *Le Mouvement social* 198 (January–March 2002): 91–110.

40. John A. Garraty and Walter Adams, *From Main Street to the Left Bank: Students and Scholars Abroad* (East Lansing: Michigan State University Press, 1959), 121.

41. Simone de Beauvoir, *America Day by Day*, trans. Carol Cosman (Berkeley: University of California Press, 1999), 281–82.

42. Karnow, *Paris in the Fifties*, 235–36.

43. "Etudiants américains à l'étranger," *Rives. Bulletin de l'Association amicale universitaire France-Amérique* 1 (April 1957): 16.

44. Eric Fassin, "Un Échange inégale: Sexualité et rites amoureux aux Etats-Unis," *Critique* 596–97 (January–February 1997): 48–65.

45. Micaela Blay-Thorup, interview by author, May 12, 2005, Paris, France.

46. Ibid.

47. Marie-José Taube, interview by author, May 13, 2005, Paris, France.

48. Ibid.

49. Gérard François, telephone interview by author, November 29, 2004.

50. "Nous entrerons dans la carrière . . . (fin). Une grande enquête de l'AAUFA," *Rives. Bulletin de l'Association amicale universitaire France-Amérique* 22 (Summer 1963): 2.

51. Gérard François, telephone interview.

52. Philippe Labro, *L'Etudiant étranger* (Paris: Gallimard, 1986), 33.

53. Elizabeth Cannon to her family, June 19, 1950, copies in the author's possession. Thanks to Elizabeth Cannon Simmons for sharing her letters.

54. Miriam Halbert Bales, letters in the author's possession and conversation with Miriam Halbert Bales, September 6, 2002, Muncie, IN.

55. Anne Rittershofer to her parents, February 12, 1957, SC, Class of 1958, box 2214. Many thanks to FlorenceMae Waldron for providing the reference to this source.

56. Barbara Boonstoppel to her family, September 13, 1966, typed manuscript in author's possession. I am grateful to Barbara Diefendorf for sharing her letters.

57. Copy of Karen Stedtfeld's final report to the Fulbright Commission, 1962, in author's possession.

58. Elizabeth E. Bacon to Mrs. R. V. L. Boname, January 21, 1963, SC JYA France, box 1133.

59. Martha Churchill to her parents, September 26, 1948, from SC, box 2172.

60. Mary Bishop Coan, telephone interview by author, January 6, 2003.

61. Mary Ann Hoberman, telephone interview by author, September 10, 2004. She felt liberated in France in other ways as well. As a Jew she felt an undercurrent of anti-Semitism at Smith College: "there was still a Jewish quota, there were all kinds of things, the clubs you couldn't get into, the parties, whatever. And then to get to France, at first we were all greeted of course, as Americans, and that was very liberating." Hoberman later discerned anti-Semitism in France as well, but overall she felt the experience had freed her in positive ways: "something had happened over there that had freed me to just be much more myself and that I had different outlooks from other people, I had different experiences, and I didn't have to conform as much."

62. Elizabeth Cannon to her mother, March 24, 1950. See note 53.

63. Anne Rittershofer to her family, November 19, 1956, SC, box 2214.

64. Anne Atheling, telephone interview by author, October 12, 2004.

65. Lucy Carr [pseudonym], telephone interview by author, January 13, 2006.

66. Barbara Boonstoppel to her mother, September 19, 1966, typed manuscript in possession of the author.

67. Laura Sherman [pseudonym], telephone interview by author, September 15, 2004.

68. Barbara Boonstoppel to her mother, September 2, 1966, typed manuscript in author's possession.

69. Carolyn Washer and Marilyn Ganetsky, "What Happened in Bordeaux," *Rives. Bulletin de l'Association amicale universitaire France-Amérique* 17 (Winter n.d. [1961]): 37.

70. Molly Debon, "On Marrying a Frenchman," *Rives. Bulletin de l'Association amicale universitaire France-Amérique* 22 (Summer 1963): 11.

71. Paul Benhamou, interview by author, April 20, 2005, West Lafayette, IN.

72. Labro, *L'Etudiant étranger*, 34–35

73. Gérard François, telephone interview.

74. Christine de Rivoyre, *The Wreathed Head*, trans. Patrick O'Brian (London: Rupert Hart-Davis, 1962 [orig. 1960]), 66.

75. Karen Stedtfeld to her family, November 7, 1961.

76. Lucy Carr [pseudonym], telephone interview by author, January 13, 2006.

77. Miriam Halbert to her mother, March 6, 1948, in author's possession.

78. Richard Robbins, "Other Cultures and Singular Pluralisms," in *The Fulbright Difference, 1948–1992*, ed. Richard T. Arndt and David Lee Rubin (New Brunswick, NJ: Transaction Publishers, 1993), 32.

79. Karen Stedtfeld to her family, October 12, 1961,

80. Karen Stedtfeld to her family, November 7, 1961.

81. Rivoyre, *The Wreathed Head*, 15–17.

82. Miriam Halbert to her mother, January 22, 1948, typed transcript in the author's possession.

83. Miriam Halbert Bales, conversation with author, September 6, 2002, Muncie, IN.

84. Copley, *Sexual Moralities in France 1780–1980*, 203, 215–21.

85. D'Emilio and Freedman, *Intimate Matters*, 289–300; Reumann, *American Sexual Character*, ch. 5.

86. Michael Seidman, *The Imaginary Revolution: Students and Workers in May 1968* (New York: Berghahn Books, 2004); Marwick, *The Sixties;* Bailey, *Sex in the Heartland*; Didier Fischer, *L'Histoire des étudiants en France de 1945 à nos jours* (Paris: Flammarion, 2000).

87. Alice Kaplan, *French Lessons: A Memoir* (Chicago: University of Chicago Press, 1993), 89.

Index

Adams, Phebe, 73, 78, 174
Algerian War, 143, 157, 188, 189
Alliance Française, 27, 36, 104
American girl, 76, 85, 86, 91, 94, 99, 100, 180, 182; as an American stereotype, 88–89, 95, 107; as a French stereotype, 88–89, 90, 94, 103, 177, 185
Americanization, 83, 129, 153, 161; in historiography, 5, 11, 31, 41, 49, 60, 126, 173, 192
Amieux, Anna, 51
Anderson, Benedict, 3, 83
Anti-Americanism, 5, 11, 41, 60, 113, 126
Anticommunism, 9, 121, 122, 123, 127, 139
Anti-imperialism, 144, 160
Appel, Paul, 66
Appiah, Kwame Anthony, 3
Arndt, Richard T., 124, 238n85
Association amicale universitaire France-Amérique (AAUFA), 150, 155, 168
Avery, Althea B., 82, 106

Bailey, Beth L., 97, 177, 190, 249n37
Bales, Miriam. *See* Halbert, Miriam (Bales)
Beauvoir, Simone de, 98–99, 101–102, 180, 186

Benhamou, Paul, 141, 153, 154, 187
Bonnet, Henri, 115, 122, 123
Boonstopple, Barbara (Deifendorf), 158–159, 183, 185–186
Bourdieu, Pierre, 81, 88, 243n36
Bragdon, Florence Elizabeth, 70, 71, 77, 91, 93
Brown, Delia, 69, 99, 176
Burgess, John W., 12, 17–18
Butler, Nicholas Murray, 18, 24

Cahill, Mary Louise, 71, 76, 91, 94, 100, 101
Carnegie Endowment for International Peace, 8, 24, 41, 65, 66
Carr, Lucy (pseud.), 157, 185, 188
Cartan, Annette-Marie, 48, 50, 51, 53, 211n34
Cattanès, Hélène, 70, 73, 90, 91, 92, 93, 94, 96, 103, 106, 176
Caullery, Maurice, 29–30, 31
Cestre, Charles, 32, 37, 63, 113, 114
Challaye, Félicien, 56, 57
Charle, Christophe, 26, 75
Charléty, Sebastien, 80
Chinard, Gilbert, 28–29, 30, 31
Churchill, Martha, 124, 132, 184, 238n84
Civil rights movement, 128, 188
Clément, Marguerite, 45–46, 48, 50

253

Coan, Mary Bishop, 134, 185
Cold War, 3, 9, 110, 126, 127, 142, 160, 177, 190; effects on study abroad, 109, 111, 120, 140, 145
Communism, 3, 77, 109, 110, 117, 120, 121, 140, 145, 207n4
Communist Party, 113, 119
Congress, U.S., 109, 117, 120, 122, 138, 166, 167, 240n11
Cosmopolitanism, 3, 23, 81, 92
Costigliola, Frank, 2, 110, 143
Cours de civilisation française, 63, 67, 86, 113, 116, 132, 133
Cultural diplomacy, 37, 83, 86, 109, 111, 116, 137

Daniels, Eleanor, 71, 78, 83, 95; on women, 94, 97–98, 99, 100, 101, 103, 107
Darlu, Jeanne, 48, 49–50, 57
Davis, Beatrice F., 69, 70, 88, 97, 105, 174, 221n88
de Gaulle, Charles, 10, 109, 142, 143, 158, 163, 241n13
Diefendorf, Barbara. *See* Boonstopple, Barbara (Deifendorf)
Donahue, Hilda, 73–74, 99
Duggan, Stephen P., 65, 66
Duhamel, Georges, 45, 58, 60, 210n23, 214n80

Ecole Normale Supérieure de Sèvres, 47, 48, 124, 228n76, 229n90
Education (higher), 3, 6, 11, 13, 144. *See also names of specific institutions*; Soldiers, American in France
Education (higher), American, 14, 38, 68, 118; appeal to foreign students, 1, 145, 169; changes since World War II, 127–128, 128–130, 142, 152; comparison/contrast with French, 29, 30, 33–34, 47–53, 73–76, 100, 130–131, 133, 151–153, 165, 192, 243n47; German influence upon, 13, 15, 18, 26, 28, 29, 31, 53, 64; reforms in American, 13, 18, 24, 75, 111; in relation to study abroad, 6, 9, 11, 24, 61, 63, 84, 134, 172; women in, 4, 7, 13–19, 19–22, 37, 43–44, 47–53, 86, 87, 95, 177, 211n32
Education (higher), French, 33–34, 36, 37, 76, 102, 219n58; reforms in French, 7, 14, 16, 25–31, 38, 43, 75, 111, 128, 134; reforms of 1968, 10, 142, 153, 160, 161, 162, 169; since World War II, 112, 127, 128–130, 151; women in, 7, 21, 88, 95, 101–102
Education (higher), German, 6, 12, 16–17, 21, 25, 31, 35; women in, 20
Ely, Richard T., 15, 19, 22–23, 24
Endy, Christopher, 2, 4
Etudiant étranger, Le (Labro), 183
Events of 1968, 141, 144, 151, 163, 164, 165, 190. *See also* Education (higher), French: reforms of 1968

Fischer, Didier, 128, 161, 190
Flack, Michael J., 148–149
Franco-American Commission, 118, 148, 156, 162, 166
Franco-American relations, 5, 7, 11, 192; late nineteenth through early twentieth centuries, 7, 15, 31, 41, 236n51; 1920s–1930s, 69, 80; following World War II, 109–110, 111, 112, 114, 116, 123, 126, 143, 144, 199n16; 1960s–1970s, 10, 186, 241n13
François, Gérard, 155, 182, 187
Fraser, Ian F., 114–115
French *jeune fille*, 86, 88, 89, 91, 95; as an American stereotype, 9, 88, 90, 103, 107; viewed by American students, 90, 91, 94, 99, 184; viewed by French, 101, 103, 104
Fulbright, J. William, 117, 151
Fulbright educational exchange program, 131, 138, 145, 156, 182, 242n26; contentions over, 121, 122, 147–148, 159, 246n87; effects of 1968 on, 161, 162–163, 165–167, 242n19; French responses to, 121, 129, 130, 150, 153, 155, 159; numbers of grantees, 118–120, 165; origins of, 9, 117–119

Gender, 37, 84, 85, 86, 177, 188, 191, 211n32, 224n14; in international relations, 7, 11, 60, 200n24; as part of national stereotypes, 9, 45, 86, 172, 177, 188, 191. *See also* American girl; French *jeune fille*; Men; Women

Germany, 6, 8, 35, 110, 145, 151; Americans studying in, 7, 12–13, 15, 16–21, 22–25

GI Bill, 9, 114–115, 131, 132, 178

Gréard, Octave, 25

Guilloton, Madeleine, 68, 93

Gullahorn, Jeanne E. and John T., 137, 138, 139, 147, 148

Halbert, Miriam (Bales), 124, 133, 135, 183, 188, 189–190

Hall, G. Stanley, 22

Hanna, Martha, 35, 86

Higher education. *See* Education (higher)

Hitzel, Edmée, 57, 58

Hoberman, Mary Ann, 185, 251n61

Holslag, Marie, 91, 106

Hovelaque, Emile, 46, 55

Hullihen, Walter, 65, 67, 68, 70, 81, 89, 106, 113, 174

Hurrey, Frances, 77, 79, 98

Institute of International Education (IIE), 1, 65, 66, 111, 118, 124, 133, 145

International relations, 85–86, 142, 148, 149, 192

Internationalism: cultural, 3, 5, 123; as espoused by Albert Kahn, 38, 42, 59; as espoused by Kahn fellows, 53, 56, 59; historical definitions of, 2–3, 14, 41; as tolerance and appreciation of difference, 3, 4, 6, 9, 11, 60, 81, 83, 106, 111, 139, 140, 192; after World War I, 62, 66, 83, after World War II, 137, 139, 146, 149, 199n16

Iriye, Akira, 2

Jambrun, Lucien, 119, 120, 162, 166

Johnson, Henry, 15, 27

Johnson, Lyndon B., 143

Johnston, Sarah (Sally), 71, 77, 94, 98, 99, 176–177

Junior year abroad programs, 4, 8, 38, 61; origins of, 62, 67–68; during interwar years, 76, 80, 84, 86, 88, 107, 108; after World War II, 112–113, 115, 117, 133, 146. *See also* Smith College Junior Year in France; University of Delaware Foreign Study Plan

Kahn, Albert, 40, 41, 54–55, 102; Around-the-World Scholarships, 7–8, 38, 39, 41, 42–44, 53, 56–57, 59

Karnow, Stanley, 131, 178, 181

Kennedy, John F., 143, 145

Kirkbride, Raymond W., 63, 64, 65, 67, 68, 70, 89, 174

Labro, Philippe, 129, 130, 182, 183, 187, 189, 250n37

Lanson, Gustave, 29, 30

Lapotaire, Alice, 49, 51

Larson, Herbert, 152, 158

Lécuyer, Carole (Christen-), 21, 52

Levenstein, Harvey, 4, 15, 173, 190

Levine, David O., 75

Linforth, Ivan, 54, 56

Lorotte, Rosine, 150, 154

Main, Anne, 55

Marshall Plan, 110, 126, 132

McNarney, Joseph T., 114

Men, 7, 20, 21, 37, 45, 48, 52, 98, 106, 179, 180, 182, 183; American, studying abroad before World War I, 12, 13, 14, 15, 16, 17, 18, 19, 34, 35, 38; American stereotypes of French, 10, 173, 176, 177, 184, 186–188, 191; as Kahn fellows, 8, 39, 42, 43, 44, 60; after World War I, 62, 84, 86, 87, 88, 89, 90, 175

Menner, Robert J., 34–35, 64

Mignon, Madeleine, 47, 49, 50, 51
Ministry of Education, French, 52
Ministry of Foreign Affairs, French, 66, 104, 107, 116, 122, 123, 176, 224n12
Moulinier, Pierre, 21, 219n58

National characteristics, American, 23, 24, 29–30, 44–45, 54; according to French persons, 5, 10, 45–46, 55, 58, 71–72, 129, 137, 140, 171–172
National characteristics, French, 88, 121; according to Americans, 5, 10, 23, 58, 69–71, 125, 127, 171; according to French persons, 31, 45–46, 55, 57, 122, 129
National characteristics, German, 22, 23, 31
National identity, 3, 11, 127, 160, 188, 192, 193; American, 7, 14, 22, 44, 46, 69, 140, 164, 167; French, 110, 160
National Office of French Universities and Schools [Office national des universités et écoles françaises], 30, 104
Nationalism, 3, 5, 40, 41, 83
Neilson, William Allan, 68, 69, 80, 89, 90, 91, 92, 94, 112, 176
1968. *See* Events of 1968
Nizan, Henriette, 132, 136, 177
North Atlantic Treaty Organization (NATO), 110, 143, 158

Offen, Karen. *See* Stedtfeld, Karen (Offen)
Open Doors, 1, 111, 144

Pace, C. Robert, 84, 139, 140
Petit-Dutaillis, Charles, 30, 80, 104, 176
Philanthropy, 40–41, 42, 59, 66
Politics, student interest in/awareness of, 5, 10, 11, 76, 77, 80, 139; in 1960s, 141, 142, 148, 151, 156, 157, 158, 160, 167, 169. *See also* Events of 1968
Price, Sarah (pseud.), 151, 156
Propaganda, 80, 109, 123; American in France, 110, 120, 121, 240n11

Race relations, 10, 57, 140, 151, 156, 157, 158, 159, 169, 176; mixed-race couples/relations, 173, 175, 188, 189
Racial discrimination, 2, 142
Reid Hall, 22, 113, 124, 162
Renauld, Jeanne, 49
Rhodes Scholarships, 8, 41, 42, 43
Richards, Mrs. Robert H., 90
Rittershofer, Anne, 127, 183, 185
Rivoyre, Christine de, 188, 189
Roberts, Leslie, 155, 157
Roche, Jean-Michel (pseud.), 150, 153, 161, 164
Roosevelt, Theodore, 44–45, 46
Rosenberg, Emily S., 2, 85
Ross, Edward Alsworth, 12, 16, 18, 23
Roussy, Gustave, 114

Sadler, Steven (pseud.), 163, 167
Sage, Marian, 69, 95, 97
Sapy, Pierrette, 51
Scanlon, Vivian (pseud.), 159, 165, 167
Seidman, Michael, 161, 190, 250n37
Sexuality, 7, 10–11, 71, 88, 97–98, 99, 172, 173, 177–178, 180, 188; American practices of, 174, 175, 179–180, 183, 187; American stereotypes of French, 173, 174, 176, 177, 178, 180, 191; French practices of, 174–175, 178–179, 187; French stereotypes of American, 173, 176; homosexual, 189–190; kissing, 180–181, 191; in relation to 1968, 190–191
Sherman, Laura (pseud.), 124, 126, 133, 186
Simmons, Elizabeth Cannon, 134, 183, 185
Smith College Junior Year in France: origins of, 8, 62, 64, 67–68, 70, 89, 176; during interwar years, 69, 80, 81, 83, 84, 86, 90, 92, 104–105, 106; during World War II, 112; after World War II, 113, 115, 116, 124, 135
Sociability, 96–97, 98, 99, 154–155, 172, 173; dating, 180–184, 188

Soldiers, American in France, 138; after World War I, 15, 31–36, 38, 61, 89; after World War II, 112, 113–115, 131–132
Stabler, Caroline Miller, 72, 103, 106
Stedtfeld, Karen (Offen), 152, 155, 184, 189
Steffens, Lincoln, 23
Stereotypes, 99, 107; American of French, 82; French of American, 93, 104. *See also* American girl; French *jeune fille*; National characteristics; Sexuality
Students, statistics on, 1, 8, 9, 26, 62, 67, 86, 111, 144, 145. *See* Education (higher); Fulbright educational exchange program; Men; Soldiers, American in France; Women
Study abroad: definition of, 4; surveys of, 81, 82, 83, 84, 104, 105, 106; after World War II, 110, 130, 137–140; in 1960s and 1970s, 10, 146–150, 168. *See also names of specific institutions*; Junior year abroad programs
Sweet Briar College Junior Year in France, 113, 115, 116, 139

Taube, Marie-José, 150, 182
Tebbets, Dorothy, 71, 73, 79, 85, 90, 96, 102, 106–107, 175
Téry, Simone, 58
Thomas, Martha Carey, 19–20
Tikhonov, Natalia, 21
Travel, 5, 15, 88, 106, 202n13, 241n13; in contrast to study abroad, 4, 8, 10, 60, 172, 192; educational, 16, 19, 24, 35, 37, 38, 64, 82, 110, 115, 134; as mode of transportation, 140, 169, 191. *See also* Kahn, Albert: Around-the-World Scholarships

United Nations Educational, Scientific and Cultural Organization (UNESCO), 116, 129, 145
United States Information Service (USIS), 110, 121

Universities: American, 1, 6, 7, 8, 13, 24, 66, 147, 148; French, 10, 39, 66, 67, 147; German, 14. *See also* Education (higher); Soldiers, American in France
University of Delaware Foreign Study Plan: origins of, 8, 62–65, 174; during 1920s–1930s, 67, 75, 80, 81, 82, 84, 103, 105, 106, 116, 139; during and after World War II, 107, 112–113, 115; policies regarding women, 86, 88, 89, 90, 91, 92–93
U.S. Information and Educational Exchange Act (Smith-Mundt Act), 117, 118, 121

Vietnam, U.S. war in, 140, 142, 143, 144, 157, 158, 159, 160, 164, 166

Weisz, George, 26
Williams, Walter, 53–54, 58
Wilson, W. Emerson, 90, 96–97, 174
Wilson, Woodrow, 24, 209n19
Women, 7, 9, 42, 45, 60; American, 6, 12, 19, 46, 51–52, 70, 84, 85, 95, 97, 124; American, and sociability in France, 184–185; American stereotypes of French, 188; education of, 13–14, 47–52, 62, 66, 87, 95, 102; French, 35, 37, 53, 95–96, 100–103; French stereotypes of American, 8, 9, 10, 37, 93, 94, 104, 171–172, 173, 185–186, 191; in international relations, 60, 85–86; as Kahn *boursières*, 8, 39, 42, 43–44, 60; motivations for studying abroad, 19, 21, 87–88, 89, 105; responses to study abroad, 9, 22, 80, 106–107, 108, 125–126, 135–136; restrictions upon, 9, 88, 90–93, 173, 184, 186; social practices of in France, 97–99, 100, 186; social practices of in United States, 10, 100; and travel, 15, 106; after World War II, 131, 134, 145. *See also* American girl; *Education (higher) in specific countries*: women in; French *jeune fille*; Gender; Sexuality

World War I, 15, 21, 22, 26, 37, 41, 47, 53, 102, 209n9, 236n51; effects on study abroad, 7, 8, 14, 31, 38, 62, 63, 77, 87; effects on U.S., 56, 59, 60, 65, 68, 75, 88, 173, 191; impact on France, 70, 72, 75, 77–79, 84, 88, 98, 103; U.S. involvement in, 55, 63, 117, 174, 217n34, 220n69

World War II, 9, 41, 59, 62, 67, 84, 86, 107, 108, 152, 172; effects on study abroad, 109, 112–115, 117, 145; impact on France, 109, 124–125

Wreathed Head, The (Rivoyre), 188

Youth, 6, 7, 11, 81, 83, 142, 144, 167, 169; American, 16, 18, 31, 88, 132, 159, 174, 241n13; culture, 11, 111, 170, 191; French, 4, 39, 42, 129, 137, 170, 178, 179, 181; revolt, 160, 249n32